Unobtrusive Evaluation of Reference Service and Individual Responsibility

Recent Titles in
Contemporary Studies in Information Management, Policies, and Services
Peter Hernon, Series Editor

Deep Information: The Role of Information Policy in Environmental Sustainability
John Felleman

Understanding Information Retrieval Interactions: Theoretical and Practical Implications
Carol A. Hert

Basic Research Methods for Librarians, Third Edition
Ronald R. Powell

Research Misconduct: Issues, Implications, and Strategies
Ellen Altman and Peter Hernon

Computer-Supported Decision Making: Meeting the Decision Demands of Modern Organizations
Charles L. Smith

Into the Future: The Foundations of Library and Information Services in the Post-Industrial Era, Second Edition
Michael H. Harris et al.

The Dissemination of Spatial Data: A North American–European Comparative Study on the Impact of Government Information Policy
Xavier Lopez

Information of the Image, Second Edition
Allan D. Pratt

Silencing Scientists and Scholars in Other Fields: Power, Paradigm Controls, Peer Review, and Scholarly Communication
Gordon Moran

The Information Systems of Inter-Governmental Organizations: A Reference Guide
Robert V. Williams

Knowledge Diffusion in the U.S. Aerospace Industry: Managing Knowledge for Competitive Advantage, Part B
Thomas E. Pinelli

Inventing the Future: Information Services for a new Millennium
Stan A. Hannah and Michael H. Harris

New Organizational Designs: Information Aspects
Bob Travica

Unobtrusive Evaluation of Reference Service and Individual Responsibility

The Canadian Experience

Juris Dilevko

Contemporary Studies in Information Management,
Policies, and Services
Peter Hernon, Series Editor

Ablex Publishing Corporation
Westport, Connecticut • London

Library of Congress Cataloging-in-Publication Data

Dilevko, Juris.
 Unobtrusive evaluation of reference service and individual responsibility : the Canadian experience / by Juris Dilevko.
  p. cm. — (Contemporary studies in information management, policy, and services)
 Includes bibliographical references and index.
 ISBN 1-56750-506-6 — ISBN 1-56750-507-4 (pbk.)
  1. Depository libraries—Reference services—Canada—Quality control. 2. Depository libraries—Reference services—Canada—Evaluation. I. Title. II. Series.
 Z675.D4 D53 2000
 025.5'2'0971—dc21   99-058739

British Library Cataloguing in Publication Data is available.

Copyright © 2000 by Juris Dilevko

All rights reserved. No portion of this book may be
reproduced, by any process or technique, without
the express written consent of the publisher.

Library of Congress Catalog Card Number: 99-058739
ISBN: 1-56750-506-6
ISBN: 1-56750-507-4 (pbk.)

First published in 2000

Ablex Publishing Corporation, 88 Post Road West, Westport, CT 06881
An imprint of Greenwood Publishing Group, Inc.
www.greenwood.com

Printed in the United States of America

The paper used in this book complies with the
Permanent Paper Standard issued by the National
Information Standards Organization (Z39.48-1984).

10 9 8 7 6 5 4 3 2 1

CONTENTS

Figures	vii
Tables	ix
Preface	xi
Acknowledgments	xiii
1 Reference Service Evaluation and Assessment	1
2 Government Documents Reference Service in Canada	25
3 What the Proxies Said About the Service They Received	77
4 Difficulty of Individual Questions	101
5 What Happens When Libraries Make Referrals?	129
6 Newspapers and the Reference Desk	147
7 Conclusion and Recommendations	177
References	207
Author Index	215
Subject Index	219

FIGURES

2-1	Frequency Distribution of Relative Difficulty of Questions Measured in Minutes	40
2-2	Daily Distribution of Questions	44
2-3	Distribution of Responses Received	45
2-4	Responses Received by Type of Depository Library	46
2-5	Types of Responses Received by Region	47
2-6	Types of Responses by Size of Census Metropolitan Area	48
2-7	Responses Received by Day of the Week	49
2-8	Responses Received by Degree of Busyness	50
2-9	Responses Received by Whether Library Had Separate Area for Government Documents Reference Service	52
2-10	Distribution of Time Spent on Each Question	54
2-11	Responses Received by Number of Minutes Spent with Patron	54
2-12	Responses Received by Method of Question Delivery	56
2-13	Responses Received by Subject of Reference Question	57
2-14	Responses Received by Class of Reference Question	58
2-15	Reasons for No/Incorrect Answer	60
2-16	No/Incorrect Answers and Referrals by Type of Library	61
2-17	No/Incorrect Answers and Referrals by Geographic Region	62
2-18	Distribution of Sources Used to Answer Questions	63
2-19	Individual Questions by Print or Web Use	65

2-20	Responses Received by Type of Source	66
4-1	Responses Received by Individual Question	102
4-2	Rank Descending Order of Questions that Were Completely Answered	103
4-3	Rank Descending Order of Questions that Received Most No/Incorrect Answers	104

TABLES

2-1	Comparison of Regional Population Distribution and Distribution of Questions	31
2-2	Modified Richardson Coding Scheme	35
2-3	Preliminary Questions Given to Pre-testers	37
2-4	Results of Pre-Tested Questions	39
2-5	Final List of Questions	41
2-6	Impact of Busyness on Type of Answers	51
2-7	Effect of Separate Area on Complete Answers	53
2-8	Method of Question Delivery and Depository Library Types	56
2-9	Comparison of Legislative and Executive Questions Generating Complete or Partially Complete Answers	57
2-10	Referrals	59
2-11	Type of Answer Received by Source	66
3-1	Descriptions of Reference Service Quality	78
4-1	Types of Answers to Individual Questions	102
4-2	Average Time Spent (in Minutes) Finding Answers	105
4-3	Types of Answers Received by Type of Library for CRTC Question	106
4-4	Types of Answers Received by Type of Library for Book Question	107
4-5	Types of Answers Received by Type of Library for Barley Question	109
4-6	Types of Answers Received by Type of Library for Lyrics Question	110

4-7	Types of Answers Received by Type of Library for Fuels Question	111
4-8	Types of Answers Received by Type of Library for Firearms Question	112
4-9	Types of Answers Received by Type of Library for Audgen Question	114
4-10	Types of Answers Received by Type of Library for Crime Question	115
4-11	Types of Answers Received by Type of Library for Magdalen Question	117
4-12	Types of Answers Received by Type of Library for Rules Question	118
4-13	Types of Answers Received by Type of Library for Refugee Question	120
4-14	Types of Answers Received by Type of Library for Garbage Question	121
4-15	Types of Answers Received by Type of Library for Photo Question	123
4-16	Types of Answers Received by Type of Library for Fisheries Question	124
4-17	Types of Answers Received by Type of Library for Africa Question	125
5-1	Resolution of External Referrals by Question	134
6-1	Summary of Most Common Responses by Question	158

PREFACE

This book began as an examination of the quality of government documents reference service at depository libraries, both academic and public, in Canada, as measured by how accurately reference staff answered fact-based questions posed by paid proxies. To say the least, such unobtrusive evaluation of reference service has aroused controversy in the past. Nevertheless, no study about the quality of government documents reference service has been conducted since the early 1980s, when Charles McClure and Peter Hernon evaluated depository libraries in the northeastern and southwestern regions of the United States. McClure and Hernon reported poor results in their study and called for improvements in the education and training of government documents specialists. They made other recommendations as well. Their book *Improving the Quality of Reference Service for Government Publications* generated much discussion in the field.

With the rapid expansion of government publications in the past two decades, I was interested in seeing how government documents reference staff members had coped in the intervening years. Had service levels at government documents reference desks improved? To be sure, a comparison between the United States and Canada is not an exact one. There are differences between these two nations with respect to the publication and dissemination of government documents to the public, yet many aspects of government documents provision are similar.

A total of 488 questions was asked nationwide, from St. John's, Newfoundland, to Vancouver, British Columbia, and including the Yukon. The results reported by McClure and Hernon were, in the main, replicated in this study. The quality of government documents reference service in Canada in the late 1990s was not high. Accuracy rates were low, and many of the staff members with whom proxies spoke were, on the whole, not models to be emulated by other librarians. About one fifth of the questions were referred to external sources, and I made a point of following up these referrals in order to trace the experience of typical users who might be referred to other locations for desired information. Certainly, some library staff were knowledgeable, courteous, and fountains of quick, accurate information. These individuals can only be commended for their exemplary and gracious service, especially in comparison with the majority of their colleagues.

As an outgrowth of the original government documents reference service study, I undertook another unobtrusive study focused exclusively on major public libraries in Canada. The focus of this second study was whether reference staff considered newspapers a rich source of information from which to answer potential reference questions. Questions dealing with important and interesting contemporary news stories were developed and were then unobtrusively asked, by telephone, at large Canadian public libraries. Again, results showed that reference staff had a difficult time providing accurate answers to a variety of questions drawn from popular newspapers. Taken together, these two studies paint an interesting picture of the amount of general and subject knowledge possessed by reference staff working in Canadian academic and public libraries at the end of the twentieth century.

Chapter 1 presents a brief philosophical discussion about some of the implications of unobtrusive reference service evaluation. Why is it the subject of almost virulent criticism? Chapter 2 is an extensive discussion of the results of the unobtrusive evaluation of government documents reference service in Canada. Chapter 3 focuses on the proxies themselves and what they experienced at depository libraries as they asked their questions. What did the proxies, all of whom were library and information science graduate students, think of the service they received? Were they satisfied with the abilities and demeanor of their future colleagues? Chapter 4 examines in detail responses to the questions asked by the proxies. Chapter 5 traces the often sinuous path of many of the referrals proxies received to their original questions. Chapter 6 looks at the value of reading newspapers for library reference personnel through another unobtrusive study of the quality of telephone reference service in large Canadian public libraries. Finally, Chapter 7 offers a series of recommendations for improving the quality of reference service in libraries.

ACKNOWLEDGMENTS

I would like to thank Professor Elizabeth Dolan of the Faculty of Information and Media Studies at the University of Western Ontario for her perpetual kindness and encouragement during the conception, planning, and writing of all parts of this book. She was instrumental in securing the grant that allowed the Canada-wide unobtrusive study of government documents reference service to be conducted, and she contributed a great deal of insight on numerous important issues. The Canadian Depository Services Program, under the very able stewardship of Mr. Bruno Gnassi, provided much of the financial support necessary to conduct a project of this scope. Mr. Gnassi was unflaggingly patient and enthusiastic at every juncture of this work. Ms. Moya K. Mason served as the Research Assistant for all parts of this book. Her ready wit, boundless energy, indefatigable work ethic, and endless patience contributed immeasurably to the completion of this project. I would also like to thank the proxies who asked questions unobtrusively at numerous government documents reference desks across Canada.

On a broader level, Professor and Vice-Provost Roma M. Harris of the University of Western Ontario graciously provided me with the opportunity, space, and time to study and explore many aspects of library work during my years in London, Ontario. She was the very model of a concerned, judicious, and good-humored mentor. I also owe much to Dean Lynne Howarth and the Faculty of Information Studies, University of Toronto, for their collective decision to offer me a teaching position. Finally, I would like to thank the individuals who became my friends during the time I lived in London, Ontario, from 1994 to the end of 1998. All of them were a precious source of fun, comfort, peace and joy, and continue to be so now. We shared much, and I continue to learn from them.

Chapter 1

Reference Service Evaluation and Assessment

In a study of the information-seeking patterns of adults in six New England states, Ching-chih Chen and Peter Hernon (1980) surveyed 2,400 residents and identified over 3,500 information needs. Excluding technical-job related information, organizational relations with supervisors and co-workers, and information about salaries and benefits, people needed information the most about, in order: consumer issues, getting or changing jobs, housing or household maintenance related matters, education, recreation, money matters, and health. Where did people go to get answers to such questions, most of which could be categorized as fact-based? For many, it was not the library. Indeed, the library ranked only ninth on the list, behind such other information sources as: own experience; friends and acquaintances; newspapers or books; someone in a store, company, or business; co-workers; professors, doctors, lawyers, or government officials; and television. Libraries, moreover, ranked fourth among institutional information providers. Among institutional providers, libraries were consulted only 17 percent of the time, while companies or businesses, for example, were used 45 percent of the time and government agencies 27 percent of the time.

Why would libraries rank so far down the list? Chen and Hernon report that 14 percent of respondents said they "didn't think libraries could help," 9 percent stated that libraries "didn't occur to me," and 7 percent noted that "in the past, I could not find what I want/need; assume same to be true in this case." By far the most cited reason, at 26 percent of total respondents, was "didn't need libraries" (p. 60). Valuable as starting points, these categories are somewhat frustrating in their lack of mutual exclusivity. Did individuals who said that libraries didn't occur to them concurrently believe that libraries couldn't help them? Did those who said they didn't need libraries feel that way because they couldn't find anything useful there on previous occasions? In sum, one could very well argue that these four categories could be combined in order to form a broad category labeled "used other sources because libraries, inherently unhelpful, would be the last place to which I would turn." This is, of course, an exaggeration, but one fact remains: many people do not consider libraries to be helpful and useful places to get diverse information. The key question is: why? What are the reasons for the existence of "never-gained" and "lost" patrons of libraries?

POSSIBLE REASONS FOR NOT FINDING LIBRARIES HELPFUL

While no single reason can be discerned with any degree of certainty, Evelyn Daniel (1987) unintentionally suggests why many people may not consider the library a worthwhile place to go when they need their questions answered. Simply put, she argues that answering short unambiguous questions has not had a long history in libraries. Libraries traditionally were not that involved in fact provision, and only began to offer such a service to patrons as an "add-on convenience to referral and provision of bibliographic information" (p. 78). She theorizes that fact provision by librarians could become a thing of the past—a short stay in the history of libraries and destined to be replaced by computer-based expert systems. "Accurate fact provision," she bluntly states, "is not perceived as a major service of the library" (p. 78). However, if people persist in wanting "accurate fact provision" from their local libraries, she proposes that such a service be offered during restricted hours only, thus ensuring that it be accorded the "lower priority" it rightly deserves. "The library might promise 95 percent accuracy in fact provision but only provide this service for a limited number of hours per week—say, three hours on a Wednesday afternoon" (p. 78). Furthermore, libraries should not be too worried about the results of unobtrusive studies showing that librarians do a poor job of answering the type of fact-based questions typically asked during such tests of reference service. Unobtrusive evaluations that necessarily focus on fact-based questions will not cause "much hand-wringing" and will lead to few "action-taking proposals" (p. 78). Daniel's evident scorn for the kinds of fact-based questions that Chen and Hernon's survey respondents had uppermost in their minds is both palpable and troubling, and may explain the reticence of some to turn to the library.

Keith Swigger (1985) thinks that findings such as Chen and Hernon's may be explained by the fact that libraries have traditionally looked upon themselves as storehouses of recorded knowledge and not as storehouses of answers to questions. Traditionally, the focus of collection development practices has been on the intellectual content of individual works. Swigger, however, argues that collection development should be geared primarily toward the actual needs of users for information. Reference questions should be viewed as indicators of community information needs, and collection development therefore must be thought of as "a process of studying users' information needs, including anticipation of future needs, so that those materials will be available that contain answers to questions patrons are likely to ask" (p. 369). Because future reference questions will likely follow the same pattern of topics as past reference questions, collection development policies should be linked more closely to the daily experiences of reference personnel. If reference staff do not have the proper collection tools with which to answer reference questions, the individuals asking those questions may, after repeated failures on the part of staff, become discouraged and turn elsewhere to meet their information needs.

Another answer to why libraries may rank so low as sources of information comes from Mary Jane Swope and Jeffrey Katzer (1972). They asked people who were sitting in the open spaces of an academic library whether they had an information need and, if so, whether they would ask the librarian for help. Forty-one percent admitted to having a possible question, but 65 percent of these individuals also stated that they would not consult with a librarian. When asked for reasons why they would not do so, 42 percent said they were dissatisfied with previous service they had received, 29 percent mentioned that their potential question was too simple for the librarian, and another 29 percent said they did not want to bother the librarian. The figure that stands out from this study is the 42 percent who were dissatisfied with service previously received. Robert Taylor (1968) observes that the decision to ask an information specialist for assistance is based "on the inquirer's image of the personnel, their effectiveness, and his [or her] previous experience with this or any other library or librarian" (p. 182). As Swope and Katzer found, the potential user can be inhibited from asking a question at a library because of past negative experiences or impressions. And even though these concepts are not further defined, they speculate that "through words and actions librarians are reinforcing the user's feelings that he [or she] is a bother or stupid" (p. 164).

KNOWLEDGE LEVEL OF STAFF MEMBERS

Whether staff are knowledgeable about the subject of reference questions, or rather, whether an individual perceives library staff to be competent, may also have an impact on whether a person chooses to approach the reference desk. But what are the factors that make one staff member knowledgeable and another one less so? Jennifer Mendelsohn (1997), in a qualitative study of two librarians and two users, found that knowledge, willingness, and time were most frequently associated with the concept of quality reference service. In addition, "lack of knowledge and time was cited as mitigating against quality service" (p. 546). Both knowledge and willingness were found to be interconnected, and without them, quality service is very unlikely. For instance, a librarian may have the knowledge, but without willingness, nothing happens, just as a librarian may be willing to help, but lacks knowledge to do so. Of course there are many types of knowledge. Mendelsohn lists 11 kinds of knowledge, including knowledge of the collections, knowledge of specific and generic reference sources, knowledge of subject headings and cataloging principles, and knowledge of the kinds of questions that are likely to recur. Nonetheless, she places subject knowledge and general knowledge at the top of her list, and quotes one of her interview subjects as saying that a knowledgeable librarian is one who knows the collections and has subject expertise in the same sort of way as "the baseline for getting an excellent teaching experience from a history professor is that they do in fact know some history" (p. 547). In one sense, subject knowledge and general knowledge include the other types of knowledge mentioned, since subject knowledge implies knowledge of collections, organizational principles of a certain field, and typical reference questions.

Another factor in being a knowledgeable librarian is actively searching for information with patrons. This allows librarians to learn new things every day and to ascertain where they can find the same kind of information for another patron at a later date. If the librarian does not accompany the user, she or he usually does not have any idea whether an answer can or cannot be found in a particular source. Here, willingness cannot be separated from knowledge, as in the example of the librarian who was asked for information about the Skydome in Toronto, Canada. After being led to a combined current affairs and business database and handed an information sheet about how to use it, the patron returned to the desk with only 11 references. As one of Mendelsohn's interview subjects recounts, "now to a reference librarian all kinds of bells and whistles should have gone off. The index was large enough and the topic was a popular enough one that there should have been way more than eleven references." Because this particular librarian just accepted the fact that there were 11 references, the interviewee characterizes her performance as "poor quality service.... That librarian, with the length of service that she had and the experience she had at that desk, should have known that that index ought to produce more than eleven references to the Skydome" (p. 548).

Willingness to learn, to continually update and expand one's knowledge in the course of work and, if necessary, outside of work, thus appears to be a key component of what differentiates a highly competent library worker from a less adequate staff member. But willingness to learn also assumes one or more of the following: that an individual realizes that he or she does not currently have sufficient knowledge to do the job; that an individual realizes that so much information and knowledge is being produced and created that he or she must constantly be in a learning mode; or that an individual realizes that he or she has made mistakes in the past that could have been correctable if she or he had had some additional pieces of information or knowledge about particular topics.

To say the least, it is difficult to admit that one does not possess the requisite knowledge about something, or about many things, or that one has made mistakes. In essence, the fact that one lacks knowledge may, in effect, be viewed as a mistake, since an individual has either (erroneously) assumed that knowledge about Topic X would not be required, or the individual believed that he or she had sufficient knowledge about Topic X when, in fact, this was not the case. Librarians and other library staff are no exception to this most human of qualities. Indeed, professions as a whole are reticent about admitting mistakes, about admitting the lack of knowledge that, theoretically, led to a mistake.

As Lydia Olszak (1991) states, the sociology of making mistakes is quite complicated, and admitting that we make them is difficult for at least two reasons. First, agreement of all parties is difficult to obtain when a mistake has been made. This is particularly true when there is an "us" against "them" mentality found in certain occupations. "Claiming superiority of knowledge and experience, members of a given occupation generally attempt to claim the right to determine if a mistake has been made" (p. 39). By admitting failure, librarians and other professionals are opening up both themselves, and their respective professions, for scrutiny, external judgment, and criticism. A weakened profession may be one outcome of admitting failure. The second reason is just as complicated and has to do with people's reluctance to point out mistakes made by co-workers. Individuals implicitly recognize that pointing out mistakes may not only be a threat to the identity and self-respect of the criticized party, but may engender criticism by others of their own mistakes at some future date.

Much like other professionals, reference librarians have adopted various strategies of "managing" their mistakes. The frequently invoked 55 percent accuracy rate of library reference staff when answering reference questions, Olszak writes, is similar to the rates in other professions. For instance, she quotes an article from the *American Journal of Sociology* that reports that watch repairers have a 50 percent accuracy rate in diagnosing simple watch repairs for their clients.

> An investigation into their behavior suggests that watch repairers often talk their customers into unnecessary repairs and cleanings in exchange for offering customers a one-year guarantee on the repair. While occupational outsiders may believe that such behavior constitutes a mistake . . . this inability to identify and correct a problem accurately is not viewed as a mistake by the repairers themselves. Instead, the repairers view this behavior as a way to establish a business relationship with a new customer. (pp. 40–41)

Olszak's point is that, within all occupations, goals and decisions are made that are not necessarily evident to the outsider. Judging reference efficiency by counting up how many correct answers are given may provide a very narrow view of the entire reference process. Olszak argues that librarians may have an ultimate goal in mind other than the provision of correct answers. For her, these goals are teaching patrons the process of finding information on their own and keeping the amount of time spent with any one patron or question to a minimum. Librarians may conduct themselves at a level that is considered above reproach in the eyes of other librarians, but still not answer a question as correctly as some would like, or to the patron's satisfaction. Much like the watch repairer, they consider themselves to have succeeded when an impartial outside observer would have judged them as having failed.

THE POLITICS OF ASSESSING SERVICE QUALITY

In other words, mistakes are in the eyes of the beholder. The question therefore becomes: By whose standards are service quality and professional competence to be judged? Should the public have something to say about it, or should it be an internal professional matter? In many ways, the issues raised by this question can be seen in the competition between an organization called Consumers Union, publisher of *Consumer Reports,* and J. D. Power & Associates, a research firm that both surveys and ranks individual companies with respect to the amount of "customer satisfaction" their products enjoy. As outlined by Timothy Noah (1999), Consumers Union "might fairly be called one of the most elitist institutions in American life" (p. 42). Its headquarters in Yonkers, New York, "stands as a kind of temple to practical science [with] its 50 laboratories housing testing machinery fussed over by white-coated scientists and technicians" (p. 44). Through stringent tests designed to simulate regular and frequent usage patterns, these "dispassionate experts" test, evaluate, and rank every possible consumer product, from shoes, to dishwashers, to tires, to computers, to breadmakers. Rankings are based on measurable criteria such as number of mechanical failures per 1,000 rinse cycles or the degree of hydroplaning for new tires. J. D. Power & Associates, on the other hand, relies on customer satisfaction surveys of competing products and services. Here, the public is the final arbiter of quality and distinction, thus allowing J. D. Power to claim that its role is "to be the public—that is, to be an accurate mirror of opinions that the public already holds" (p. 45). Moreover, J. D. Power has established minimum sample sizes for each rated product—for instance, 250 customer responses per car model—while Consumers Union buys only a few samples off the shelf and then puts these through rigorous tests.

Whose opinion is worth more? Each method of evaluation has its virtues and drawbacks. Can technicians and scientists come to any conclusion about how products are used in the real world by creating artificial, often exacting, test conditions that may never be replicated by actual users? Do consumers really know the technical details of each product they purchase? Who fills out the questionnaires? Are they filled out by people who are relatively indifferent "to the subtle benefits of one consumer product or service as compared with another" or are they "the same folks who go through life sending their steak back because they wanted it medium well, not medium?" In either case, surveys become skewed: "people who care too much about being satisfied customers don't necessarily have a tighter grip on reality than people who care too little" (p. 44). On the other hand, it was J. D. Power's survey of the first thousand buyers of Mazdas equipped with the new Wankel rotary engine that not only revealed that "one in five Mazdas that had been driven more than 30,000 miles experienced major engine trouble," but also sounded the death knell of the rotary engine as an automotive innovation.

Whom to trust? A sample of consumers with subjective impressions based on widely varying personal experiences, or measurable standards and tests which can be used to compare one product or service with another? By its very nature, the sample of consumers is disparate: Each person has bought a particular product for a different reason, has different expectations with regard to its performance, and will probably put it to different uses. Satisfaction will therefore vary accordingly. For example, if, coming out of our office building one afternoon, an individual suddenly and unexpectedly finds that it is raining heavily, she or he may purchase an inexpensive umbrella at the corner store, knowing full well that it will likely keep her/him from getting wet while walking to the fast-food restaurant up the street, but that it will not be serviceable much beyond that. Expectations are reduced, the quality of the umbrella is low, but the individual is satisfied nonetheless insofar as he/she did not get soaked during the lunch hour.

LEVELS OF EXPECTATION

In the library world, the question of expectations has only tangentially been addressed. What do patrons have a right to expect when they ask a question? One approach to this issue lies in examining what patrons think about the individuals whom they see working at library. Numerous studies have shown that patrons simply do not know who, among the staff, is a professional librarian or who is a paraprofessional. Patricia Dewdney and Catherine Ross (1994), for instance, report that only 15 of the 72 proxies involved in their study knew whether they had been helped by a librarian or a clerk. Mary Tygett, Lonnie Lawson, and Kathleen Weessies (1996) found that students in an academic library complained about not being able to distinguish between professionals and paraprofessionals. Joan Durrance (1989) asks "[h]ow long must the library user interact with an unidentified library staff member at a desk that may not even be marked and that only sometimes identifies the type of occupant and even less often its specific occupant and virtually never indicates their credentials" (p. 36)?

The satisfaction level with service received depends on what a patron or customer gauges the qualifications and skills of the person dispensing the service to be. In the absence of any identifying signs or tags, and without any clear notion of the educational or expertise level of librarians, patrons may assume that the most visible tasks of library work—circulation and reshelving—are the defining components of the job descriptions of all library staff. And because, often, pages, students, and paraprofessionals are hired to fill front-line positions, library users, unconsciously, may get the fuzzy notion that the educational requirements needed to hold a job as a library worker are not very high. As a result, their expectations about the level of service they should be receiving may decrease. With lower expectations, any amount of help from library staff, even the most general or merely directional, is highly appreciated. Libraries who rely on surveys showing high levels of user satisfaction as an indication that they are serving their customers well may be getting the wrong picture.

Consider the following statement from one of Mendelsohn's (1997) interviewees about service at an academic library: "I'm reluctant to say that quality service is just when the student feels satisfied, because you can satisfy some people with a lot less than you know you can give them. I mean it's quite spooky actually when you think about it. . . . Students use what you give them. And if you give them anything they're satisfied" (p. 549). It is important, therefore, not to define quality service in terms of the satisfaction level of the student on leaving the reference desk, because that student is not aware of "what the possibilities are," if they have been given "the right things, the best things," or merely something that is most convenient or less taxing for the librarian (p. 549). In this example, a professional librarian has skimped on the service that, theoretically, could have been provided. The patron goes away happy, but what happens three months later, for example, when the patron discovers, on her own, a treasure trove of sources on the exact question she asked at the reference desk three months ago? What will this patron think now of the service she received then? Disappointment might be tinged with a little bit of anger, and she may file away in the back of her mind, for future use, the notion that library staff are not as competent as she originally thought, that they are not to be relied upon in crucial situations. The cycle leading to lower expectations has begun. However, what happens when patrons with high expectations about the skill level of librarians and knowledgeable about their professional training ask questions at library reference desks? The standard against which the received service is measured becomes necessarily more exigent. Expectations are higher; after all, the user knows that he or she is dealing with a professional who has undergone graduate-level training.

In the competition between Consumers Union and J. D. Power & Associates, each side criticizes the other for the perceived shortcomings of its methodological approach. But what if it could be possible to combine the best of both worlds? That is, if people knowledgeable about the mechanical and technical intricacies of products or knowledgeable about the complex factors, requirements, and relative difficulty involved in delivering a particular service (the "white-coated scientists and technicians" of Consumers Union) could be surveyed to the extent that J. D. Power & Associates surveys the general public?

THE VALUE OF UNOBTRUSIVE PROXY-BASED EVALUATION

From one perspective, unobtrusive testing by library and information science students acting as proxies who ask questions designed to elicit the knowledge and accuracy levels of library reference staff fulfills the above condition. They know what competent librarians *should* be able to do; they know what they themselves are trained to know and to accomplish during their course work in graduate-level programs. To be sure, their demands and expectations are high, partly because they have been asked to do much during their own university years, but also partly because they understand that to be an information professional at the beginning of the 21st century, when the infrastructure of local, national, and transnational economies is heavily dependent on knowledge and information exchange, is to be an important and vital part of social and technological progress.

In general, reference staff should take it for granted that expectations are high, and they should welcome evaluation that, theoretically, allows them to display their acquired skills. A study by Vicki Coleman, Yi Xiao, Linda Bair, and Bill Chollett (1997) on service quality shows just how high expectations of patrons are with regard to the skills they expect of library staff and the disappointing reality of the service received. One of the dimensions of service quality they measured was "assurance," defined as "the knowledge and courtesy of employees and their ability to convey trust and confidence." Three of the four questions that comprised this dimension speak directly to reference desk workers: (a) employees who instill confidence in customers; (b) employees who have the knowledge to answer customers' questions; and, (c) assuring customers of the accuracy and confidentiality of their transactions. Survey respondents were requested to indicate a minimum service level, a desired service level, and the actual service level of the library studied for each of the above aspects. In order, the desired levels of service, on a 10-point scale, were 7.5, 8.4, and 7.9. The minimums were, again in order, 5.6, 6.7, and 6.3. The actual scores on these three aspects for the library in question were consistently below or just barely above the minimum scores, thus revealing a significant gulf between the desires of patrons and their lived experience. In other words, knowledge and accuracy, and the confidence in one's own skills that knowledgeable and accurately delivered service in the past confers on library workers in the present, are very important for patrons in library interactions, especially in reference work. But patrons, at least in this library, are not getting what they deem to be important.

Studies such as this one offer evidence that there should be nothing wrong with testing for the ability to answer reference questions knowledgeably and accurately, as a means of measuring service quality and customer satisfaction. If patrons expect high levels of knowledge and accuracy from library staff, including reference personnel, what better way to measure the competence of reference staff than by testing a key component of their daily work? Shortcomings in their knowledge and skill levels can be identified, and work can be started to try to improve accuracy and knowledge levels. If staff can't answer short, fact-based, unambiguous reference questions accurately and knowledgeably, if they aren't willing to explore further why a patron, for example, only retrieved 11 citations for a common topic such as the Skydome in a major business and current affairs database, what are they doing working at a reference desk? Unobtrusive reference testing is a valid measure of both knowledge and accuracy, even if it is confined to the type of unambiguous fact-based questions library staff say is a very small part of their total work load at reference desks. I mention the Skydome question here for a specific reason. Some library personnel may argue that they get more Skydome type questions, that is, questions where patrons want broadly based information about a certain topic, than short, fact-based questions. But the Skydome question can also be construed as a fact-based question. What if the user asks for "*all* the citations to Topic X in Database Y" because she is doing a content analysis of the portrayal of Topic X in the media covered by Database Y? Is the librarian who gives the patron an information sheet about how to search Database Y and then, when the patron returns to say that she only found 11 citations, remarks that "[w]ell, if that's what it says there are, then that's what there are" (Mendelsohn, 1997, p. 548) providing knowledgeable and accurate service? My point here is that all questions, on some level, are fact-based questions. To be sure, some take longer to answer than others, some involve more steps than others, some are more ambiguous than others, but, at the end of the day, patrons are seeking knowledge from the mass of assembled facts present at, or accessible from, the library.

Thus, when Thomas Childers (1987) criticizes unobtrusive reference evaluation for not being robust enough to take into account questions such as "Can you help me prepare a comprehensive bibliography . . . on genetic engineering?" or "Can you give me an idea of what distinguishes Theatre of the Absurd from other kinds of drama?" (p. 74), he is missing the point. The answers to these questions involve starting with unambiguous facts, then, if necessary, expanding outwards. At each stage of outward expansion, another series of unambiguous questions may arise. Take the example of the genetic engineering bibliography. The patron may, at some point, decide that additional citations about the bioethical aspects of genetic engineering are required in order to make the bibliography truly comprehensive. She then can return to the reference desk and ask another unambiguous question about the types of sources and databases and web sites she should be looking at in order to find out detailed information about such ethical issues. On some occasions, the fact, or discrete piece of information, is itself knowledge; at other times, knowledge has to be distilled from, or chained together from, facts and information, broadly conceived. In either case, a patron's search begins with the presence of facts that have been unambiguously inscribed and stored, whether in a book, in a database, on a video or CD, or on web sites. Unobtrusive evaluation studies typically based on short-fact based unambiguous questions should not be cavalierly dismissed; rather, they should be an alert to staff and management that there is something seriously wrong with reference service provision.

THE POLITICS OF CUSTOMER SATISFACTION STUDIES IN LIBRARIES

John Budd (1997), however, objects to the focus on customer satisfaction and service quality in assessing the worth of libraries, arguing that such emphasis conceals a disturbing tendency to emphasize "the exchange value of libraries and their services" to the detriment of "embracing use as a value of libraries (that is, a human purpose or utility underlying the thing) . . ." (p. 313). Simply put, libraries are focusing on customer service not because they care for the customers *qua* customers, but because customer service is "worth something material to the library." The library's service becomes "a means of garnering a larger piece of the budgetary pie" rather than being an end in and of itself (p. 313). Thus, the satisfied customer or consumer is "sometimes seen as a source of material gain for the library" (p. 314). As John Budd and Douglas Raber (1998) discuss further, unambiguous and quantifiable measures of performance, because they "sustain an unexamined certainty regarding the purposes, methods, and results of the evaluation mechanisms," create the library in the image of a "machine, equipped with governors that can regulate its performance" (p. 70). The application of performance standards to library service, and the positioning of these standards as a means to better serve the customer, masks the actual goal of libraries, which is "instrumental gain through the potential increase in resources that customer satisfaction can lead to" (p. 74). On this reading, quantifiable measures have very little place in the assessment of libraries, because such measures have the unintended consequence of commodifying knowledge to the extent that, following Jean-François Lyotard, "knowledge is and will be produced in order to be sold [and] it is and will be consumed in order to be valorized in new production" (Budd, 1997, p. 320; Budd and Raber, 1998, p. 60). Knowledge thus loses use value and assumes only exchange value.

What commentators such as Budd overlook are the very real library patrons who make use of reference services on a daily basis. As Brenda Dervin (1992) has shown, each of these individuals may be thought of as experiencing a gap in her or his understanding of a particular situation, whether intellectual, psychological, emotional, practical, or recreational. They have a discontinuity in their knowledge about something, and they are unable to continue on their journey of achieving knowledge without obtaining "gap-bridging" information (p. 68). The knowledge gap functions as a barrier to further progress in a desired direction. For all intents and purposes, they are "stopped." According to Robert Taylor (1968), the individual goes through three stages of information need: the visceral level, defined as a vague sense of having need of information; the conscious level, where the individual is able to mentally form a picture of the need, but is still unable to articulate it clearly; and the formalized level, where the need is presented in a coherent fashion to an intermediary. Being "stopped" may take a number of forms, and Dervin (1992) employs transportation metaphors to differentiate these various "stops." For instance, there is a decision stop (a choice needs to be made between two or more options), a problematic stop (a person, having chosen one path, discovers that the chosen path is not the right one), a spin-out stop (no road to follow), a wash-out stop (a person travelling on a road finds that it has suddenly disappeared), and a barrier stop (someone or something has blocked the chosen road) (p. 75). No matter the kind of "stop" experienced by the individual, it creates a knowledge gap that must somehow be bridged. After having experienced one of Dervin's "stops" and after having gone through Taylor's visceral and conscious levels, the individual may reach out for help to a library reference desk. Individuals in any of these stopped situations have real needs, real aspirations, and real hopes of finding solutions to their unique dilemmas. If they had no such hope, why would they bother going to the library in the first place? Moreover, this sense of hope is embodied in the person at the reference desk. Patrons want to use any information, or "gap-bridging" knowledge, that they may be given to help solve their difficulty, to take steps toward a final resolution of their problematic circumstances.

In effect, Budd wants to dismiss the unique human element from the reference encounter. He forgets that each reference question comes with a complex history and, often, a psycho-social context that is fraught with bewilderment, emotional uncertainty, confusion, and pain. Accurate and knowledgeable reference service may be the first step to alleviating such bewilderment and situational difficulty by giving the patron a useful start and a bridge toward even more useful information, but inaccurate and ill-informed service will do nothing to help the patron toward problem resolution. Accurate reference answers are therefore very much used in some way; they become invaluable pieces of information that allow the individual to move forward in some aspect of his or her life, or to reach a point where a better question can be formulated. To use Dervin's (1992) terminology, reference staff may be instrumental in a series of "helps" that can assume such diverse forms as initiating a new idea or a new way of looking at things; offering a sense of direction; assisting in the development of a new skill; regaining control; moving out of a bad situation, obtaining support, comfort, or reassurance (p. 75). Carol Kuhlthau (1993), moreover, sees the librarian as a counselor who establishes, with the patron, an ongoing dialogue "that leads to an exploration of strategy and to a sequence of learning" (p. 144). Typically, the dialogue may be reformulated, redefined, and nuanced throughout the many stages of the information-seeking process, as librarians "facilitate understanding, problem solving, and decision making" (p. 188). Reference staff who provide inaccurate information make no contribution to helping people achieve their disparate goals; in fact, they may be hindering the gap-bridging process, since the patron will no longer have confidence in the ability of the library worker to help effectively. Seen from this perspective, evaluating reference service through unobtrusive testing and quantifying accuracy rates is something that should be done on a regular basis by libraries who understand the complex human dimension behind each reference question, no matter how simple and straightforward it may seem at first.

FACT-BASED, UNAMBIGUOUS REFERENCE QUESTIONS AS SURROGATES

Evaluating library performance by testing reference accuracy rates through proxy-administered unobtrusive questions serves another purpose. It allows the fact-based "ready-reference" question to function as a surrogate for a more in-depth knowledge of various subjects. In the fall of 1999 during the extended Republican and Democratic primary campaigns, George W. Bush, the 2000 Republican Presidential candidate and son of former President George Bush, was asked to name the leaders of four countries: Chechnya, India, Pakistan, and Taiwan. Bush was only able to name one of them, thus raising questions about his grasp of international affairs. Predictably, his performance was analyzed, re-analyzed, and then analyzed again. On the one hand, some commentators decried the "gotcha" journalism of the Boston television reporter who asked Bush the question; editorial writers pointed out that the "kind of quiz-show questioning" Bush was subjected to "offers little chance for illumination" about his ability as a future president. On the other hand, there was real concern that Bush might become president. Susan Buchman (1999) remarked that "[t]he saddest part of all this is that Mr. Bush could have sailed through the questions if he had taken 30 minutes to memorize the names of some world leaders, but apparently he is not willing to make even the most superficial attempt at understanding world affairs." Daphne Philipson (1999) was disappointed that Bush "appears to have no empathy for the places in question and no apparent interest in their future and how they could affect the citizens of the United States." Maureen Dowd (1999), observing that the questions asked were "not trick questions about obscure spots like Burkina Faso . . . [or about] the difference between Iran and Irian," wrote that, if Bush "had been reading the newspapers closely the last few weeks, he could have aced his quiz. India and Pakistan were central to the recent debate on the nuclear test ban treaty, and India's prime minister . . . has been in office a year and a half. Chechnya [has] long [been] one of the diciest pieces of the crumbling Soviet empire." For Dowd, Bush's stumble not only showed him to be "willfully clueless" and behind in his homework, but also as someone who really "doesn't care about the gaps in his knowledge," perhaps feeling that such questions are beneath him.

Why are the trials and tribulations of George W. Bush relevant for library reference staff and methods of reference assessment? As mentioned previously, one of the reasons many librarians disparage unobtrusive proxy-based evaluations is that, according to them, only the most simplistic, not to mention artificial, questions can be asked in such circumstances. Such questions, they continue, cannot fairly be used as a basis of evaluation because, for the most part, they do not represent the type of questions reference staff answer, and in no way should be taken as representative of their knowledge and ability. The types of questions they deal with are, instead, more source based, more along the lines of "where would I look for topic X?," or "could you help me find something on topic Y?" In broad terms, this is exactly what Bush's spokesperson told the media: "For the American people . . . the relevant question isn't how many names of foreign leaders a candidate knows, but whether he has a strategic vision for America's role in the world." Don't ask me fact-based ready-reference questions, ask me about the "big picture!"

But the spokesperson's comment is revealing in an unintentional way, given Bush's attempt to talk his way around the fact that he couldn't remember the name of Pakistan's leader. "The new Pakistani general, he's just been elected—not elected, this guy took over office. It appears this guy is going to bring stability to the country and I think that's good news for the subcontinent." From one perspective, Bush's lack of knowledge about the name of General Pervez Musharraf is a synecdoche for his lack of awareness of larger geopolitical issues. His statement does not build confidence in his ability to handle complex situations. So it is too with library reference personnel who are unable to answer ready-reference questions. Their failure in this respect does not augur well for their ability to assist patrons with more substantive questions, nor does it instill confidence in patrons to ask questions, whether simple or complex. As Peter Hernon and Charles McClure (1987) note, if reference staff members can answer factual questions accurately only 55 percent of the time, "what degree of accuracy can be expected for questions requiring in-depth analysis. . . ?"(p. 70).

Bush's inability to name international leaders is instructive for librarians from another vantage point. After the jokes died down, commentators such as Thomas Friedman (1999) began to urge Bush to demonstrate knowledge about substantive and pressing foreign policy questions. As Friedman remarked, citizens may very well forgive Bush for not keeping the names of international leaders in his head at all times, but they have a right to know "how he feels about these countries in his gut. We have to know if *that* tank is empty too" [original emphasis] (p. 15). In other words, his failure on simple questions has engendered suspicion that he does not have a very clear grasp of larger issues. Friedman therefore proposed 10 questions Bush should be asked, ranging from his views on the best way to engage China to whether the United States should "intervene in regions where our interests are ambiguous, but the human tragedy is unambiguous," to his views on promoting democracy in Saudi Arabia and Egypt and the extent to which NATO should be expanded.

Not surprisingly, Bush himself realized that he needs to know more about international affairs. One aide recalled Bush telling him "I've got to take some questions given to me by people who are pretty good at it and get dirtied up a bit." To this end, Frank Bruni and Eric Schmitt

(1999) report that, "for more than two hours on Monday afternoon, and then again on Monday night, and then again on Tuesday afternoon," Bush's leading advisors and aides tutored him on world trouble spots such as Russia, China, North Korea, and Iraq. Their avowed goal was Bush's "ongoing education" about international affairs. Among his staff, there was a palpable sense of urgency, since each knew that "the scrutiny given to Mr. Bush's words on this topic would only intensify over the next few pivotal days and weeks." Background information to each of Friedman's 10 foreign policy questions was provided, and his advisors were encouraged when Bush displayed inquisitiveness: "Some people can ask you the first question, but I was more impressed when he asked a follow-up and another and another. . . . He's honing his views." In addition, Bush revealed that he now reads four newspapers every day: *The New York Times*; *The Wall Street Journal*; *The Dallas Morning News*; and *Austin American Statesman*.[1]

Certainly, the position of a librarian is nowhere near that of a presidential candidate in terms of public exposure and overall responsibility, but the situation experienced by Bush is replicated, on a smaller scale, on a daily basis in libraries all across North America. Patrons ask millions upon millions of questions each month at reference desks, many of which are of the ready-reference kind. After a short period where each person is given the benefit of the doubt, library staff who cannot answer such questions may become less trusted by patrons. Staff have two choices. They can do nothing and carry on as before or they can, quite literally, take the Bush approach: study, read more, and learn more. It can only be hoped that they choose the latter avenue. If they do, poor results on proxy-administered unobtrusive evaluations at library reference desks may have a salutary effect because they may encourage librarians to make concerted efforts to improve their in-depth knowledge, so that the embarrassment of having to say "I don't know" to a ready-reference question is something that will happen only rarely, if at all, in the future.

IMPROVING THE INTELLECTUAL ENVIRONMENT

Durrance (1989) challenged librarians "to consider altering [their] environment with the aim of increasing reference success and creating an environment that better serves the public" (p. 36). The term "environment" should be thought of in the broadest terms possible. First, it should encompass the intellectual environment. Each library staff person should constantly be asking herself or himself such questions as: What did I do today to improve my skill and knowledge level so as to better serve potential reference patrons; did I browse my own reference collection; did I discover something new; did I read about something that may prove useful to me in my work; did I improve my knowledge about an area in which I knew very little before? If patrons never receive service that they consider to be exemplary from reference personnel, they either grow accustomed to low service levels, or they stop asking questions and rely on their own skills. Recall that in the study conducted by Swope and Katzer (1972), 65 percent of those interviewed said they had a question to ask, but would not approach the librarian with it.

The standards library reference staff set for themselves are the cornerstone by which the public will judge library service, whether academic or public. To be sure, striving to make personal improvements in one's own general knowledge about diverse subject areas is a solution that does not take into account the numerous structural and systemic factors that may inhibit the delivery of quality reference service, but it is a solution that has the psychological virtue of not blaming other forces, often beyond the control of the individual, for problems, shortcomings, and failures. If even a small portion of the energy expended analyzing and complaining about external factors affecting library work were directed towards self-improvement and a firm dedication to meeting respectfully and completely the informational needs of reference patrons, no matter how complex, arcane, or seemingly impossible, library staff may discover that a better rate of success at the reference desk increases self-respect, which may lead to a concomitant increase in one's sense of professionalism.

THE NEED FOR PERSONAL RESPONSIBILITY

Accordingly, one of the main benefits of unobtrusive testing is that it allows librarians, individually and collectively, to debate and define what it means to be a professional, what it means to provide good service. If, on the one hand, a professional is satisfied with, or rationalizes, a 55 percent or lower success rate in doing something she or he is specifically trained to do, then the entire profession suffers from the myriad consequences such acceptance entails. Librarians may as well start thinking of themselves as watch repairers. This is not to criticize watch repairers. It is merely to point out that librarians should not be surprised if the public accords them the stature of watch repairers—essentially technicians—rather than highly educated information professionals. If, on the other hand, low success rates are perceived as early warning signs and as an impetus that could lead to significant improvements in the skill levels of staff and service delivery, thus improving success rates in the future, unobtrusive testing will have fulfilled its function. The debate about the utility and appropriateness of unobtrusive reference testing is really a discussion between those who do not wish to challenge themselves personally to take individual responsibility for improving service in their own library and those who, despite the many obstacles in their way, wish to do so.

Improvement in reference service in libraries must be seen as an incremental process, one library staff member at a time. The profession is only as strong as its weakest link. If each librarian acts to improve herself or himself locally, then global, structural changes will become that much easier. President George Bush (1989–1992) was, in certain circles, castigated and mocked for his "thousand points of light" slogan, yet the essence of his thinking has applicability for librarians, as it does for other professionals, including teachers. If each individual strives "to be all that he or she can be," to become one of the thousand points of light, the resulting network of improved librarians and libraries, teachers and schools, will be its own testament to the validity of such an approach. Certainly, one can laugh at the pastiche of clichés and advertising slogans in this paragraph, smirk at the naïveté of the writer, argue that library work is much more than the provision of unambiguous facts at reference desks, and conclude that it is impossible for each library worker to know something about everything and to be a walking encyclopedia; yet by doing so we implicitly convince ourselves that positive change is beyond our means and ability to effect, that personal commitment and hard work will not ameliorate the quality of service delivery at reference desks. At best, this is a defeatist attitude, one that accepts the status quo, argues that nothing much can be done given present circumstances, and is essentially self-serving and egotistical—self-serving because increasing one's knowledge level about a variety of subjects takes time away from potentially more pleasurable activities, and egotistical because it suggests that one's current level of knowledge is sufficient.

The real question is: Why should librarians and reference paraprofessionals stop wanting to improve their general knowledge of history, bioethics, or contemporary art, to name only a few possible topics of interest? Librarians should be voracious acquirers of a broad array of subject knowledge. They should be constantly reading print materials, exploring Web sites, making notes about what they find, always thinking about how the heterogeneous bits of information and data they come across could be of potential use to the next person making an inquiry at the reference desk. Library workers may object that they already take upgrading courses, that they are great believers in the concept of continuing education. But, as Margaret Stieg (1980) noted, the over-reliance on formalized continuing education courses "can provide illustration of librarianship's worst faults: a mindless borrowing from other subjects and professions without proper understanding; an eagerness to do something just because it is different; and a tendency to make means ends in themselves" (p. 2551). While she admits that there are some virtues to continuing education courses, she also makes it clear that they can never be a substitute for private reading and study, or for time spent in a university setting pursuing "a year of graduate study in the liberal arts and sciences" (p. 2551). Not everyone can afford the time or expense to undertake "a year of graduate study," but the habit born of constant reading, simply for the sake of reading and discovering the heretofore unknown, can bear immeasurable fruit on a daily basis, especially at a busy reference desk.

In one sense, librarians should strive to become what Harlan Cleveland (1985) calls "the knowledge executive." Cleveland was thinking about business and government leaders, not librarians, when he coined this phrase, but what he considers to be one of the most vital characteristics for successful executive leadership has thought-provoking applicability to librarians. The best leaders, Cleveland writes, are the generalists, those individuals who "get-it-all-together" (pp. 1–18). After plumbing the depths of their specific branch of knowledge, they can become "knowledge executives" because of their ability to make connections between disparate fields. They realize, too, that "it's not mainly our capacity to dig out facts, but rather the educated intuition and practical experience to arrange them in meaningful patterns" that is most valuable. Still, the executive leader, or knowledge executive, is "very likely to be unsuccessful unless he or she has, earlier in life, been a first-rate specialist" (p. 11). That is to say, unless he or she has dug out facts. Cleveland approvingly quotes from *A Bibliography on America for Ed Dorn* (1964) by the American poet Charles Olson.

> Best thing to do is to dig one thing or place or man until you yourself know more about that than is possible. . . . It doesn't matter whether it's Barbed Wire or Pemmican or Paterson or Iowa. But exhaust it. Saturate it. Beat it. And then U KNOW everything else very fast: one saturation job (it might take 14 years). And you're in, forever.

Of course, leaders do not stop learning and accumulating new general knowledge once they have reached the executive stage. They must constantly be asking questions, talking with people, reading books, making connections, accumulating new information so that they will maintain their position as leaders. For librarians, "knowledge executive" is an appropriate description, since they work in an institution that does, indeed, purport to bring diverse facts together, to "get-it-all-together."

But if librarians are to become "knowledge executives," a heightened sense of responsibility for one's own work performance is called for, in much the same way that being a high-level business executive calls for constant attention to one's own continuous development and personal growth. The key point is, as Olson puts it, to have knowledge about one thing, not so much for the fact of knowing about that one thing, but because it allows the individual, from that point forward, to acquire general knowledge about other things very quickly, to start down the road of becoming the "get-it-all-together" type of person praised by Cleveland. As librarians evolve into "knowledge executives," it is imperative that they constantly strive to expand their subject knowledge as much as possible. While they are not responsible for the growth of a particular business, they are responsible to all the people in their community, who look to librarians and the library as a source of opportunity, personal growth, and problem resolution.

THE HISTORY OF FACT-BASED REFERENCE SERVICE

Daniel (1987) was of the opinion that ready-reference assistance did not have a long history in libraries and should not be a main focus of library work. Samuel Rothstein (1953), however, points to the example of the Providence Public Library (PPL) in Rhode Island as evidence that reference service providing a wide range of help was a central part of a library's mission as early as the 1890s. In 1890, William Foster, the head of PPL, petitioned the trustees to create a position specifically devoted to reference service. "One of the most pressing needs of the library," Foster wrote, "is the appointment of a regular clerk whose distinct business it shall be to answer questions on special subjects . . . [because] few can adequately conceive to what extent the inquiries made at the library have become specialized and require trained facility and research, and time to devote to it" (p. 14). As Rothstein shows, Foster's conception of reference service had, by 1890, evolved from an earlier model, where librarians provided "reference lists" and assistance primarily as "a means of raising reading tastes" (p. 13). By 1891, Foster had convinced the trustees to open an "information desk," and in 1892 he remarked that the information desk has "gradually becom[e] the center of the library's life; a favorite resort for the reader who is perplexed in his search for some elusive material, and who is sure of finding here interested and intelligent assistance; the natural starting point of the reader who comes with the purpose of pursuing as thoroughly as possible some line of investigation" (p. 15).

By juxtaposing Foster's statements in 1892 about the importance of the reference desk for finding "elusive material" with Daniel's (1987) disdain for "accurate fact provision" (p. 78), it is possible to see why Chen and Hernon (1980) discovered that the library was only the ninth most likely place a person would seek information. Daniel claims that librarians are, and should be, doing more important work than mere fact-retrieval. This attitude supposes that fact-retrieval is not to be considered interesting work, that librarians have moved beyond the mere looking-up of facts. Or, it could suggest that she knows that accurate fact-retrieval is difficult, that the 55 percent reference accuracy rate paints a true picture, and in order to protect the image of librarians, it is necessary to dispense with the "add-on convenience" of fact-provision service. Either way, Daniel does not see the patron from the perspective of Dervin (1992) and Kuhlthau (1993). Instead, she sees patrons and users as so many impediments to a smoothly functioning library, to be shunted aside into a special three-hour time slot on Wednesday afternoons where "accurate fact provision" will be offered. The unintended implication is that, during all other times, inaccurate fact provision is the norm.

But if libraries are not in the business of providing answers to ready-reference questions for patrons, what are they in the business of doing? Each question, whether ready reference or not, has a tangled personal history attached to it and emanates from a situation where a person is at a loss about how to move forward. How can the librarian presume to judge that one question is a mere fact-based one to be treated lightly and without much consideration, while another question or problem calls for the application of more sophisticated skills, which, in essence, legitimize it as a worthy question to be entertained and worked on by library personnel? Yet, to the individual asking, no question is a simple one. One explanation for Chen and Hernon's (1980) findings may therefore be that people needing information know intuitively that library staff are not that interested in helping them with their very real problems.

Foster, however, observes that the individuals staffing his information desk were intelligent and interested in finding "elusive material" for a never-ending stream of patrons. Of course, an objection may be made that Foster's definition of "elusive material" does not include fact-based reference questions. We will never know for certain, but let us suppose, for the sake of argument, that Foster's librarians and clerks did answer fact-based ready-reference questions as part of the "elusive material" they found for patrons. What qualities did they possess that made the information desk at the Providence Public Library a very busy and important place? Foster mentions two characteristics: intelligence and interest. In this regard, it is useful to compare an early reference handbook, James Wyer's (1930) *Reference Work* with William Katz's (1982)

Introduction to Reference Work from the standpoint of what each says about the most important mental traits for librarians. In 1930, Wyer listed intelligence, accuracy, judgment, professional knowledge, and dependability as the top five mental traits for a librarian. "Interest in work" was in tenth place, "mental curiosity" was twelfth, and "interest in people" was thirteenth. In 1982, Katz, in his introductory subsection entitled "The Reference Librarian," opted to mention only professional knowledge, judgment, speed, imagination, and perseverance as the five important mental traits for reference librarians (Richardson, 1992, p. 81). Certainly, Katz would no doubt agree that all 28 traits listed by Wyer are important for reference work in some degree, but, from the discourse analysis perspective recommended by Bernd Frohmann (1992), his choice of five traits is revealing, especially because of what is not there. The characteristics of intelligence and interest that both Foster and Wyer held in high esteem are not present; neither is Wyer's second highest quality of accuracy. These omissions are suggestive of a shift in the priorities of library educators and librarians—a shift that may, in some significant, though little understood way, be correlated with the 55 percent accuracy rate in reference work. This is not to say that librarians are no longer intelligent, accurate, and interested in their work or the people they serve. It is merely to observe that these mental traits may no longer be considered as vital as they once were, for reasons having to do with the evolution of the profession and the rapid growth of knowledge and information sources. Yet, if current library and information science educators emphasize, through their syllabi, teaching strategies, and attitudes, the top five mental traits as put forward by Katz (1982) without giving significant attention as well to Wyer's (1930) list of necessary characteristics, they may be training a generation of librarians who are not unduly concerned about their lack of general and subject-specific knowledge and who are confident that their "professional knowledge" will be sufficient to provide high-quality reference service. Such librarians may find it difficult to improve on the 55 percent accuracy rule. If, throughout the 21st century, librarians want to assume a key place in the information economy and be true "knowledge executives," it may be well to reflect on the similarity between Cleveland's top two mental traits and the characteristics that Foster and Wyer found indispensable for good librarians. For Cleveland, they are a genuine interest in people and intellectual curiosity, defined as "self-induced continuing education" (pp. 161, 165). In other words, he is not so very far from what Foster and Wyer identified as key characteristics for librarians, but he is far from what Katz identified as the most important trait.

Cleveland speaks, too, about the importance of having a sense of personal responsibility for one's work, of understanding how one's knowledge, or lack thereof, can affect the organization of which one is a part as well as others beyond the organization. For reference librarians, having a sense of personal responsibility for one's job means understanding how important it is to keep up with general knowledge in all its manifestations, because a patron walking in the door tomorrow or three months hence may need to know just that piece of news or information you, as a librarian, read or heard about last night, last week or last month. Having a sense of personal responsibility toward one's place of employment means understanding how disappointing it is to admit that only 55 percent of the time does a customer or patron walk away from the reference desk with an accurate answer, and trying to do something, on a personal level, to raise that rate. Of course, knowing everything is impossible. Still, as Cleveland maintains, "it is still a healthy ambition to be *interested* in everything" [original emphasis] (p. 164). For librarians, there can be no better way to assume personal responsibility for the quality of their work and their contribution to their organization and community than by being "interested in everything," by having the kind of familiarity with a broad range of subject areas that can only be gained through daily sustained reading and careful study of a multiplicity of print and electronic sources.

NOTE

1. Kristoff, Nicholas D. (2000, March 3). Rival Makes Bush Better Campaigner. *The New York Times*, A15.

Chapter 2

Government Documents Reference Service in Canada

Unobtrusive evaluation studies concerning the efficacy of library reference service have consistently shown that librarians are able to offer complete and satisfactory answers to patrons about 55 percent of the time (Hernon & McClure, 1986) and that five variables (library expenditures, volumes added, fluctuations in the collection, size of the service population, and hours of operation) "reveal a consistent moderate association with reference accuracy" (Saxton, 1997, p. 281). However, only Charles McClure and Peter Hernon (1983) have focused on the unobtrusive evaluation of government documents reference service. Their study examined academic libraries located in the northeastern and southwestern regions of the United States. Results indicate that library staff members answered government documents questions with an overall accuracy rate of 37 percent. Reference staff in the Northeast did considerably better than reference workers in the Southwest; the former answered questions correctly at a rate of 49 percent, while the latter did so only 20 percent of the time (p. 35). Question delivery that occurred by phone was more successful than in-person questions. In the Northeast, for instance, phone questions were answered correctly 64 percent of the time, while in-person questions achieved a 35 percent success rate (p. 37). This lower success rate for government reference questions may reflect the more specialized and difficult nature of the subject matter.

Hernon and McClure received a great deal of criticism for their unobtrusive study. These criticisms are summarized in Hernon and McClure (1987), and range from the contention that correctness alone is not an adequate gauge of service quality, to the objection that the sampling frame of 17 libraries was too small, to the concern that the questions were too difficult or unrepresentative, that there was no guarantee that it was a professional librarian who fielded the query, and that proxies were instructed to act in too passive a manner (pp. 165–167). Joan Durrance (1989) and David Tyckoson (1992) argued that a more qualitative approach to evaluation of reference services was needed, one that would take into account the often complex interaction between librarian and user by concentrating on behavioral aspects of the reference process. The results of such studies have suggested that reference success rates are much higher than the 55 percent rule. For instance, June Parker (1996) reports a 72.3 percent satisfaction rate, while Carolyn Jardine (1995) points to a 99 percent success rate, as measured by whether the patron would return to the same library staff member with another question.[1] Patricia Dewdney and Catherine Ross (1994) also used "willingness to return" as a measure of success in reference interviews, but, unlike Jardine, found that 40.3 percent of the proxies would not be willing to return. Their study thus seems to be in agreement with the research stating that patrons receive incorrect information 45 percent of the time. "It seems that no matter which outcome measure is used—accuracy, user satisfaction, or willingness to return—and no matter what type of library is observed, reference service is still not meeting the goals of effective information service in 40 to 45 percent of cases" (p. 223).

Patricia Hults (1992) notes that studies that explain low success rates by pointing to the complex nature of librarians' job responsibilities "beg the question" because what the library community "really needs to address" is the question of whether a 55 percent accuracy rate "is acceptable [and] if not, what priority do libraries place on improving that rate" (p. 143). She observes that many public and academic libraries have adopted policies in which unobtrusive testing of the service provided by reference staff is a vital part of self-evaluation studies. Certainly, there are many ways to evaluate the quality of reference service, but "accuracy of information . . . seems the baseline to work from" (p. 143). Ellen Altman (1982) goes even further, arguing that the dismal results uncovered by unobtrusive studies "call into serious question the quality of information services currently provided" (p. 174). Who, she asks, would trust a doctor "who could affect a cure for only half of the patients," or an accountant whose work was audited "as defective" half the time by the Internal Revenue Service? Libraries, she concludes, have a responsibility "to render a service equal in quality to what we expect to receive from other professional groups" (p. 175). Simply stating that any perceived problem is "much more complex" than at first sight fails to recognize that any benefits of a service "cannot occur if elements in the delivery system break down along the way." Accordingly, if librarians are "not willing to accept measures that can point up deficiencies as well as the strengths of our information services, then we should have the integrity to stop discussing measurement and evaluation" (pp. 181–182).

Peter Hernon and Ellen Altman (1998) point to a study of Fortune 1,000 executives indicating that "accuracy was the most important factor in determining service quality." In a library setting, they argue, key measures of accuracy are whether "shelves are regularly read for misplaced or hidden books," whether "items returned are discharged properly so that customers are not charged fines," and whether "answers to reference questions are correct and complete, which means that the library must ensure that information about current situations is kept up to date" (pp. 176–177). Hernon and Altman maintain that statistics about patron satisfaction should therefore be understood through the prism of work conducted by Katharine Johnston (1996), who suggests that "customers who are merely satisfied with a company or service [are] in a zone of indifference toward a continuing relationship with company or service" (p. 7). Libraries should thus try to avoid a situation where "library performance is poor and expectations are low, but customers appear indifferent or satisfied (Hernon & Altman, 1998, p. 15). Hernon, Nitecki, and Altman (1999) stress that customer satisfaction and overall service quality should not be confused. The former is a "transaction-specific . . . short-term measure [that] focuses on a personal emotional reaction to service," while the latter is a long-term measure relating to the expectations not only of actual customers, but also "lost customers" and "never-gained" customers" (pp. 11–12).

Accuracy, in other words, is a key component in evaluating library service quality. Unlike the analysis of other aspects of the reference procedure such as question negotiation, search strategies, and subject analysis, unobtrusive testing emphasizes the user's perspective and can offer useful insights into the quality of service provided to library patrons (McClure & Hernon, 1983, p. 11). Among the benefits of unobtrusive testing identified by F.W. Lancaster (1977) are the following: Staff members are observed under operating conditions assumed to be normal; the success with which staff members answer various types of question can be measured; and there is an opportunity to make conjectures about the reasons for incorrect answers (pp. 77–136). Hernon and McClure (1987) note that 22 unobtrusive evaluations of reference service were conducted at various types of libraries between 1968 and 1986. Since 1986, Hults (1992) reports that many public and academic libraries have adopted policies in which unobtrusive testing of the service provided by reference staff is a vital part of self-evaluation studies. Vanessa Czopek (1998) describes how a public library in California took advantage of a "mystery shopper" service offered by the local chamber of commerce to aid businesses in evaluating service quality.[2]

BACKGROUND AND PURPOSE OF RESEARCH

Governments at all levels are rapidly moving to the electronic dissemination of official information through Web-based protocols. By the end of 1997 and early 1998, many departments and agencies had already achieved impressively successful results in transferring their documentation to electronic supports. The United States and Canada have been leaders in implementing digital access to government publications (Aldrich, 1998; Beamish, 1999; Clausing, 1999; Farrell, Davis, Dossett, & Baldwin, 1996; Ryan, 1997). Systematic examination of the readiness of federal depository libraries to effect a smooth transition to electronic formats is essential if the public is to benefit from rapid, cost-effective, and timely availability of a profusion of rich resources. To this end, in the fall of 1996, the Depository Services Program (DSP) in Canada funded the first extensive examination of the state of readiness of depository libraries in Canada to adopt new electronic technologies. Elizabeth Dolan and Liwen Vaughan (1998) and Vaughan and Dolan (1998) reported and analyzed the results of a project to investigate the technological capabilities and related services required by depository libraries to provide permanent public access to Canadian federal government information in electronic form. The study was conducted through a self-administered questionnaire that was sent to all full and selective depositories in Canada and abroad in order to collect both quantitative and qualitative data. Results of this work indicate that while a majority of the libraries surveyed consider official publications to be very important or essential parts of their collections, depositories are severely pressed by the demands of developing new methods of handling documents in electronic form, providing help to patrons in the use of the new technologies, and meeting the associated costs. Respondents to the survey acknowledged the potential of the Internet for timely access to government information, but expressed reservations in the following areas: inadequate bibliographic control and archiving, the threat of inequitable access if fees for service are imposed, the transfer of publishing costs from the government to libraries if they are expected to download and print documents available only on the Internet, and the demands of staff training and costs of maintaining and replacing equipment. The study also found a significant degree of uncertainty among depositories about the future use of government information when it is available primarily in electronic form. Recommendations were made for further study of related issues, among them the nature of adequate reference service associated with collections of official publications. In late 1997, the DSP funded a second inquiry, this time focusing on the reference process in Canadian full and selective depository libraries.

Effectiveness in providing accurate answers to reference queries is a central element in the provision of public access to official information. This chapter reports on the results of an unobtrusive examination of reference encounters carried out in full and selective depository libraries in all five geographic areas (Atlantic Provinces, Québec, Ontario, Prairie Provinces, British Columbia and the northern territories) of Canada. Full depository libraries, of which there are 48 in Canada, automatically receive all publications listed in the *Weekly Checklist* of Canadian government publications. Typically, full depositories are located in public libraries in large urban centers and in major academic research libraries. Full depositories have the financial and staff resources to house, maintain, and provide professional access to federal government information. The 754 selective depositories in Canada choose items they wish to order for their collections from the *Weekly Checklist*. Selective academic libraries are typically located in undergraduate university libraries and in community college institutions, while selective public depositories are typically located in smaller urban centers. This chapter reports on the first unobtrusive study of government documents reference service since McClure and Hernon (1983) and Hernon and McClure (1987), the first nationwide evaluation of government reference service in Canada, and the first to be conducted in an age of electronic government information provision.

For this investigation, 15 government document-related questions were developed in order to elicit the following information:

- the accuracy of the answers;
- the extent to which library staff used electronic sources, especially the web;
- the degree to which staff members engaged in referral;
- the types of questions that tended to be referred;
- the effect of asking questions over the telephone;
- the value of separate government document reference desks; and
- the level of knowledge of official sources and expertise in using them displayed by the librarians and other staff members to whom the queries were addressed.

The test questions cover major categories of Canadian federal documents of interest to various sectors of the public and were modeled after actual queries, such as those compiled by the Inquiry Desk of the Transport Canada Library and Information Center (Canada, 1986).

The purpose of this study is to investigate how well library staff in Canadian federal depository libraries answer government documents reference questions and whether they are using Internet-accessible and Web-based sources to do so. The key research questions are:

- What is the degree of accuracy of government reference service in Canadian academic and public libraries that participate in the Federal Depository Services Program, as measured by the number of complete answers supplied by library personnel to specific questions?
- To what extent do staff members in these libraries use electronic information sources such as CD-ROMs and the range of Web sites made available by the Canadian federal government?
- Which categories of government reference questions are the most difficult to answer for library staff personnel at depository libraries?

While there are legislative libraries with full depository status in most provinces, public access to government documents is most readily achieved through public and academic libraries. Accordingly, the research questions developed for this study were examined through the lens of four categories of Canadian depository libraries: academic full depositories, academic selective depositories, public full depositories, and public selective depositories.

METHODOLOGY

This study was conducted using paid proxies. Quality of reference service was operationally defined as the percentage of complete or combined complete and partially complete answers to 15 government documents questions. Selection of tested libraries was based on a proportionally stratified cluster sample. On the first level, proportional stratification was effected on the basis of the five geographic areas of Canada. On the second level, clusters of cities and towns within the geographic areas were identified, and a convenience sample of public and academic depository libraries was taken to reflect the proportion of these libraries in the depository system as a whole. Fifteen questions were asked 488 times at 104 libraries in 30 metropolitan census areas as defined by Statistics Canada. Each proxy package consisted of 15 different questions and a brief survey form. Proxies were recruited from students enrolled in a Masters of Library and Information Science (MLIS) program at a major Canadian university. Questions were asked from December 10, 1997, to February 10, 1998—a period during which many students traditionally return to their hometowns for the holiday season.

Questions asked in each of the five geographic areas reflect approximately the population distribution of Canada as determined by the 1996 Census. Seventy-five questions (15.3%) were asked in the Atlantic region; 105 (21.5%) in Québec; 165 (33.8%) in Ontario; 90 (18.5%) in the Prairie Provinces; and 53 (10.9%) in British Columbia and the northern territories. In order to ensure complete national coverage, questions were asked in *each* province and in at least one of the territories. As a result, the Atlantic and Prairie regions are slightly over-represented. Atlantic Canada is over-represented not only because of the inclusion of libraries in Prince Edward Island, but also because Moncton, New Brunswick, was chosen as a test site to take into account the demographic reality of a francophone population outside of Québec. Consequently, British Columbia, Ontario, and Québec are slightly under-represented in relation to their national population percentage. Table 2-1 shows the extent of this under- and over-representation.

Since the sampling frame was confined to public and academic libraries that make up 88.9 percent of the total number of depositories, the proportion of questions asked was made to conform approximately to the proportion of public libraries and academic libraries, respectively, within the sample. Public libraries make up 50.8 percent of Canadian federal depositories, academic libraries constitute 38.1 percent, and legislative libraries make up the remainder.[3] Thus, 296 questions (60.7%) were asked at public libraries, while 192 questions (39.3%) were asked at academic libraries. Some 49 percent of the questions were asked at public selective depositories, while 26 percent were asked at academic

Table 2-1
Comparison of Regional Population Distribution and Distribution of Questions

	% of National Population	% of Questions Asked	Under- or Over-Representation
Atlantic	8.1	15.3	+7.2%
Québec	24.7	21.5	−3.2%
Ontario	37.3	33.8	−3.5%
Prairies	16.6	18.5	+1.9%
BC/North	13.2	10.9	−3.3%

full depositories. Put another way, 38 percent of the questions (186 questions) were asked at full depositories (public and academic), while about 62 percent (302 questions) were asked at selective depositories (public and academic).

Since there are 790 depository libraries in Canada, of which only 48 enjoy full depository status, the study disproportionately concentrates on full depositories. But because full depositories, whether public or academic, tend to be concentrated in major population centers, they are accessible to a large percentage of the total Canadian population and thus provide good indicators of the type of reference service that is available to a significant number of Canadians. Conversely, many of the public selective libraries are in small towns, and often do not opt to carry a wide range of official publications.

The choice of cities to which proxies were sent was based on the 25 most populous metropolitan census areas as defined by Statistics Canada in the 1996 Census. In selecting cities, the following factors were taken into account: the availability of student proxies who were traveling to their hometowns over the holidays, the presence of a full depository library in those 25 most populous census metropolitan areas, the fact that a geographical distribution that approximated the regional diversity of Canada was required, and the necessity of asking questions in all provinces and in one of the territories.

In total, proxies were sent to 30 different metropolitan census areas. Twenty-three of those areas were among the 25 most populous metropolitan census areas as reported by the 1996 Census. The three largest centers were assigned two proxy packages each. Smaller centers were assigned one half of one proxy package. And, in order to include at least a few small public selective depositories, two students whose holiday itineraries would cause them to travel between two major metropolitan centers were asked to make stopovers at some of the public selective libraries in towns on the path between the two major centers. In total, 10 questions were asked at such small public selective depositories. The populations contained in these metropolitan census areas include 61.8 percent of the total population of Canada. Of the total 488 questions, 105 were asked in metropolitan areas having over 1 million inhabitants; 80 were asked in metropolitan areas having a population between 500,000 and 999,999; 75 were asked in areas having a population between 250,000 and 499,999; 172 in metropolitan areas with between 100,000 and 249,999; and finally, 56 questions were asked in those areas with a population of less than 100,000.

Fifteen government documents questions were developed and tested before they were given to the proxies. McClure and Hernon (1983) established 20 different types of United States government documents for their unobtrusive study. Some of these types are: statistics, administrative reports, directories, maps, bills, laws, regulations, debates, agencies/boards, and periodicals. Fifteen of their categories were chosen and adapted where necessary to suit the Canadian context. Appropriate questions were then developed for the present study. All questions could be answered using either print or Web-based sources. Five questions were designated as phone questions, while the remaining 10 questions were in-person questions.

In addition, the questions were divided into two groups: one dealing with documents emanating from the legislative branch of government (i.e., bills, statutes, debates, and parliamentary procedure) and one pertaining to those produced by the executive branch (i.e., departmental reports, statistics, directories, and periodicals). Questions were also classed according to whether they dealt primarily with data retrieval or document retrieval. Although recognizing the fluid nature of almost all reference questions, Katz (1996) writes that this is "[a] useful method of distinguishing types of queries" (p. 18). Data-retrieval queries are those for which individuals ask "specific questions and expect answers in the form of data." Document-retrieval queries are those for which patrons "want information, not just simple answers," and the information is "usually in the form of some type of document" (p. 18).

Proxies were provided with printed forms containing one reference question each. A full proxy package consisted of 15 reference question forms. Information about whether the question was an in-person question, telephone question, a legislative branch question, or an executive branch question was printed on the form. In addition to providing the reference questions themselves, the forms asked the proxies to supply some answers about selected institutional variables and question variables. Institutional variables included the type of depository library and whether it had a separate area or desk designated for government reference service. Question variables included day of the week and time of day when the question was asked, time spent by library staff member with proxy, and the degree of busyness at the reference desk where the question was asked. Whenever proxies received an answer, they were asked to state as fully as possible the answer itself and the source used to provide it. Moreover, even if they did not receive an answer or were referred, proxies were asked to write down everything that happened during the reference interview. Proxies did not know the correct answers to the questions that they asked. This was a conscious decision taken in order to simulate as closely as possible a real situation in which a reference question would be asked by a member of the public.

Proxies were recruited during the late part of November 1997 in order to take advantage of the traditional holiday season when many students travel to their various hometowns. It was not possible to recruit proxies from MLIS students for several selected cities with full depositories. In these cases, students were asked to contact friends or family members residing in those identified cities, and to ask them if they would be willing to participate in the study. A $200 honorarium was paid for the completion of each proxy package. A training session was held in December 1997, when the proxies were provided with extensive instructions about all aspects of the study. Proxies unable to attend the training session were provided with detailed written instructions about the purpose, conduct, and procedures of the study. Each proxy was provided with a complete set of printed question forms and a list of libraries at which the questions were to be asked. Beside each named library on this list was a library type designation—whether the library in question was an academic full depository, an academic selective depository, a public full depository, or a public selective depository. Proxies were repeatedly told *not* to indicate the actual name of the visited or telephoned library on their question forms; rather, they were merely to indicate the *type* of library at which each question was asked. Any questions that the proxies had about the nature of the study were discussed and answered in order that proxies understand clearly what they were expected to do. Stress was put on the importance of providing as completely as possible the source of any answer to each reference question, whether it was a CD-ROM product, a book, or a Web address. Proxies were told that they could visit or telephone the library on any day of the week and at any time of the day of their choosing between December 10, 1997, and February 10, 1998. To preserve institutional and individual anonymity, there was no linkage of specific test sites with results. The issue of informed consent and debriefing was addressed through a message sent by the DSP to the directors of all depository libraries.

A research assistant entered the data. For most items, such as constitutional region, day of week question was asked, and time spent with patron, data entry was straightforward. Particular attention, however, was paid to coding for the *type* of answer the proxies received in response to each question asked. The primary reason for this was that the proxies merely recorded whether they received an answer; they did not record whether it was a complete or incorrect answer. The coding scheme adopted for this study is a modified version of a grid developed by John Richardson (1998), itself a modification of Ralph Gers and Lillie Seward (1985) and Chery Elzy, Alan Nourie, F.W. Lancaster, and Kurt Joseph

(1991). Richardson's definitional descriptions were retained, but his evaluation levels were reworked and simplified into four categories. Richardson's categories of "excellent" and "very good" were collapsed into the category of "complete answer;" his categories of "good" and "satisfactory" were collapsed into the category of "partially complete answer;" his category of "fair/poor" was retained intact, but was renamed "referral." Finally, Richardson's bottom three categories of "failure," "unsatisfactory," and "most unsatisfactory" were categorized as "no/incorrect answer." Table 2-2 summarizes the modifications.

Of interest, too, was the location to which a proxy was referred. Types of referral were coded as follows: another non-government library; government or legislative library; government department; external non-government agency or establishment. Data were entered into an electronic file (Microsoft Excel, Version 7), and charts were generated in various versions of Microsoft Excel. Results of statistical analysis are reported in aggregate form only.

Many of the results of the study are analyzed and reported so that separate figures are provided for "complete answers" and for "complete or partially complete answers." This reflects the two types of reference service identified by Katz (1982) and described as "liberal" and "conservative." A liberal philosophy of reference service is defined as one in which the librarian "give[s] the greatest amount of help to people" and where it is understood that "[t]he primary function of a reference librarian is

Table 2-2
Modified Richardson Coding Scheme

Coding	Definition
Complete answer	Referred to single source, complete and correct answer OR referred to several sources, one of which gave complete and correct answer.
Partially complete answer	Referred to single source, none of which leads directly to answer, but one which serves as a preliminary source OR referred to several sources, none of which leads directly to answer, but one of which serves as a preliminary source.
Referral	No direct answer; referred to external specific source or person or institution.
No/Incorrect answer	No answer; no referral (I don't know) OR referred to single inappropriate source OR referred to several inappropriate sources, none of which answers question correctly.

to answer questions [by] giving total service." A conservative philosophy, on the other hand, is characterized by a librarian who "points rather than assists," that is, showing the patron a possible direction and path, and then leaving the patron to locate the final answer (pp. 32–33). Results designated "complete answers" reflect the liberal approach to reference service, while those termed "complete or partially complete" exemplify the conservative philosophy.

A preliminary list of 32 questions was developed and tested by two students enrolled in an MLIS program. The students were approximately halfway through the program; both students had some knowledge of Web sources and Internet searching skills. One student (Student A) was enrolled in a Government Documents course; the other (Student B) had never taken such a course. The reason for this procedure is as follows: One criticism levied against McClure and Hernon (1983) was that their proxies did not know whether the people to whom they talked at library reference desks were government documents specialists, generalist reference librarians, or paraprofessionals. McClure and Hernon felt that this criticism was unfair. After all, members of the public do not know about the distinctions between library staff members, nor inquire about them at the reference desk. Patrons simply want their questions answered. To take into account criticisms about this aspect of the McClure and Hernon study, questions were chosen that could be answered by individuals who had had special training in government documents as well as those who had not had such special training. The students were told they could use either electronic or print sources to find the answers to these questions; each chose the Internet. In order that the project not take them away from their schoolwork for an overly long period, they were advised to spend no more than 15 minutes searching for the answer to each question. This preliminary list of questions is shown in Table 2-3.

Results shown in Table 2-4 indicate that Student A found the answers to 26 out of 32 questions (81.3%), while Student B found 23 answers (71.9%). Both found all their answers in Web documents. For the 26 questions that Student A answered completely, the average time spent researching each question was five minutes. For the 23 questions that Student B answered completely, the average time spent on each question was 8.2 minutes. The high success rate of the students in finding complete answers to these questions in relatively short periods showed that almost all of these questions could be answered by *all* library personnel, no matter their level of specialization in government sources.

The choice of the final 15 questions to be used during the study

Table 2-3
Preliminary Questions Given to Pre-testers

1. Who is the Chair and who are the other full-time members of the CRTC (Canadian Radio-Television and Telecommunications Commission)?
2. What is the cost of *Aboriginal Self-Government* by Jill Wherrett, published in 1996?
3. Where can I find the government publication that lists forgotten bank accounts?
4. I'd like to get a copy of the bill that says criminals can't profit from books they may write about their crimes.
5. What did Preston Manning say in Parliament in response to the Speech from the Throne?
6. Can you help me find the regulations attached to the Canada Student Loans Act?
7. I'd like some government figures about circulation and sales of Canadian magazines, or What is the percentage of French lyrics in Canadian-content sound recordings for 1990–1994?
8. I'd like to see the 1997 Commons committee report on draft regulations on firearms.
9. I'd like to get the text of the act that talks about unconventional fuels.
10. I'd like ordering information and price lists for an aerial photograph of our cottage and lake.
11. Who chaired a Royal Commission on Newspapers in the 1980s?
12. How many total workers went on strike in Canada in the 1950s?
13. I'd like a copy of the statement made by the Foreign Affairs Minister this fall about the treaty banning land mines.
14. Has Health Canada produced a fact sheet on electromagnetic fields?
15. Has anything been said in the House of Commons about closing the marine radio station on the Magdalen Islands?
16. I'd like the list of everything the Senate did for all its sessions in October 1997.
17. What are the rules for oral questions in the House of Commons?
18. What are the export sales for electricity for Québec in the 1980s?
19. Did the Auditor General say something about forest management practices of natives in the 1992 report?
20. Are there any contracts for work hauling garbage for the federal government?
21. I'd like to see the evidence from December 11, 1996, of the House of Commons subcommittee on sustainable human development.
22. What are the names of all the members of the House of Commons born outside Canada?
23. Where can I rent artworks from the government for my company offices?

continued

Table 2-3 (*continued*)

24	I'd like to know about river drainage into Hudson Bay for about the past 30 years.
25	I'd like some information about an application filed by the Bank of Montréal in 1995 before the Competitions Tribunal.
26	Who were the witnesses that appeared before the Senate Committee on Legal Affairs when it had hearings in 1996 about changes to the names of electoral districts?
27	What were the final payments per bushel of No. 2 Canada Western Amber Durum Wheat for 1995–96?
28	Is there an official document about the possibility of immigrating to Canada because of gender persecution?
29	Did the Senate Special Committee On Euthanasia say anything about palliative care?
30	I'd like the committee minutes for the first 25 meetings of the House of Commons Standing Committee on Canadian Heritage in the 35th Parliament.
31	Are there any regulations attached to the Fisheries Prices Support Act?
32	Does the government publish any newsletters or bulletins about business opportunities in Africa?

depended on two factors. First, there had to be as close to a statistically normal distribution as possible with respect to the time needed to answer the questions. Second, a broad cross section of types or categories of government questions, as defined by McClure and Hernon (1983), was felt to be desirable. Seven of the questions could be answered in less than 10 minutes; five questions could be answered in a period of time ranging from 10 to 14 minutes; and only three questions required more than 15 minutes to answer.

As shown in Figure 2-1, the curve is very close to being normal, with a mean of 9.26 minutes, a median of 10 minutes, and a modal value of 10 minutes. In other words, the mean time spent answering these questions by the two student pre-testers was a little over nine minutes. Twelve of the 15 questions were completely answered by both student pre-testers; two questions were answered by one of the pre-testers; and only one question was unanswered by both students. Table 2-5 presents the final choices for the 15 questions. Questions 1–5 were telephone questions, while questions 6–15 were in-person questions.

The column labeled "Type of Question" provides three pieces of information. First, it indicates the specific type of government document in which the answer can be found; second, it indicates whether the ques-

Table 2-4
Results of Pre-Tested Questions

Question	Did Student A Find Right Answer?	No. Minutes Spent by Student A	Did Student B Find Right Answer?	No. Minutes Spent by Student B
1	Yes	2	Yes	2
2	Yes	15	Yes	10
3	Yes	2	No	Time out
4	Yes	5	Yes	15
5	Yes	3	Yes	5
6	Yes	5	Yes	5
7	No	Time out	Yes	11
8	Yes	15	Yes	15
9	Yes	5	Yes	5
10	Yes	2	Yes	13
11	No	Time out	No	Time out
12	No	Time out	No	Time out
13	Yes	5	Yes	10
14	Yes	15	Yes	2
15	Yes	5	Yes	15
16	Yes	2	Yes	5
17	Yes	3	Yes	4
18	No	Time out	No	Time out
19	Yes	3	Yes	4
20	No	Time out	No	Time out
21	Yes	5	Yes	10
22	Yes	2	Yes	10
23	Yes	1	No	Time out
24	No	Time out	No	Time out
25	Yes	4	Yes	5
26	Yes	2	No	Time out
27	Yes	15	Yes	5
28	Yes	5	No	Time out
29	Yes	2	Yes	15
30	Yes	2	Yes	15
31	Yes	10	Yes	1
32	Yes	5	Yes	8

tion deals with the executive arm or legislative branch of government; and third, it classifies the question as to whether it is primarily a data- or document-retrieval question. To be sure, historical questions are not included here, but a number of questions about government services were included. Questions 2 and 13 deal with ordering various govern-

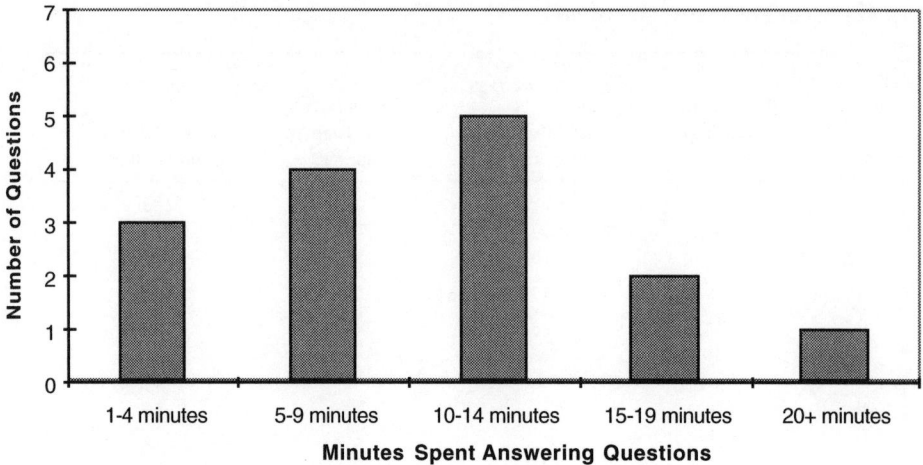

Figure 2-1 Frequency Distribution of Relative Difficulty of Questions Measured in Minutes

ment products, while questions 12 and 15 deal with employment and business opportunities.

LIMITATIONS

One limitation of this study derives from the fact that each depository library did not have an equal and independent chance of being selected for inclusion in the study. *All* public full depositories and academic full depositories in Canada, with the exception of one, were visited by proxies for the purposes of this study. The inclusion of many public selective and academic selective libraries in the sample therefore depended on the presence of a full depository library in a particular census area. Random selection of depository libraries therefore did not take place. However, the sampling frame was large and national in scope; external validity is therefore present. Another limitation stems from the fact that there was little control over the exact wording used by individual proxies asking questions at various reference desks. While they were told in each case to stress that questions were government related and to ensure that they mentioned all key concepts in each question, it is logical to expect that there were differences in emphasis from one proxy to another when individual questions were asked. As McClure and Hernon (1983) noted in their study, "it is possible that proxies failed to provide accurate renditions of the test questions" (p. 22). Proxies were also instructed, during phone questions, to systematically ask for a source. This may have

Table 2-5
Final List of Questions

	Type of Question	Short Name	Full Wording of Question	Avg. No. Minutes Spent by Pre-Testers
1	Directory; Executive; Data	CRTC	Who are the Chair and other full-time members of the CRTC (Canadian Radio-Television and Telecommunications Commissions?	2
2	Bibliography; Executive; Data	Book	I want to order a copy of *Aboriginal Self-Government* by Jill Wherrett, published in 1996. I'm sure it's a government document, and I specifically want to know how much it costs and any ordering instructions.	12.5
3	Agency or Board Report; Executive; Data	Barley	I'd like to know what the total payments were per bushel of barley for 1995–1996? Specifically, I'm interested in the category "select two-row" of designated barley.	10
4	Statistics; Executive; Data	Lyrics	I'd like to know how many new Canadian-content sound recordings (albums, tapes, CDs) released during 1990–1994 have French lyrics?	15.5
5	Statute; Legislative; Document	Fuels	I'd like to get the text of the act that requires crown corporations to power their motor vehicles with fuels that do not harm the environment. How many of their vehicles have to use these non-conventional fuels?	5
6	Committee Report; Legislative; Document	Firearms	There was a Parliamentary sub-committee on the draft regulations on firearms that submitted a report to the House of Commons in January or February of 1997. I'd like to see a copy of this report.	15
7	Administrative Report; Executive; Document	Auditor-General	I'd like to know if the Auditor-General said something in the 1992 annual report about forest management practices of natives, specifically about the good job done by the Stuart Trembleur Lake Band.	3.5
8	Bill; Legislative; Document	Crime	I'd like to see a bill that was introduced into the House of Commons this past fall. It has to do with the profits convicted criminals might make if they were to publish books about their crimes.	10

Table 2-5 (*continued*)

	Type of Question	Short Name	Full Wording of Question	Avg. No. Minutes Spent by Pre-Testers
9	Debates; Legislative; Document	Magdalen Islands	I'm doing a class project about the Magdalen Islands, and there was talk about closing the marine radio station there. I'd like to know if anything was said in the House of Commons about this topic in the last year, and if anything has been decided about its fate.	10
10	Procedures; Legislative; Document	Rules	I'd like to know the complete set of rules that govern Question Period in the House of Commons.	3.5
11	Admin Guidelines; Executive; Document	Refugee	I want to know if there is any official document about the possibility of immigrating to Canada as a refugee because of persecution based on gender.	12.5
12	Contracts; Executive; Data	Garbage	Someone I know is looking for work hauling garbage. Would there be any specific opportunities to put in bids for contracts in this field with the federal government?	20+
13	Maps; Executive; Data	Photo	My mother's birthday is coming soon, and I want to order a color enlargement of an aerial photograph of the lake where my parents have their summer cottage as her present. Could I have a price list for the enlargements, and information about what I need to do to order such a photograph?	7.5
14	Regulations; Executive; Document	Fish	Can you help me find any regulations or enabling statutes associated with the Fisheries Prices Support Act?	5.5
15	Periodicals; Executive; Document	Africa	Does any government department put out any newsletters or bulletins about business opportunities in Africa? If so, I'd like a copy of the latest one.	6.5

been seen as an uncommon request by some staff members, although none of the proxies reported problems in this area.

McClure and Hernon (1983) and Hernon and McClure (1987) have carefully and thoroughly established the validity and reliability of unobtrusive testing in measuring the quality of documents reference service.

Yet some scholars argue that fact-based questions of the type used in unobtrusive studies account for a small proportion of the total number of reference queries. Childers (1987) suggests that queries with factual and unambiguous answers make up only about one eighth of the volume in reference departments. In an obtrusive study of five northern California libraries, Jo Bell Whitlatch (1989) found that factual questions were only asked 11.3 percent of the time at reference desks, while bibliographical questions were asked at a rate of 18 percent and subject/instructional questions were asked 70.7 percent of the time. The success rate for factual questions in this study was 78.6 percent; for bibliographic questions and subject-instructional questions, the success rates were 70.5 percent and 62.6 percent, respectively. Compiling the results of 71 Wisconsin-Ohio Reference Evaluation Program surveys, Marjorie Murfin (1995) found that fact-based transactions represent 21 percent of all in-person reference questions at academic libraries and 18 percent at public libraries (p. 235).

The choice of time period in which to ask the questions could also be faulted. Levels of expertise may be reduced during the holiday season, since key staff may have priority in release time over this period and thus may not be available for desk duty. On the other hand, holidays may be taken at any time during the calendar year, and so there does not exist a perfect time to conduct a study such as this one. Indeed, the December-January holiday season may be less busy than usual at libraries—a circumstance that might provide more time for staff members to answer reference questions.

One of the central issues in this study deals with the extent to which depository libraries are able to cope with reference questions by using the Internet. Queries requiring the use of retrospective sources were not included since most Web documents have been produced very recently. This explains the absence of historical questions. Relationships between, on the one hand, institutional variables (e.g., budget, collection size, staffing, and education levels of staff) and, on the other, success in answering proxy-administered questions, were not explored. Information of this kind could lead to the collocation of unique data. Instead, each of the four types of depositories are roughly characterized by a general institutional profile. As mentioned previously, public full depositories are in large public libraries in large urban centers, and thus typically have large budgets and extensive professional staffs. Full academic depositories are typically located in major research universities. Selective academic depositories are located in smaller undergraduate universities or community colleges, while public selectives are located in public libraries in less-populated urban centers.

RESULTS

Overall Accuracy Rate

Proxies were not given instructions about the day of the week or the time of day when they were to ask questions. Yet the distribution of questions across the week (Monday to Saturday) is relatively uniform. Proxies asked 14 percent of their questions on Monday. As shown in Figure 2-2, the peak times for questions were Tuesday, with 20 percent of the total, and Wednesday, with 18 percent. On Thursday and Friday 14 percent and 12 percent of the questions, respectively, were asked, while on Saturday, 17 percent of the questions were asked. By far the lowest percentage of questions, only 5 percent of the total, was asked on Sunday. Just over two thirds of the questions (67.8%) were asked in the afternoon (331 questions), while about a quarter of the questions (23.2%) were asked in the morning (113 questions). Only about 9 percent of questions were asked in the evening (44 questions). The skew towards afternoon questions may not represent typical usage patterns.

On the other hand, because many libraries have staggered shifts for their professional staff, librarians may work a regular 9:00 A.M. to 5:00 P.M. shift one day, but an evening shift of 1:00 P.M. to 9:00 P.M. the following day. Thus, the optimum time to ask a reference question would seem to be in the overlapping afternoon period. Budget cuts in the past several years have occasioned cutbacks in the number of weekly hours public libraries are open to users, and some public libraries have elected to close on alternating weekday evenings and weekday mornings. For both of the above reasons, optimum access times for reference questions may be in the afternoon. The fact that over two thirds of proxy questions

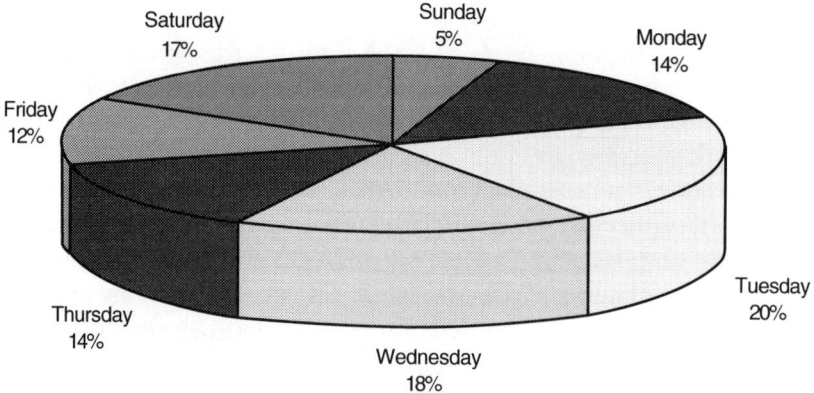

Figure 2-2 Daily Distribution of Questions

were asked during this afternoon period offers confidence about the validity of the results.

Complete answers were provided to 29.3 percent (143 questions) of the 488 questions. When complete and partially complete answers are taken together, reflecting the conservative philosophy of reference service, the success rate climbs to 42.4 percent (207 questions). Library staff referred 20 percent (98 questions) of the 488 questions. No answers or incorrect answers to questions were received 37.5 percent of the time (183 questions). Figure 2-3 displays the results.

Type of Depository and Geography

While the overall rate of complete answers was 29.3 percent, there were statistically significant differences among the four types of depository libraries ($\chi^2 = 29.13$, df = 9, $p < .01$, Cramér's $\varphi_c = .141$). The highest rate for complete answers was achieved by academic full depositories, at 39.4 percent (50 out of 127 questions). Public full depositories provided complete answers 32.2 percent of the time (19 out of 59). Academic selective depositories performed at 29.2 percent (19 out of 65), and public selective depositories lagged behind, with 23.2 percent (55 out of 237). When complete and partially complete answers are taken together, academic and public full depositories show an almost identical rate—51.2 percent (65 out of 127) and 50.9 percent (30 out of 59), respectively. Both types of selective libraries also gave either complete or partially complete answers at about the same level of success—37.1 percent

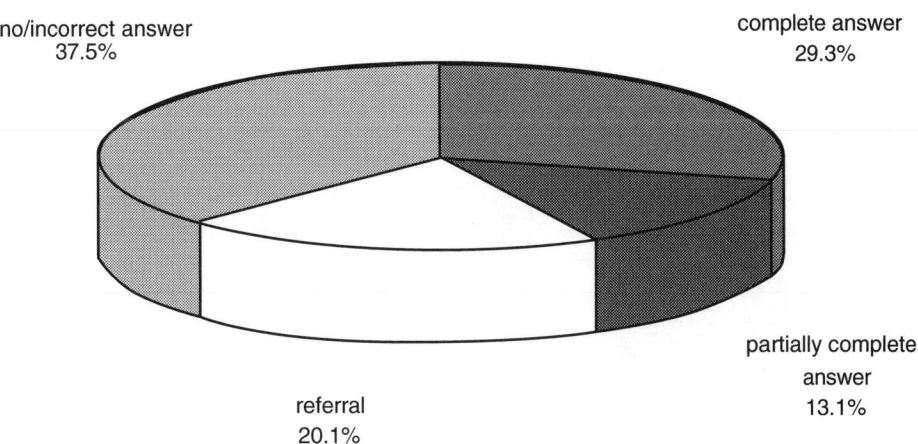

Figure 2-3 Distribution of Responses Received

for public selectives (88 out of 237) and 36.9 percent for academic selectives (24 out of 65). See Figure 2-4.

The data were also analyzed by geographic area. Figure 2-5 summarizes these findings. Ontario displays the best performance, with a rate of 38.2 percent complete answers (63 out of 165 questions) and a rate of 57.6 percent for combined complete and partially complete answers (95 out of 165). Depository libraries in British Columbia (including one location in the northern territories) provided complete answers 35.9 percent of the time (19 out of 53), and at a rate of 45.3 percent for complete and partially complete answers (24 out of 53). Depository libraries in the Atlantic Provinces gave complete answers to 28 percent of the questions (21 out of 75); combined complete and partially complete answers were given 41.3 percent of the time (31 out of 75). Ontario and British Columbia provided complete or partially complete answers at or above the national rate for complete answers, and for combined complete and partially complete answers. Atlantic Canada conformed to the national average.

The Prairie Provinces and Québec fall below the national average for complete and partially complete answers. In the Prairies, staff at depository libraries were able to answer questions completely at a rate of 23.3 percent (21 out of 90 questions), while combined complete and partially complete answers were provided 32.2 percent of the time (29 out of 90). In Québec complete answers were given at a rate of 18.1 percent (19 out of 105), while combined complete and partially complete answers were elicited 26.7 percent of the time (28 out of 105). Differences across regions are statistically significant ($\chi^2 = 33.54$, df = 12, $p < .01$, Cramér's $\varphi_c = .151$).

Success rates were also analyzed by region and type of library. In the

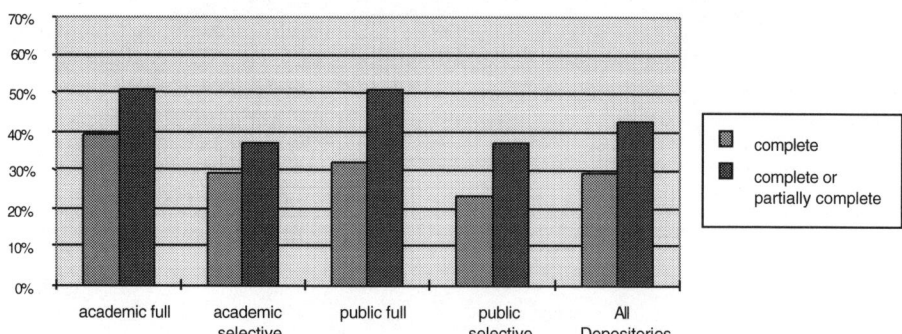

Figure 2-4 Responses Received by Type of Depository Library

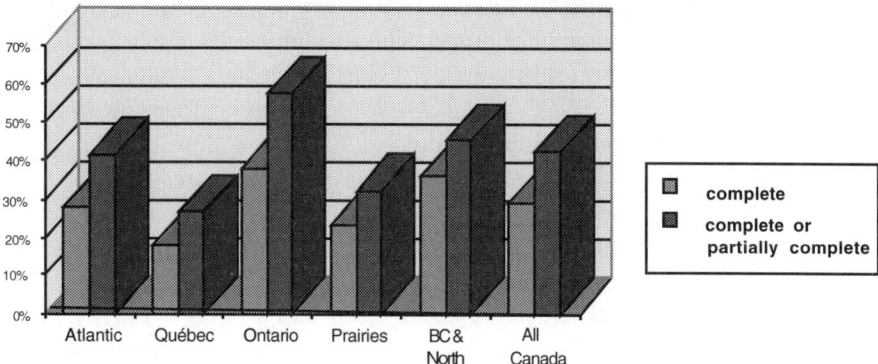

Figure 2-5 Types of Responses Received by Region

Atlantic Provinces, for example, 43.1 percent of public selective library answers were complete or partially complete (19 out of 44 questions), while 42.1 percent of academic full depository answers were complete or partially complete (8 out of 19). Academic selective depositories in Atlantic Canada answered completely or partially completely 33.3 percent of the time (4 out of 12). No public full depositories exist in Atlantic Canada, but results suggest that in this region equally good service for government reference questions is available at public selective libraries and academic full libraries, while academic selective libraries lag behind.

In Québec, academic full depositories answered 47.8 percent of the questions completely or partially completely (11 out of 23). By contrast, academic selectives provided 10.5 percent of such answers (2 out of 19). Taken together, public full and public selective libraries gave complete or partially complete answers 23.8 percent of the time (15 out of 63). In Québec, academic full depository libraries answered government reference questions most effectively. Public depositories and academic selective depositories in Québec were notable for poor success rates.

In Ontario, academic full depositories answered 55.8 percent of the questions completely or partially completely (29 out of 52); academic selective libraries, 58.3 percent (7 out of 12); public full depositories, 61.1 percent (22 out of 36); public selective depositories, 56.9 percent (37 out of 65). Proxies in Ontario received markedly similar and relatively high levels of government documents reference service no matter what type of depository library they visited.

In the Prairie Provinces, both academic full and selective depositories provided complete or partially complete answers 47.1 percent of the time (8 out of 17 questions each). Taken together, public full depositories and public selective depositories give such answers 23.2 percent of the time (13 out of 56). Results from Québec and the Prairie Provinces are strikingly similar. Academic libraries in the Prairies successfully answered questions at twice the level of success of public depository libraries in that region. In British Columbia and the North, academic full depository libraries provided complete or partially complete answers 56.3 percent of the time (9 out of 16), while the performance for academic selective libraries was 60 percent. Both types of public libraries provided such answers 37.5 percent of the time (12 out of 32).[4]

Results show that the level of government documents service is associated with region and type of depository library. In general terms, a patron in Québec, the Prairies, and British Columbia might be well advised to seek out an academic depository library, preferably an academic full depository, for government information. In Atlantic Canada and Ontario, however, similar levels of government information service are provided by all four types of depository libraries, with the exception of academic selective depositories in Atlantic Canada.

Depository libraries are located in census metropolitan areas of varying sizes. Data in Figure 2-6 show whether the size of a particular census area has an impact on the level of government documents service provided. Results are statistically significant ($\chi^2 = 30.71$, df = 12, $p < .01$). Two main findings emerge. First, the lowest number (7 out of 56 questions, 12.5%) of complete and combined complete and partially complete answers (13 out of 56 questions) (23.2%) to government reference questions was given in cities with fewer than 100,000 inhabitants. The best chances of receiving complete or partially complete answers were in census areas with a population either over one million (53 out of 105 questions) or between one quarter and one half million inhabitants (43 out of 75 questions). Census areas of both sizes had complete or partially

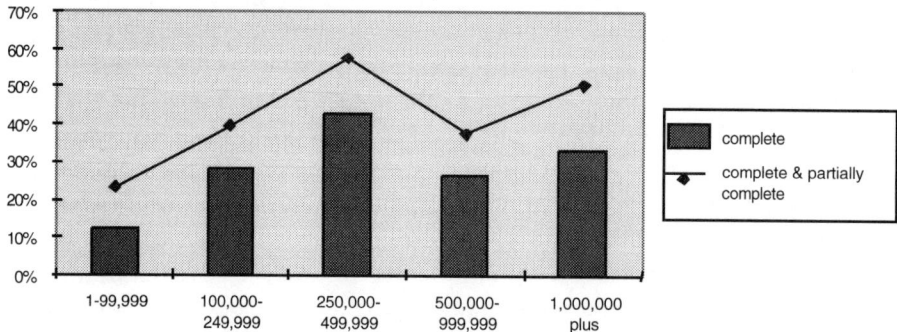

Figure 2-6 Types of Responses by Size of Census Metropolitan Area

complete answer rates of over 50 percent. It may seem counterintuitive that there is a decrease in service levels in the two largest categories of census areas, but this may in part be explained by the exceptional results that were obtained in libraries in two of the cities with a census area population of between 250,000 and 499,999.

One explanation for the low success rate in small localities may be that these small centers generate fewer government documents questions, and therefore library staff are more likely to have only a more generalist knowledge of the field. They may also not have as many opportunities to participate in training sessions or be exposed to the latest government publications and information sources.

Day of the Week and Degree of Busyness

Did the day of the week on which proxy questions were asked make a difference in type of answers received? Figure 2-7 addresses this point. On most days of the week—Monday, Wednesday, Thursday, Friday, and Saturday—the level of service was remarkably similar. On these five days complete answers were provided at a rate of between 24.7 percent and 28.8 percent, whereas complete and partially complete answers were provided at a rate of between 39.1 percent and 43.9 percent. On Sundays, however, the rate for complete answers fell to 13 percent, and the rate for complete and partially complete answers is 21.7 percent. Proxy questions that were administered on Tuesdays were answered completely 41.7 percent of the time, while such questions received complete or partially complete answers 53.4 percent of the time. The relatively low level of reference service on Sunday may be explained by the fact that regular professional staff may not be working on this day.

Did the degree of busyness at government documents reference desks

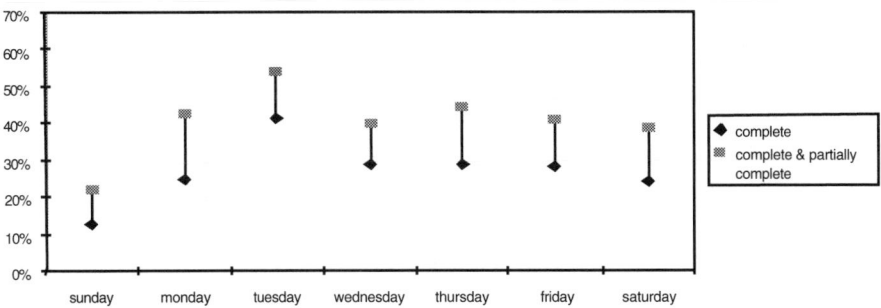

Figure 2-7 Responses Received by Day of the Week

have an impact on the quality of answers received? Proxies were requested to make a judgement about whether the reference desk was busy, very busy, or not busy at the time each question was asked based on "such indicators as the number of people waiting in line to ask questions or whether the library staff member was answering questions by phone or performing other duties." In total, proxies approached reference desks with their questions during busy times at a rate of 29.7 percent (145 questions), at non-busy times at a rate of 65.9 percent (322 questions), and at very busy times at a rate of 4.3 percent (21 questions). Figure 2-8 summarizes these findings.

What is apparent here is that depository library reference desks provided the same level of service, as measured by complete, partially complete, or no/incorrect answers, when they were busy and when they were not busy. For example, complete answers were provided 29.5 percent of the time (95 out of 322 questions) when the reference area was not busy, and 31 percent of the time when it was busy (45 out of 145 questions). Partially complete and complete answers were provided at a rate of 45.5 percent during busy times (66 out of 145 questions) and at a rate of 41.6 percent during non-busy periods (134 out of 322 questions). There is no statistical significance in these variations ($\chi^2 = 5.34$, df = 6). A similar trend is evident for no/incorrect answers; both at busy times and not busy times, no/incorrect answers were received 37 percent of the time. Only when the reference desk becomes "very busy" did the level of service substantially decline. Thus, complete answers were received 14.3 percent of the time (3 out of 21 questions) when the reference area was very busy, a drop of some 50 percent in success rates from busy or not busy periods. A similar 50 percent drop was experienced when complete and partially complete answers are taken together. The rate of no/incorrect answers,

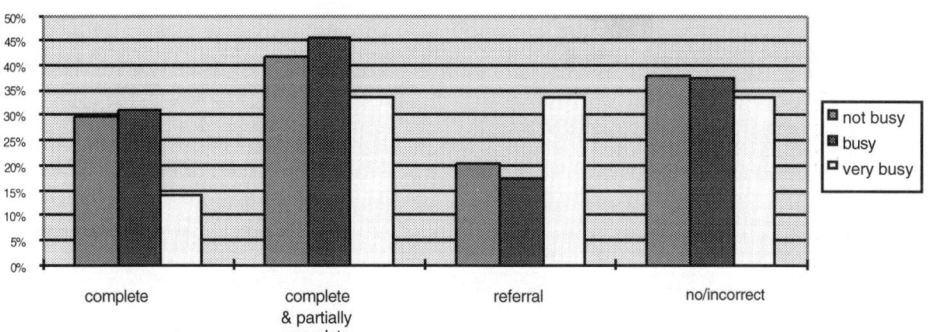

Figure 2-8 Responses Received by Degree of Busyness

however, stays approximately the same during very busy, busy, or not busy periods. Another interesting point is that while referral rates are approximately the same during busy and not busy times, referral rates soar to 33.3 percent during very busy periods.

When complete and partially complete answers are further analyzed by type of depository library and degree of busyness, results as displayed in Table 2-6 emerge. Notwithstanding whether they are busy or not busy, academic full depositories provided complete and partially complete answers at the same rate of about 50 percent and public selectives do so at a rate of between 36 percent and 41 percent. The quality of reference service, however, declines significantly at academic selective depositories when the degree of busyness increases, although the small sample size (n = 14) of academic selectives during busy periods may be a factor in this finding. Paradoxically, the quality of reference service, as measured by complete and partially complete answers, increases substantially at public full depositories as the degree of busyness rises. This last finding may also be explained in part by the small sample size of public full depositories (n = 23 at not busy times; n = 29 at busy times).

From an overall perspective, the degree of busyness does not seem to be an important factor in whether a patron receives a complete or partially complete answer. One possible explanation for this is that library staff members at most libraries attempt to accord each reference question a respectful degree of attention no matter how stressful long line-ups or ringing phone lines may be. The question, after all, is equally important to the patron asking it when there are few people in the library as when the library is serving hundreds. Although those library

Table 2-6
Impact of Busyness on Type of Answers

	Complete And Partially Complete Answers	
	Not Busy	Busy
Academic full	48/92 (52.17%)	16/32 (50.00%)
Academic selective	21/51 (41.18%)	3/14 (21.40%)
Public full	8/23 (34.78%)	18/29 (62.07%)
Public selective	57/156 (36.54%)	29/70 (41.40%)

staff members who were experiencing busy times at the reference desk achieved high rates for complete and partially complete answers, it might be expected that others who were not so busy might have spent more time with patrons.

Separate Government Information Area

A likely determinant of the level of government documents reference service is the presence of a specific area or reference desk that deals solely with government reference questions. Having such a special area may indicate the availability of specialist librarians who devote some or all of their time to official publications. Proxies asked 44.3 percent of questions (216 questions) at depository libraries that had separate government reference areas and 52.6 percent at depository libraries that did not have such separate areas (257 questions).[5]

As indicated by Figure 2-9, depository libraries without separate areas for government documents reference service answered 24.9 percent of the questions completely (64 out of 257). They provided complete or partially complete answers 39.3 percent of the time (101 out of 257). Depository libraries that had separate areas for government documents reference service provided 35.2 percent complete answers (76 out of 216) and 47.2 percent complete or partially complete answers (102 out of 216). These dif-

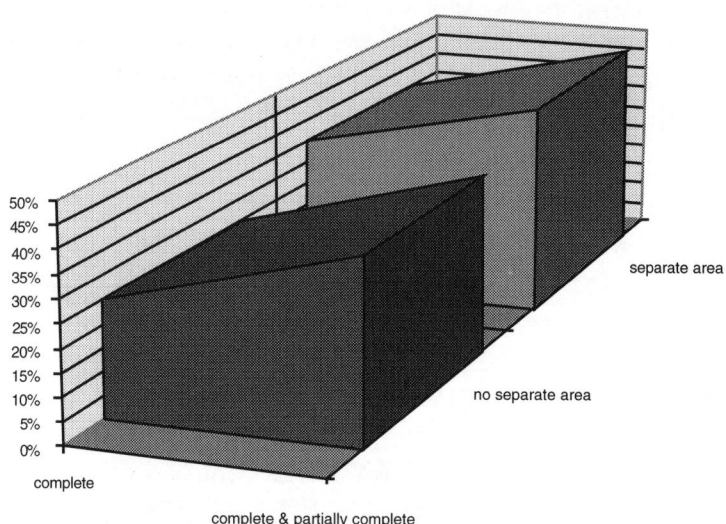

Figure 2-9 Responses Received by Whether Library Had Separate Area for Government Documents Reference Service

ferences are statistically significant when complete and partially complete answers are placed in one category, while no/incorrect answers and referrals are placed in another category ($\chi^2 = 4.85$, df = 1, $p < .05$, Cramér's $\varphi_c = .102$).

Table 2-7 summarizes the impact of a separate government documents reference area on complete answers by type of depository library. Those full depositories that have separate reference areas for government questions tended to provide more complete answers than did those institutions without such areas. The tendency was most pronounced in public full depositories, although the difference in academic full depositories was also noteworthy. Similarly, public selective depositories with a separate reference area for government documents provided complete answers at a rate of 29.6 percent, while those without performed at 20.9 percent. For academic selective libraries, the difference between those institutions that do and do not have separate areas was very small.

Time Spent Answering Questions

Proxies gathered information about how long library staff members spent with them in answering their questions. Minutes were grouped into the following categories: 0–4 minutes; 5–9 minutes; 10–14 minutes; 15–19 minutes; and more than 20 minutes. As shown in Figure 2-10, library staff spent up to 4 minutes with each patron 32.8 percent of the time (160 questions); 5–9 minutes, 24.4 percent of the time (119 questions); 10–14 minutes, 16.4 percent of the time (80 questions); 15–19 minutes, 8.8 percent of the time (43 questions); 20 minutes or more, 9.4 percent of the time (46 questions). Phone-back situations arose on 40 questions (8.2%).

Table 2-7
Effect of Separate Area on Complete Answers

	Complete Answers	
	Separate Area	*No Separate Area*
Academic full	30/67 (44.8%)	19/54 (35.2%)
Academic selective	8/30 (26.7%)	9/29 (31%)
Public full	17/48 (35.4%)	2/11 (18.2%)
Public selective	21/71 (29.6%)	34/163 (20.9%)

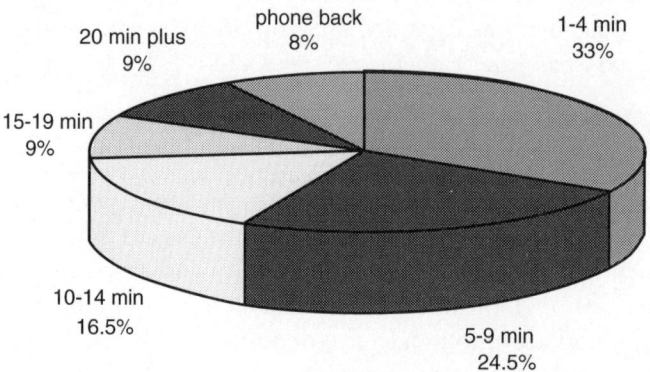

Figure 2-10 Distribution of Time Spent on Each Question

Another point of interest was the relationship between time spent with patrons and complete or partially complete answers. Differences in types of answers received are statistically significant ($\chi^2 = 70.29$, df = 15, $p < .01$, Cramér's $\varphi_c = .219$). In those reference encounters where a staff member spent up to four minutes with a patron, complete answers were received only 11.3 percent of the time (18 out of 160 questions), while complete or partially complete answers were received at a rate of 21.3 percent (34 out of 160). Figure 2-11 shows that as the amount of time spent with a patron increased, the number of complete or partially complete answers also increased. For example, spending between five and nine minutes with a patron is associated with complete answers 31.9 percent of the time (38 out of 119), and with complete or partially complete

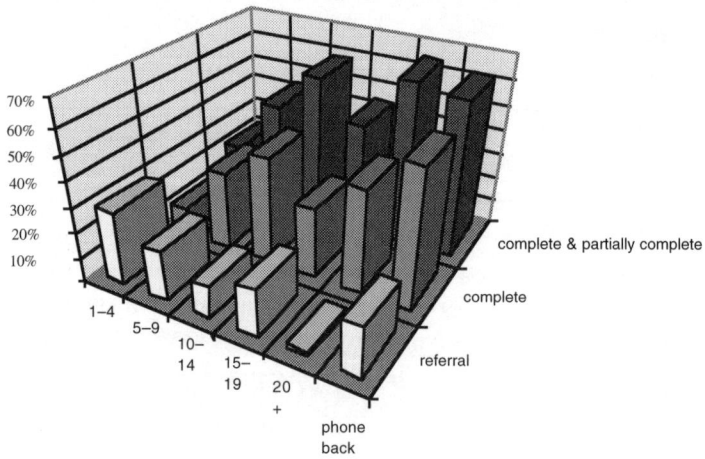

Figure 2-11 Responses Received by Number of Minutes Spent with Patron

answers 43.7 percent of the time (52 out of 119). In those instances when a staff member spent more than 10 minutes with a patron (i.e., the categories 10–14 minutes, 15–19, and 20 or more), the rate of complete or partially complete answers rose to 56.8 percent (96 out of 169). Moreover, when staff members devoted 20 or more minutes, the rate of complete or partially complete answers rose to 65.2 percent (30 out of 46).

As might be expected, the opposite tendency was observed with referrals. When up to four minutes were spent with a patron, referrals account for 29.4 percent of all answers (47 out of 160). When a staff member spent more than 10 minutes with a patron (i.e., the categories of 10–14 minutes, 15–19, and 20 or more), the referrals fell to 11.2 percent (19 out of 169), and when more than 20 minutes was devoted to a question, the referral rate was 2.2 percent (1 out of 46). In phone-back situations, where the staff member might be under less pressure in searching for an answer, the rate of complete or partially complete answers was 62.5 percent—approximately the same rate as when the staff member spent more than 20 minutes assisting. In sum, the more time a staff member spends with a patron, the greater the chances that a patron will receive a complete or partially complete answer.

Results suggest that, given sufficient time and opportunity, library staff are able to achieve very high rates of complete and partially complete answers. One troubling finding does emerge from a further parsing of the data. When staff members were judged by proxies to be not busy, and when these staff members subsequently spent only one to four minutes answering proxy-administered questions, the rates for complete and partially complete answers were very low—19.1 percent and 17.9 percent in academic depositories and public depositories, respectively.

Delivery Method of Questions

Proxies asked their questions either by telephone or in person at a government documents reference area. A total of 163 telephone questions were asked over the phone, while 325 questions were asked in person. Figure 2-12 shows the effect of question delivery method on the type of response received. More complete or partially complete answers were received when questions were delivered in person (45.9%) than by telephone (35.6%), in contrast to McClure and Hernon's findings (1983). Conversely, more referrals were given to telephone questions (23.9%) than to in-person questions (18.2%). These results are statistically significant ($\chi^2 = 4.68$, df = 1, $p < .05$, Cramér's $\varphi_c = .098$).

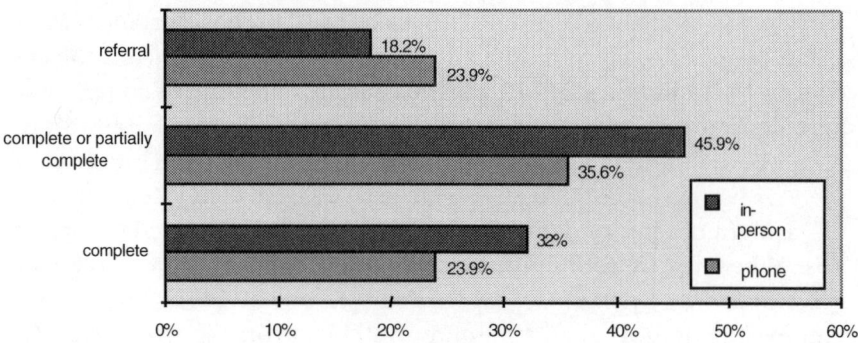

Figure 2-12 Responses Received by Method of Question Delivery

And, as Table 2-8 shows, the findings from Figure 2-12 hold true when results are broken down by type of depository library. Telephone questions were answered less successfully than in-person questions in all types of libraries. The greatest divergence occurs in public full depositories, where complete or partially complete answers were given to in-person questions 57.5 percent of the time, but only 36.8 percent of the time when asked by telephone. A similar gap exists at academic full depository libraries. Selective depositories showed smaller differences.

Subject Matter of Questions

In total, proxies asked 324 executive branch questions and 164 legislative questions. As indicated in Figure 2-13, complete or partially complete answers were provided to legislative questions at a statistically significantly higher rate than to executive questions ($\chi^2 = 24.92$, df = 3, $p < .01$,

Table 2-8
Method of Question Delivery and Depository Library Types

	Complete and Partially Complete Answers	
	In-person	*Phone*
Academic full	46/80	19/47
	(57.5%)	(40.4%)
Academic selective	18/48	6/17
	(37.5%)	(35.3%)
Public full	23/40	7/19
	(57.5%)	(36.8%)
Public selective	62/157	26/80
	(39.5%)	(32.5%)

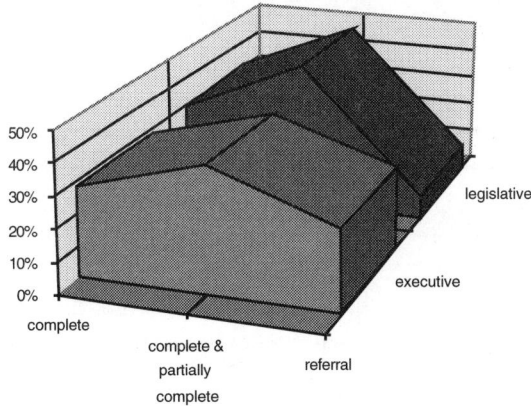

Figure 2-13 Responses Received by Subject of Reference Question

Cramér's φ_c = .226). While legislative questions were completely or partially completely answered by all libraries 48.2 percent of the time (79 out of 164), executive branch questions received complete or partially complete answers 39.5 percent of the time (128 out of 324). Moreover, legislative questions were referred at a substantially lesser rate (26.2%, 85 out of 324) than were executive branch questions (7.9%, 13 out of 164).

Whereas selective depositories provided complete or partially complete answers to legislative and executive questions at about the same rate, the difference between the two types of questions is most apparent in public full and academic full depositories. Table 2-9 shows that full depositories provided complete or partially complete answers to legislative branch questions

Table 2-9
Comparison of Legislative and Executive Questions Generating Complete or Partially Complete Answers

	Executive	Legislative
Academic full	35/75	30/52
	(46.7%)	(57.7%)
Academic selective	15/40	9/25
	(37.5%)	(36%)
Public full	16/38	14/21
	(42.1%)	(66.7%)
Public selective	62/171	26/66
	(36.3%)	(39.4%)

(academic full at 57.7%; public full at 66.7%) at a greater rate than to executive branch questions (academic full at 46.7%; public full at 42.1%).

Retrieval Types

There is a distinction prevalent in the scholarly literature of librarianship between data-retrieval questions and document-retrieval questions. Is this distinction germane for government-based reference questions? As mentioned above, Katz (1996) defines data retrieval questions as those in which individuals ask "specific questions and expect answers in the form of data," while document-retrieval queries are those in which patrons "want information, not just simple answers," and this information is "usually in the form of some type of document" (p. 18). As shown in Figure 2-14, document-retrieval questions received slightly more complete answers (31.7%, 93 out of 293) than data-retrieval questions (25.6%, 50 out of 195).

When complete and partially complete answers are combined, document-retrieval questions scored 45.4 percent (133 out of 293), and data-retrieval questions scored 37.9 percent (74 out of 195). Moreover, data-retrieval questions (31.3%, 61 out of 195) are referred more than twice as often as document-retrieval questions (12.6%, 37 out of 293). The above differences are statistically significant ($\chi^2 = 25.86$, df = 3, $p < .01$, Cramér's $\varphi_c = .230$).

Referrals

In total, 98 questions (20%) were referred to various governmental and non-governmental institutions (Table 2-10). Half of the referrals (49

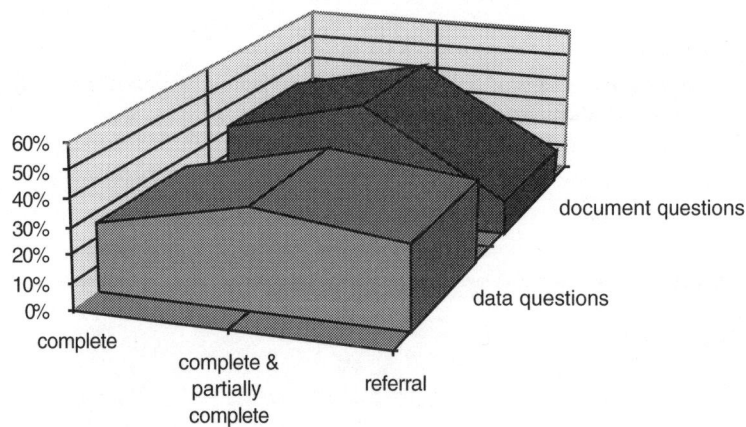

Figure 2-14 Responses Received by Class of Reference Question

Government Documents Reference Service   59

Table 2-10
Referrals

Patron referred to . . .	Frequency
Another government department	49 times
Non-governmental libraries	28 times
Non-governmental agencies or commercial establishments	14 times
Governmental or legislative libraries	7 times
Total number of referrals	98 times

questions) were to government departments. Another 7 percent were to governmental or legislative libraries (7 questions). Proxies were referred to other non-governmental libraries, usually at a university, 29 percent of the time (28 questions). In addition, 14 percent of the time they were referred to external non-governmental agencies or establishments that were not libraries (14 questions).

Of the referrals made to government departments, 65.3 percent were made by public selective depositories. This should not be surprising given that many public selective libraries do not collect a wide array of government documents. More interesting is the fact that both academic full depositories and public full depositories each referred to government departments at a rate of 16.3 percent despite their holdings of a vast range of official publications. Of the referrals to other non-governmental libraries, 71.4 percent of the time such referrals were made by public selective depositories and academic selective depositories. The success rates for referrals are discussed in more detail in Chapter 5.

No/Incorrect answers

No/incorrect answers were received by proxies 183 times, that is, at a rate of about 38 percent. As Figure 2-15 demonstrates, the most common explanation for a proxy's receiving a no/incorrect answer was that the library staff member simply did not know how to find the needed information. This happened in 37 percent of the cases in which a no/incorrect answer was given (67 out of 183). The next most common reason for a no/incorrect answer was that the library staff member provided an answer, which, unfortunately, was inaccurate. This happened 21 percent of the time that a no/incorrect answer was provided (38 out of 183). Ten percent of no/incorrect answers (18 out of 183) were the result of the unwillingness of library staff members to answer proxy questions—a circumstance that may, of course, mean that library policy precludes providing a certain type of service over the phone, or to those not

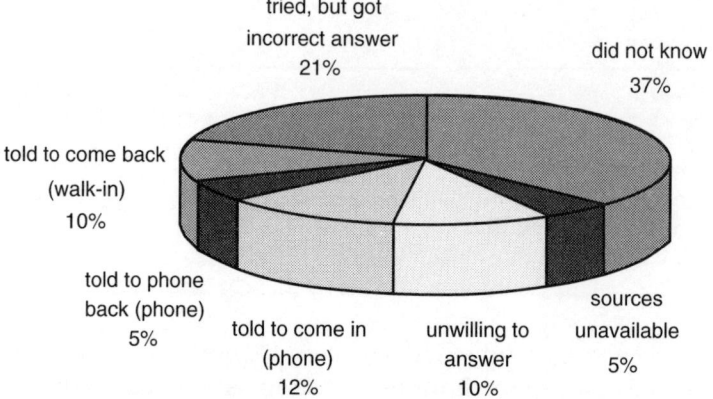

Figure 2-15 Reasons for No/Incorrect Answer

perceived to be primary clients. Indeed, in the case of telephone queries, where the patron cannot see the selection of available resources, some libraries may have a specific policy to refer telephone questions quickly to a government contact. As a last point, 27 percent of the time that a no/incorrect answer was provided, proxies were told either to come into the library, phone back, or come back at a more opportune time (49 out of 183). Again, some libraries may have policies that encourage users to come in and decide for themselves which resources best fit their needs, or to work through what a staff member may have thought was a complicated reference interview. Sources were unavailable nine times (5%). Two other reasons occurred.

Staff members at public selective depositories accounted for 52.2 percent (35 out of 67) of the "did not know" category. More problematic is the fact that staff members at academic full depositories told proxies that they "did not know" at a rate of 20.9 percent (14 out of 67). Staff at public full depositories accounted for 9 percent of the "did not know" category (6 out of 67). The type of question that most received a "did not know" reply (46 out of 67 questions) was an executive branch question (68.7 percent of the time), as opposed to a legislative branch question (21 out of 67) (31.3 percent of the time).

Staff members at public selective depositories accounted for 47.4 percent of the "tried but got incorrect answer" category (18 out of 38). Their counterparts at academic full depositories fell into this category at a rate of 21.1 percent (8 out of 38). Staff at public full depositories accounted for 13.2 percent of the "tried but got incorrect answer" category (5 out of 38). The type of question that most received a "tried but got incorrect answer" reply (25 out of 38) was an executive branch question (65.8 percent of the time), as opposed to a legislative branch question (34.2 percent of the time).

Figure 2-16 addresses the question of whether the type of depository library had an impact on the rate of referrals and no/incorrect answers. Academic full depositories, public full depositories, and public selective depositories gave no/incorrect answers at approximately the same rate, which hovers between 34 percent and 36 percent. Academic selective depositories provide no/incorrect answers at a significantly greater rate—53.9 percent. Referrals were provided by academic full depositories, academic selective depositories, and public full depositories at an approximately equal rate, ranging from 9 percent to 15 percent. Among the four types of depository libraries, public selectives referred patrons at an almost 30 percent rate. Not surprisingly, those depositories that had full collections of government documents were less likely to provide no/incorrect answers or to make referrals.

Figure 2-17 provides a detailed look at referrals and no/incorrect answers by geographical area. Depository libraries in Ontario provided no/incorrect answers at a rate of only 25.4 percent (42 out of 165 questions) and referred patrons elsewhere only 17 percent of the time (28 out of 165 questions), clearly the best record in Canada. Depository libraries in the Atlantic Provinces gave no/incorrect answers at a rate of 37.3 percent (28 out of 75 questions), while these libraries referred questions elsewhere 21.3 percent of the time (16 out of 75 questions). British Columbia is much like Atlantic Canada in this respect. Depository libraries in British Columbia provided no/incorrect answers at a rate of 39.6 percent (21 out of 53 questions) and referred at a rate of 15.1 percent (8 out of

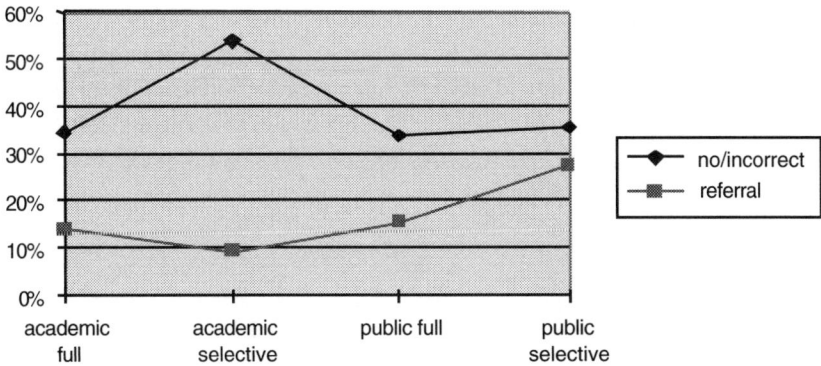

Figure 2-16 No/Incorrect Answers and Referrals by Type of Library

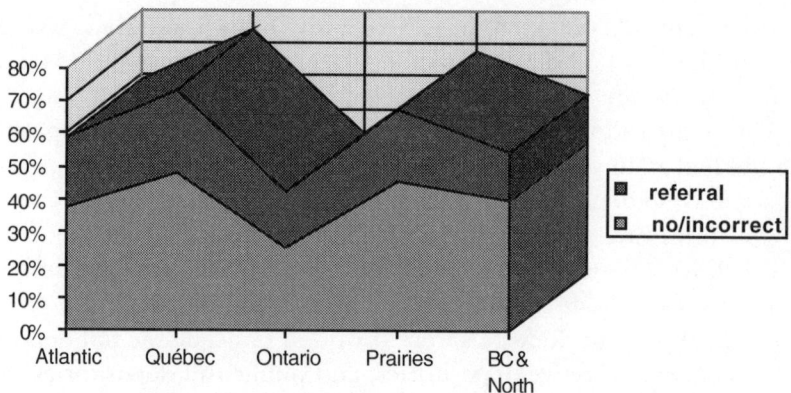

Figure 2-17 No/Incorrect Answers and Referrals by Geographic Region

53 questions). The Prairie Provinces and Québec had no/incorrect answer rates of 45.6 percent (41 out of 90 questions) and 48.6 percent (51 out of 105 questions), respectively. Referral rates for the Prairies and Québec were 22.2 percent (20 out of 90 questions) and 24.8 percent (26 out of 105 questions), respectively.

The relatively high levels of no/incorrect answers and referrals revealed in this study are a cause for concern. One explanation may be found in a study conducted by Roma Harris and Victoria Marshall (1998). They provide evidence, based on interviews with Canadian library directors, that restructuring imperatives occasioned by budget constraints have led to the increased use of paraprofessionals in reference functions. Since paraprofessionals may not have the necessary background knowledge and specialized skills to answer government documents questions, a certain deskilling of reference work may be taking place. In addition, Harris and Marshall note that library directors envision librarians as primarily managerial material—a circumstance that may result in high-quality reference librarians being taken away from desk duty and placed in exclusively administrative roles. Further study is needed to determine the impact on patrons of no/incorrect responses and referrals. Do patrons become discouraged? Frustrated? Do they follow up on referrals or give-up? Do they turn to other sources for needed information?

Sources Used

As indicated earlier, all 15 questions could be answered using Web resources. Dolan and Vaughan (1998) report that by the end of 1996, 89 percent of depository libraries had Internet access and that of the 11 percent that did not have Internet access in December 1996, some 70 percent were planning to have such access within one year. When the present study was conducted in December 1997, it was not unreasonable to suppose that Internet access was available in some 96 percent of federal depository libraries. Dolan and Vaughan also report that print sources are used much more frequently in depository libraries than are electronic sources. A question of interest in this study was therefore the extent to which library staff turned to various types of sources to answer patron questions. Figure 2-18 summarizes source use.

Print-only sources constituted by far the largest single source (45.7%) used to answer proxy questions (223 out of 488 questions). The Web alone was used 11.5 percent of the time (56 questions), and the Web in combination with another source, 5.5 percent (27 questions). Thus, in whole or in part, use of the Web hovered around 17 percent (83 questions). About 23 percent of the time "no sources" were consulted (112 questions), and in an additional 9.6 percent of cases (47 questions), the only source used was a library on-line public access catalogue (OPAC). CD-ROMs or databases were used 3.7 percent of the time (18 questions); and microforms, just over 1 percent (5 questions).

Of the 112 questions for which "no sources" were used, 55 were in-person questions and 57 were telephone questions—an almost equal division. However, 325 questions were asked in person, while only 163 questions were asked by telephone. Accordingly, "no sources" were used in 34.9 percent of telephone questions, but only in 16.9 percent of in-person questions. If the 15 questions are ranked by the number of times

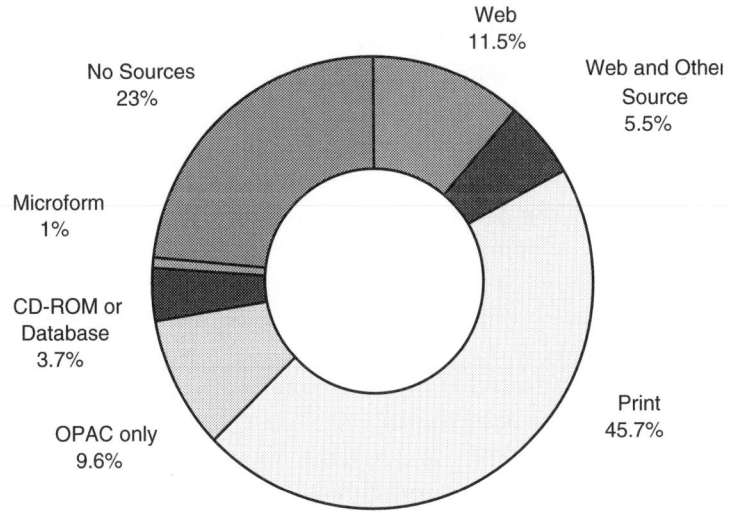

Figure 2-18 Distribution of Sources Used to Answer Questions

"no sources" were used in answering them, three of the top five were telephone questions: lyrics (17), fuels (14), and barley (11). From a different perspective, four of the top five are executive branch questions, and four of the top five are data-retrieval questions.[6] There was a difference among depository libraries in their use of "no sources." On these 112 occasions when proxies indicated that "no sources" were consulted by library personnel, 48.2 percent of the time this occurred at public selective depositories, 30.4 percent of the time at academic full depositories, 14.3 percent of the time at academic selectives, and only 7.1 percent of the time at public full depositories.

Minor variations were observed in the sources used, depending on the type of depository library. Use of the Web at academic full, academic selective, and public full depository libraries ranges from 21.1 percent to 25.2 percent—statistically indistinguishable rates. Public selective libraries, however, used Web-based sources significantly less—12.2 percent of the time ($\chi^2 = 22.45$, df = 12, $p < .05$, Cramér's $\varphi_c = .123$).[7] Use of print sources at public full depositories and public selective depositories is around 53 percent, while in academic full and selective depositories print use hovers around 40 percent.

Is there a difference in types of sources used in different regions of Canada? Depository libraries in Ontario, the Atlantic Provinces, and British Columbia made use of the Web significantly more than depository libraries in Québec and on the Prairies ($\chi^2 = 51.41$, df = 20, $p < .01$, Cramér's $\varphi_c = .162$). Depositories in Atlantic Canada made use of the Web at a rate of 22.7 percent (17 out of 75 questions), those in Ontario used Web resources at a rate of 21.2 percent (35 out of 165), while those in British Columbia employ the Web 18.9 percent of the time (10 out of 53 questions). These results are, for all intents and purposes, indistinguishable. In Québec, however, Web use in depository libraries drops to 13.3 percent (14 out of 105 questions), and on the Prairies, use of Web resources declines to 7.8 percent (7 out of 90). Nonetheless, all regions of Canada, except the Atlantic Provinces, use print sources more than twice as much as they use Web-based resources. In Atlantic Canada, print-only sources are used 41.3 percent of the time (31 out of 75). Depository libraries in the Prairie Provinces use print-only sources at a rate of 55.6 percent (50 out of 90), more than depository libraries in any other region. Depository libraries in Ontario also have a high rate of print use (53.3%, 88 out of 165).

Were there certain types of questions for which Web sources were more popular than print sources? Figure 2-19 tracks sources by individual questions. In general, it is apparent that for most questions, print-only sources were more popular than Web-based sources. A slight trend

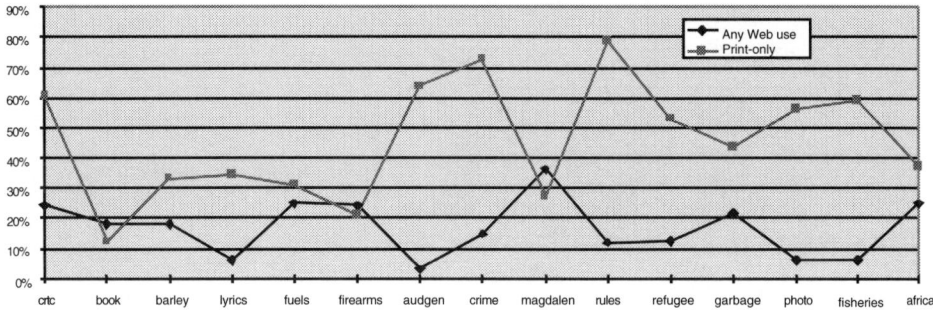

Figure 2-19 Individual Questions by Print or Web Use

may nevertheless be discerned. There are four questions for which either Web use was greater than print use or print and Web sources were used approximately the same: the Hansard question about the Magdalen Islands, the question about a committee report on firearms legislation, the question about the Alternative Fuels Act, and the bibliographic question about the price of a government-published book.

Three of these four questions deal with legislative-branch issues. Relatively high Web use (in comparison with print use) in searching for answers to these questions may indicate that staff members in depository libraries are familiar with the extensive legislatively based information available on the Canadian Parliamentary Web site. At the same time, library personnel do not appear to be sufficiently familiar with the range of executive-branch information that is also available on the Web, since in nine out of the 10 questions dealing with the executive branch, they employed print sources to a greater extent than they did Web sources. For the five legislative branch questions taken as a group, staff used Web sources 24.5 percent of the time, while for the 10 executive branch questions, they employed Web sources 14.7 percent of the time. Still, print sources were by far the most preferred source for both types of questions. Indeed, use of print sources was more than double that of Web sources for legislative and executive questions.

Depository library personnel clearly favor print sources by a wide margin over Web sources. Such practice may be based on long-standing habit and experience as well as the conviction that complete answers may be found more readily in print sources. Are these two beliefs accurate? Figure 2-20 shows complete and partially complete answers by type of source used. A good place to begin is with complete answers—perhaps the best indication of the value of individual sources. When print sources alone are used, complete answers are found 39.9 percent of the time (89 out of 223 questions). When Web sources alone are used, however, complete

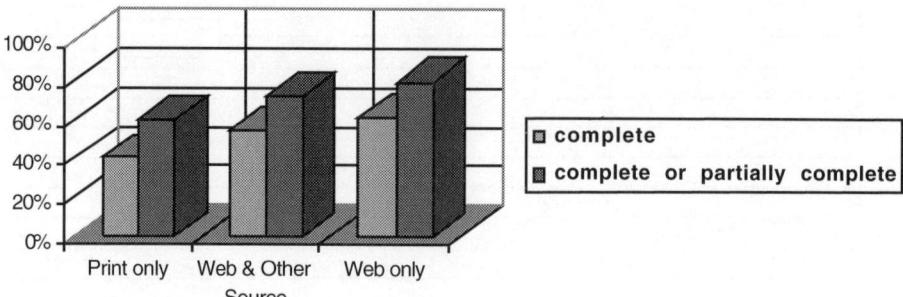

Figure 2-20 Responses Received by Type of Source

answers soar to 60.7 percent (34 out of 56)—an approximately 50 percent increase. Complete or partially complete answers occur 78.6 percent of the time (44 out of 56) when Web sources are used alone, while complete or partially complete answers are provided 60.1 percent of the time when only print sources are employed (134 out of 223).

In sum, Figure 2-20 shows a step-like progression in efficacy rates. Print is the least effective for achieving either complete or partially complete answers. The second most efficacious results are achieved when the Web is used in combination with another source. Best results are achieved when the Web is used as the sole source for government information retrieval. As shown in Table 2-11, these differences are most pronounced in public selective libraries and academic full depositories. In public selective depositories, for instance, Web sources, when used alone, led to complete or partially complete answers 84.2 percent of the time, while print sources produced the same type of answers 52.9 percent of the time. The difference is more muted in academic full depositories and public full depositories, although still important. Web sources, when used alone, resulted in 81 percent complete or partially complete answers in academic full depositories, while print sources pro-

Table 2-11
Type of Answer Received by Source

	Complete and Partially Complete Answers	
	Web Alone	*Print Alone*
Academic full	81%	70.8%
Academic selective	62.5%	65.2%
Public full	75%	67.7%
Public selective	84.2%	52.9%

vided 70.8 percent complete or partially complete answers. In public full depositories, Web sources resulted in complete or partially complete answers 75 percent of the time, while print sources did so 67.7 percent of the time.

Even though the Web as a storehouse of information and knowledge was still, in the late 1990s, in its infancy, this study offers some evidence to suggest that it has surpassed print sources as a means of retrieving complete or partially complete answers to government documents reference questions. These results are not inconsistent with Janes and McClure (1999) who, in a study of the success with which "quick fact reference questions" could be answered using freely available Web sites, found that "the people using Web resources performed slightly better" in terms of accuracy than those using print sources (p. 33).

DISCUSSION

The level of service and knowledge suggested by a 29.3 percent complete accuracy rate or a 42.4 percent complete and partially complete answer rate is disquieting given the emphasis the DSP places on the depositories' role as the public's center of expertise for finding, accessing, and retrieving federal information. It may be that the complexity and sheer quantity of official documentation from all sources is overwhelming depository libraries. It may also be that depository staff members are not confident enough to move through the labyrinth that many perceive government documents to be. Or it may be that the package provided to depository libraries by the DSP may be lacking in consistency, indexing, and accompanying training material. No text or manual giving guidance in the use of federal documents has been published since the appearance of Olga Bishop's *Canadian Official Publications* in 1981.

In the past decade libraries have been forced to suffer painful budget cuts. Respondents to the survey conducted by Dolan and Vaughan (1998) reported that libraries are suffering from an absence of funding, a dearth of training programs, and a lack of available time for maintaining or improving staff expertise in the area of official publications; in addition, depositories are especially in need of knowledgeable personnel to assist with electronic access. This last point is of particular relevance for the present study.

Full depositories perform at a higher level than selective depositories. Complete answer rates ranged from 39.4 percent at academic full depositories to 32.2 percent at public full depositories to 29.2 percent at academic selectives to 23.2 percent at public selective depositories. This should not be surprising, given the fact that full depositories have access to the entire range of DSP publications. Moreover, they are typically located in large urban areas or at major universities across the country and have the benefit of staffing and funding levels that are much higher than selective depositories. This latter circumstance suggests that full depositories may either have more specialized government documents reference personnel than selective libraries, more practice in answering questions than selective libraries, or both.

Libraries that had separate government reference areas typically performed better than those with common reference areas. Dolan and Vaughan (1998) report that 29 percent of depository libraries in Canada have separate government documents collections, while 55 percent have a mixed arrangement. Whereas only 14.7 percent have integrated their government holdings into either their main collections or their reference collections, 16.1 percent have moved to merge their collections since 1986. Although an integrated government documents collection does not preclude the existence of a separate government documents reference area, and there is not necessarily a relationship between the organization of a government documents collection and the presence (or absence) of a government documents reference area, the findings presented in Table 2-7 and Figure 2-9 suggest that, even if the trend to consolidate government documents collections continues, depository libraries should seriously consider retaining separate government documents reference areas. This finding substantiates that of Philip Van De Voorde (1989), who reports a slight decline in the quality of reference service at a single merged area that dispenses both general and government reference service. Atifa Rawan and Jennifer Cox (1995), however, suggest that "the loss of specialization is countered by the gain in awareness of the [government documents] collection by library staff" (p. 261), and Frazer, Boone, McCart, Prince, and Rees (1997) report that merged reference departments continue to be implemented. Still, integration of government reference service into the main reference area may devalue the specialist knowledge that government documents librarians possess. The retention of a separate government documents reference area may serve to maintain and valorize this specialist knowledge; it may also act as a stimulus to the development of higher levels of expertise as specialist librarians continually update and refine their skills.

Legislative questions were typically answered more successfully than those questions defined as pertaining to the executive branch. One reason for this phenomenon may be that legislative questions are more homogeneous than executive branch questions. While the subject matter of legislative questions can be as broad as executive branch questions, the sources in which the answers to legislative questions can be found are limited in number. For instance, once a librarian knows how to find one statute, one bill, or one comment in Hansard, then the answer to any subsequent questions dealing with statutes, bills, or debates will be found in the same location. It should also be noted that the questions themselves often include clear references to appropriate sources, e.g. "Where can I find a bill about Topic X?" Executive branch questions, on the other hand, are heterogeneous not only in regard to subject matter, but also in regard to potential sources.

Although academic depositories and public full depositories used Web sources approximately twice as much as public selective depositories, this study indicates that library personnel turn to print sources more frequently than to Web-based resources. Reasons for this may be many. Some library staff may feel that government servers are too slow, that government search engines are ineffective, or that the necessary information is contained in Adobe Acrobat files that are either inaccessible or too large to print. Another reason for this may be the philosophy put forward by Brendan Devlin (1997) that the Internet should be chosen as an information source only if the question is unlikely to be answered elsewhere, or if other sources have been unsuccessful, or if a comprehensive search is required. Devlin's approach may be valuable for many general reference questions, but his searching strategy model may not be appropriate for government documents questions. Government information on the Web is usually reliable since it is posted by government departments and agencies themselves. Moreover, Allen Benson (1995) suggests that if a previously identified, credible Internet source has been located, it should be consistently used as an information source. Canadian government documents are readily available on well-established and stable Web-based platforms. Library reference departments may want to consider adopting a service policy stating that if a question seems to be a government documents question, a staff member should consult Web-based sources early on in the search. More frequent use of the Web at academic and public full depositories may be due to higher bandwidth connections to the Internet, which facilitates speedy access to Web pages. As more public selective depositories become part of a telecommunications infrastructure supporting high bandwidth, their use of Web resources may increase.

There are a number of issues, however, that need to be addressed before library staff make full and complete use of Web resources as a matter of natural course. The authority of electronic sources is one such major concern. Many departments decree that print versions are the authoritative versions of texts. One government Web site, for instance, clearly states that "In the event of a discrepancy between the electronic version and a hard copy publication, the hard copy will be considered the accurate version." Another site warns that "inadvertent errors can occur for which no responsibility is accepted. In addition, staff have reported important missing elements, especially tables and charts, from electronic copies of publications. In these circumstances, it is logical to expect library staff to turn to print sources before they turn to Web sources until such time as digital signatures become accepted. Authority of information on government Web sites is therefore a serious issue that should be addressed. Another concern is the question of use restrictions on government sites, although some sites allow the downloading of "one copy of the materials on any single computer for your personal, non-commercial home use only."

A number of technical issues surrounding government sites may also inhibit staff members from turning to Web-based sources. For instance, the use of frames and graphics, as well as PDF formats and proprietary software such as FOLIO, are problematic, especially where public service sites have multiple functions. Reference staff may also feel that search engines are less than adequate, given that some departments still use HARVEST and that other engines only search HTML documents and do not pick up PDF documents. Moreover, some library personnel, having become accustomed to sophisticated Web-site search engines that contain such features as exact phrase, word proximity, date or database limitation, and truncation features, may find government search engines to be lacking in some of these areas.

Many government sites do not contain all-important accompanying metadata, despite the existence of basic standards for Internet publication within the government. Archiving policies are still not yet in place; the result is documents that appear and then disappear. For librarians trained in the integrity and reliable accessibility of information, this circumstance is disquieting. A final issue is that some government Web sites and Web addresses are not stable, resulting in confusion for the library community and much extra work in updating electronic bookmarks.

Dolan and Vaughan (1998) present evidence to suggest that staff preparedness to help patrons with electronic access and competent delivery of electronic government publications is lacking because of the absence of funding, the dearth of training programs, and the lack of time available for acquiring and passing on expertise in dealing with electronic sources of government information. Along the same lines, Stephanie Ford (1997) notes that serious problems in staffing in some regional U.S. depositories is inhibiting public access to electronic government information. Training of library personnel in electronic sources of government information may be especially crucial, given the fact that the use of Web sources to find government information is associated with a better reference efficacy rate, as measured by complete and partially complete answers.

CONCLUSIONS

The Canadian federal government is moving to implement a plan in which the preferred delivery platform for government information will henceforward be electronically based through the Web. One consequence of this will be that the distinction between a full depository library and a selective depository library will disappear. Indeed, all computer-owning individuals will have the same access to publications provided by the federal government as the largest library in the country. However, not everyone will have access to a computer and the Web. Moreover, those individuals who do have such access may not be very proficient at finding their way around this new information medium in their search for specific government publications and data. Depository libraries therefore still have an important role to play as intermediaries between government information and the general public, but if and only if they are able to provide superior reference service in government publications. And if they are to offer superior levels of service, one requirement must be increased attention to systematically training staff members in efficiently locating government publications and data.

McClure and Hernon (1983) concluded that there is a strong likelihood that "the individual staff member is the *single most significant factor* affecting the quality of reference service for government documents," and suggested that "concentrating on the skills and competencies of individual staff members may well upgrade the quality of reference service" (p. 111, original emphasis). They called for an increased knowledge of basic and advanced government documents reference sources and "a *program* of education for the documents depository staff, as well as a program that develops learning opportunities for other library staff members" (p. 143, original emphasis). Specifically, they recommended formal programs of study in political science and history, and internships in federal agencies.

More than 15 years later, a similar recommendation can be made. To make use of Canadian government Web resources effectively, it is vital that library staff members are fully aware of the structures, functions, and evolution of both the legislative and executive branches of government. Staff members need to know what programs are available and who is responsible for which program in the federal government.[8] In short, library staff should be knowledgeable about who does what and how things work within the many departments, agencies, and other administrative entities of the federal government. Even better service might be provided if library personnel possessed substantial knowledge about what services are offered by which level of government; that is, in the Canadian context, either federal, provincial, or local (municipal and regional), or in the American context, federal, state, and local. Once staff members can readily identify a potential question as falling within a particular governmental realm through their knowledge of "who does what," it may become much easier to identify the electronic site where the desired information may be found. Within the Canadian context, the Depository Services Program (DSP) may be the logical agent to institute such a formal training program.

When all is said and done, the key issue is whether library staff should be satisfied with the accuracy rates described in this study. Hernon and Altman (1998) have suggested that accuracy is a key indicator of overall service quality in the eyes of business executives. To be sure, a library is not a business, yet should library patrons be expected to accept a level of service that they may not necessarily countenance from a business establishment? Moreover, a lack of accuracy and success in answering reference questions may be a leading indicator of other shortcomings in a particular library.

Furthermore, library staff should understand that patrons who may have turned to their local public or academic library for help with government information now have alternatives. There are numerous toll-free phone numbers in both Canada and the United States that connect directly to government departments, agencies, and help lines. And, as Rita Beamish (1999) reports, many government departments in the United States have instituted programs whereby government officials accept questions, and provide answers, through e-mail. For instance, the Environmental Protection Agency has "two dozen librarians fielding as many as 1,500 such e-mail questions each month, with a typical response time of fewer than five days" (p. D8). Many other departments have electronic messaging departments staffed with specially trained individuals who provide "precise information, complete with citations and details" in e-mail messages that are "as chipper as a happy-face sticker" (p. D8). Given the existence of these new messaging departments, depository libraries may wish to re-examine all aspects of their government documents reference service in order to improve accuracy and success rates.[9]

In addition, depository libraries now have to compete with a service such as govWorks.com, which provides impressive access to a complete range of federal, state, and local government information through its "consumer portal." Founded in 1998, govWorks.com also provides members of the public with a free 24-hour hotline and e-mail service which "will work around the clock to get you the right information for any interaction with government [a]nd we'll get it to you within one business day." Certainly, the free information service is subsidized by other for-free services: consumer online tax, bill, and ticket payments; e-government services which include "co-branded Web sites powered by govWorks"; and tools for business-to-government (B2G) electronic transactions. Although nestled within a commercialized service, the free govWorks hotline is another way for individuals to have a convenient access to a plethora of government information from the comfort of their home.

Given these various forms of competition, reference service improvements at libraries are vital, for there is still a strong need for government documents reference service at depository libraries. There are at least three reasons for this. Beamish (1999) reports that many government departments, hoping that users will find the information themselves, do not encourage them to send them e-mail requests. She quotes a high-level official in the Emerging Information Technology Policies division of the General Services Administration as saying that "[t]he ideal web site answer[s] as many questions as possible, so the last option is to send an E-mail which requires a person to intervene and answer a question" (p. D8). However, the sheer complexity of some government Web sites may inhibit information retrieval by untrained users. Thus, the expertise of trained government documents reference personnel will be even more important. Second, many individuals may not want to wait to receive certain government information. Again, trained staff at libraries could reduce waiting times. Third, fee-based cross-departmental and cross-agency search services may be on the horizon to deal with the vast and ever-expanding universe of government information (Clausing, 1999). Many people will not be able to afford such services from their homes. Depository libraries, functioning as free or partially subsidized gateways to government sources, will therefore continue to play a significant role in ensuring equitable access to government information for all citizens, no matter their socio-economic status.

Hernon, Nitecki, and Altman (1999) point to 16 reasons why libraries and library staff may resist criticisms about their work. Three of the main reasons are that "a focus on improvement implies an initial baseline of *inferior* or *substandard* service," that service quality concepts can only be associated with "commercial service settings," and that libraries "need not be concerned about competition" (pp. 13–14, original emphasis). As discussed above, the last point no longer holds for libraries providing government information. The challenge for government documents reference staff at depository libraries in Canada is therefore to see themselves as part of a competitive information-provision marketplace. To this end, studies comparing the accuracy and service levels of depository libraries, government telephone help centers, information provision centers such as govWorks, and e-mail messaging departments should be undertaken on a regular basis. Hernon, Nitecki, and Altman endorse the general practice of comparative benchmarking, suggesting, for example, that interlibrary loan departments attempt to match state-wide "best practices" or "even commercial delivery services such as United Parcel Service (UPS)" (p. 12). Just as depository libraries should be encouraged to meet performance standards, they should also be open to guaranteeing such standards as part of their service commitment to patrons. The findings of the present study lend support to McClure and Hernon's (1983) call for a "certification process whereby [depository] libraries must show evidence of meeting specific criteria" and where the individual in charge of the government documents collection must also meet "specific *performance-related* criteria to direct the collection" (p. 160, original emphasis). It may even be worthwhile to extend the certification process to all staff who regularly provide government documents reference service. In addition, serious thought should be given to a stringent recertification process of reference librarians, as recommended by Hernon and McClure (1987) who point out that health sciences librarians must be recertified every five years (pp. 152–56).

Certainly, such a recommendations are controversial, yet the increased complexity of the government information universe, combined with the low accuracy levels found in this study, calls for a serious reappraisal of government documents reference delivery in depositories. Such a reappraisal seems all the more urgent, given that service levels at depository libraries have not improved since McClure and Hernon (1983). While McClure and Hernon (1983) investigated the situation in two regions of the United States, the present study focused on a wide range of depository libraries across Canada. Yet, the findings of these two studies are similar. Providing government information to the public, no matter the country, is an arduous task. Indeed, the task will become even more difficult in the future, with the creation of supra-national organizations that impact directly on national social, economic, and political life. For instance, rulings of the World Trade Organization (WTO), as well as the political and economic compromises that will have to be reached because of these rulings, will assume an increasingly prominent place in the daily lives of large corporations, small businesses, and ordinary citizens.[10] In another example, courts in the United States are increasingly accepting jurisdiction over cases, filed under the Alien Torts Claim Act, that employ international human rights statutes and international environmental accords such as the Rio Declaration.[11] Although some attention has always been paid to international documents in depository libraries, the tendency has been to treat them as a specialized, often separate, component of the collection. Now, however, many international documents are, in effect, becoming national and local documents. Accordingly, depository reference staff have another level of information to master. More than ever, such circumstances warrant a concerted effort by depository libraries to improve government documents reference service in the 21st century.

NOTES

1. An intriguing study that falls on the midpoint of the spectrum between unobtrusive reference evaluations and user-satisfaction studies was conducted by Thomas Childers (1997). After interviewing 57 library patrons in a public library as they left the reference area, he reports that, of the 32 people who sought staff help, 20 (63%) received a complete answer to their question (p. 161). The remaining 25 patrons did not seek staff help, yet they were able to find a complete answer 40 percent of the time. Childers goes on to point out that, of the patrons who did seek staff help, 72 percent declared that the information located was very useful, while only 54 percent of those who did not seek staff help stated that the information they found was very useful. Given the small sample size, the 63 percent figure for patrons receiving complete answers may be seen as close to the acknowledged figure of 55 percent success. Childers also reports that 17 people chose not to participate in the interviews after they were initially approached. Although this study was conducted at a single public library in an affluent community, Childers' methodology has a number of merits, especially if his 11-question survey instrument could be made more detailed.

2. Unobtrusive testing has recently been in the news in Canada, as attested by a report in *The Globe and Mail* describing Health Canada's effort to discover whether retailers are complying with a law that forbids the sale of tobacco to minors (McIlroy, 1998, pp. A1, A10). An account in *The New York Times* offers another example: undercover shoppers, posing as customers, are paid by marketing agencies to grade service in stores so that retailers can evaluate themselves (Steinhauer, 1998, pp. C1, C23).

3. Legislative libraries were excluded from this study because members of the general public do not generally use them.

4. Public full depository and public selective depository figures are reported together for Québec, British Columbia, and the Prairies because in each region there is only one public full depository library. Identification of this library would therefore be possible. Anonymity is preserved by conflating results for both types of public depositories.

5. Proxies were unsure of whether a library had a government reference area 3 percent of the time.

6. All questions received at least one "no sources" reply. The following is a list, in descending order, of the number of times a particular question received a "no sources" answer. The short name of the question is used. Refer to Table 2-5 for the full question, as well as for information about whether each question was categorized as being: in-person or telephone, executive or legislative, data retrieval or document retrieval. The list is as follows: Lyrics (17), Fuels (14), Photo (12), Barley (11), Garbage (11), Book (10), Africa (7), CRTC (5), Magdal (5), Refugee (5), Audgen (4), Fish (4), Firearms (4), Rules (2), Crimes (1).

7. This chi-square test and the chi-square test in the next paragraph are calculated using the five major sources used by depository libraries (print, Web only, Web combined, OPAC, no sources) and a category called "other," which includes database, CD-ROM, and microform sources. These three sources (23 instances in total) were combined due to cell size criteria.

8. It is also important for staff to know the history of departments and changes in ministerial responsibilities. In Canada, various programs and administrative entities may migrate from department to department, depending on political circumstances.

9. Although Beamish (1999) focuses exclusively on developments within the United States, it is not improbable that the innovations she mentions will become current in Canada in the near future.

10. See, for example: Moberg, David. (1999, February 21). Going bananas. *In These Times, 23*(6), 14–16; Vittala, Kalyani. (1999, May 27). U.S.-Canada agreement on magazines. *The New York Times,* C5 [National].

11. See Press, Eyal. (1999, May 31). Texaco on trial. *The Nation,* 11–16.

Chapter 3

What the Proxies Said About the Service They Received

After completing their round of questions, the proxies participating in this study were also requested to describe how they felt about the service they had just received at the reference desks of depository libraries. They were asked to write down their overall impressions, concentrating both on the positive and negative aspects of their experiences when searching for government information. In this part of the study, the proxies were not given a specific set of evaluative questions to answer; nor were they channeled in a particular direction by preliminary instructions; nor were they asked to produce, on a deadline, a certain amount of commentary, as measured by page counts. Rather, a deliberate choice was made to allow the proxies to speak about their concerns in an environment free of pressure or time constraints. In this way, proxies were given the chance to reflect on their experiences and emphasize the most salient features of their library visits. In addition, proxies were *not required* to submit written comments. They were merely urged to do so, and payment of honoraria did not depend on the submission of comments. This was done in order that the proxies would not feel obligated in any way to produce accounts of their visits just for the sake of receiving payment. Such coerced testimony might have been tainted insofar as proxies may have unconsciously believed that payment was contingent on a set of expected responses.

Of the 30 proxies participating in the study, 21 opted to submit written responses that ranged in length from three paragraphs to three pages. All written statements were received within two months of completion of the study, and most were received between three and four weeks after the proxy had returned the package of questions. In other words, ample time had elapsed so that first impressions could be tempered by a certain amount of perspective.

The range of emotions expressed in the proxy accounts covered a broad spectrum. Table 3-1 summarizes the frequency with which proxies used certain adjectival descriptions of the service they received. The most common adjective employed to describe government documents reference service was "helpful," followed by "friendly" and "disappointing." Although the number of positive adjectives (32) is almost equal to the number of negative adjectives (36), there were numerous accounts, almost all of them negative, that could not be classified by adjectival description. These accounts provide an insight into the depth of anger and frustration that proxies experienced when confronted with library staff who provided less than adequate service. To be sure, some proxies had both good and bad experiences with government documents reference staff, and two proxies had nothing but positive comments. Some proxies made useful recommendations, while others were adamant that they would never again make use of library personnel when searching for government information.

The main themes raised by the proxies are discussed in the following sections, and are grouped according to whether they believed library personnel were or were not helpful at the reference desk. Separate sec-

Table 3-1
Descriptions of Reference Service Quality

Positive Descriptions	Frequency	Negative Descriptions	Frequency
Helpful	11	Disappointing	7
Friendly	7	Rude	6
Nice	3	Indifferent	3
Efficient	2	Quite poor	3
Polite	2	Uncaring	3
Professional	1	"Trying to get rid of me"	2
"Go the extra mile"	1	Appalling	2
Worked very hard	1	Not useful	1
Caring	1	Not interested	1
Courteous	1	Not courteous	1
Wonderful	1	Not cordial	1
Pleasant	1	Abrupt	1
		Dreadful	1
		Bewildered	1
		Hostile	1
		Unpleasant	1
		"Half-assed"	1

tions discuss the lack of subject knowledge displayed by reference staff, the overall feelings proxies had at the completion of the study, and salient recommendations made by proxies. Indeed, their comments about the various ways in which government documents reference staff failed to provide adequate service are remarkably similar to the experiences categorized by Catherine Ross and Patricia Dewdney (1998), who identify 10 strategies of "negative closure" by which staff members end a reference transaction without satisfying the information needs of the user (p. 151). Ross and Dewdney contended that a key goal for library reference staff is processing users through the system in as expeditious fashion as possible. "Increasingly harried as fewer people do more work and face longer line-ups of users," librarians "win" the reference game "when the transaction is completed and [they] can move on to the next question" (p. 154). While such strategies of "negative closure" allow staff to deal with more information requests, users are frustrated at the quality of service they have received. The 10 strategies in question are:

1. Unmonitored referral, defined as "a situation in which the reference librarian gives the patron a call number or refers the patron to a source within the library but makes no effort to check that the source is ever found, or, when found, actually answers the question" (Ross & Dewdney, 1998, p. 151; Murfin & Bunge, 1984, pp. 175–182).
2. Reference personnel "immediately refer the user somewhere else . . . to another floor within the library or to another agency altogether" (Ross & Dewdney, 1998, p. 155).
3. The librarian "implies that the user should have done something else first before asking for reference help" (Ibid.).
4. Staff members try "to get the user to accept more easily found information instead of the information actually needed" (Ibid., pp. 155–156).
5. The librarian "warns the user to expect defeat because the topic is too hard, obscure, large, elusive, or otherwise unpromising" (Ibid., p. 156).
6. Staff members "encourage the user to abort the transaction voluntarily" (Ibid.).
7. Librarians signal "nonverbally that the transaction is over by tone of voice, turning away, or starting another activity" (Ibid.).
8. Staff state "explicitly that the search has reached a dead end" (Ibid., p. 156).
9. The librarian "claims that the information is not in the library or else doesn't exist at all" (Ibid.).
10. The librarian "goes off to track down a document but then never returns" (Ibid.; Durrance, 1995, pp. 243–265).

As shown below, all of these negative strategies, originally identified when patrons were not asking government documents reference questions, were also employed by government documents reference personnel.

NEGATIVE IMPRESSIONS OF REFERENCE SERVICE QUALITY

Many proxies commented on the minimal level of help they received after initial contact with a staff member. Typically, the patron was given a Web site address, and nothing more. In effect, this action amounts to the librarian "point[ing] in the direction of the shelves, but . . . giv[ing] no indication of where the user should look" (Ross & Dewdney, 1998, p. 155). To be sure, proxies were sometimes pointed in the right direction, but they were subsequently left on their own. Accordingly, the "unmonitored referral" is alive and well in the electronic age. Instead of sending users to book shelves, staff now vaguely send them to the Web. One proxy wrote:

> For many of the questions I was led to the Federal Government web page but there was little to no help after they found my initial starting point. In almost every case the librarian did not actually find my answer. He/she would lead me to where they thought I should look and then leave me. Off they would go to help another patron. If I was having difficulty the librarian would not have known because they never, not once, came to see if I found what I was looking for. I had to wave at them to come over to my terminal, or go back to the desk if I was having problems. On one occasion the librarians were just sitting at the desk chatting while I and other patrons were trying to find the answers to our questions. If my mother were asking these questions she probably would not have been so persistent and she probably would not have been able to work on her own.

Particularly troubling in this report is the picture of librarians "sitting at the desk chatting" while patrons unsuccessfully search for relevant information. The attitude of the reference staff in this example not only displays a marked insouciance toward customer satisfaction, but also a disquieting unprofessionalism. The body language of the staff members here is tantamount to telling patrons that, first, the minimal amount of help that was initially provided should be sufficient and, second, if the information still cannot be located, then the problem lies with the patron and not with the initial set of instructions. Chatting among coworkers here takes precedence over proactive helping behaviors that may alleviate patron stress and confusion; roving reference service is not offered. Patrons are left to fend for themselves as best they can. Some may find what it is they are searching for, others will no doubt spend long periods of time exploring unfruitful avenues, and still others will become frustrated and give up. Would it have been so difficult for one of the staff to periodically make a short trip to the computer terminals and ask each individual, however briefly, whether she or he was successful in finding necessary materials?

Staff assume that the mere act of providing a single gateway Web address constitutes good service. However, electronic sources of information are no less complex than print sources, and not all patrons, especially older adults such as the proxy's mother mentioned in this example, are adept at navigating Web pages, let alone understanding the structure and authority of Web documentation. Two other proxies had similar experiences with staff who assumed that their job was done the moment a single Web address was given.

> A number of times the librarian would provide me with a web site address rather than a printed source. That was fine except that often it seemed like they were trying to get rid of me by supplying a piece of an answer with little evidence that the response would actually be there—and there would be no follow-up if the response was not found on the Web site and no alternatives were supplied.

In this instance, it would appear that a Web site address is being used as a shortcut response intended to "get rid of" a patron, with no follow-up and no suggested alternatives, should the original Web address fail to meet an information need. Noteworthy, too, is the proxy's feeling that staff is unsure of whether a response *really* exists in the source to which they direct patrons. Nonetheless, in this example, the patron was at least provided with a starting point. Other patrons were not so fortunate. One proxy noted: "On several occasions, I was directed to the Web with no direction or actual URL to go by. I feel that the average patron would be at a disadvantage in this case, because often the [required] information was buried and required some internet skills to retrieve."

Again, the Web seems to be functioning as a "one-size-fits-all" source. There is no indication, in the above three quotations, that library staff are aware of the problems that patrons may encounter in finding information on the Web. Moreover, there is little indication that staff are prepared to aid patrons in finding their way in the electronic realm. Staff treat the Web as a potentially rich mass of material that, because of its vast extent and unfamiliarity, is *likely* to contain the sought-after information. But what is the difference between telling a patron that her answer could be found in any one of thousands of books physically housed in the library, and telling that same individual that her answer is probably located on the Web? Library staff seem to be missing an opportunity to establish themselves as indispensable guides to, and teachers of, the intricacies and organizational structure of Web-based documents.

Reference personnel may argue that the relatively recent introduction of Web tools, as well as their constant evolution, makes it more difficult to provide detailed and knowledgeable reference service using electronic sources than using traditional sources. Yet, the same lack of concern shown to patrons directed towards the Web in search of an answer to a government documents reference question was also in evidence when library staff did not suggest using the Web as an information source. "I was often pointed towards a stack of shelves and told to 'Check there' with little or no direction as to which texts may be of help," wrote one proxy. Another lamented that "we were merely pointed towards what [staff members] thought might contain the answers and left to our own devices. In one case [my boyfriend] asked a question at the public library and the reference person told him that they didn't have that information and never even looked at him." Still another proxy states that the library staff "pretty much put a very small effort into looking the subject up on the library computer, which listed the library's stocks, and then they said, well you can check there if you like, I doubt if you'll find what you need. . . . There was a bit of an attitude that I should be able to find what I needed myself."

In sum, the unmonitored referral occurs both with traditional print sources and electronic sources. From one perspective, it is even easier to invoke the seemingly "magical" names of the Web and Internet as a solution to all problems than it is to jot down, on a slip of paper, a series of call numbers of books that the patron is to browse in the hopes of locating a piece of necessary information. After all, the Web is imbued with a mystique of omnipotence, and the mere mention of it may induce, in some patrons, a feeling that immediate help is moments away. But, as one proxy states, this tactic may be a sign of a more fundamental problem, namely, reference personnel who are attempting to hide their lack of skills. She relates how, "[o]n some occasions I was met with hostility and rudeness. This, I believe had less to do with me than it had to do with the librarian[s] realizing their own ignorance and inability to deal with the situation. . . . On two occasions at the public library, I was told that I might want to check the internet for myself."

Referring a user "somewhere else, preferably far away" was another common tactic employed by reference staff answering government documents reference questions. One proxy asking about Parliamentary procedure wrote: "The reference gentleman told me that he thought there were some books on the rules governing the House of Commons but these were on the first floor. No attempt was made to leave his post or explain further where I was to look; he did offer to call a friend of his who worked at the provincial legislature who might have a more ready

What the Proxies Said About Service   83

source." A number of other proxies were told that questions of this type were best answered at the local university. When they went to the university, they found that government documents reference service was provided only during very limited hours. Another proxy wrote that even when she persisted, she was given only the vaguest of referrals.

> For a full depository with a well staffed government documents reference desk, I was disappointed in the service. For all of the questions asked, the librarians couldn't care less if I found the correct answer or not. It seemed as if their main drive was to give me something and do it quickly. When I asked about the aerial photographs, the lady looked at me and said, "I have no idea." The funny part was that she intended to leave me with this answer but when I didn't go away, she realized that maybe she should give me something. If I recall correctly, she gave me a phone number that I later discovered was out of service.

Staff also tried to suggest to users that they should have done something else prior to asking their question, as illustrated in the following statement.

> I felt that several of the librarians were not interested in helping me, and in fact resented the fact that I had so little information on each question. Many of the librarians expected me to know more about my questions than I would expect of the average user: i.e. they expected me to know the Act or Bill numbers and claimed that without said numbers they were unable to produce an answer.

Another proxy, when asking a question about the price farmers in Canada receive for barley, was pressed for clarification as to whether he wanted prices, payments, or subsidies. The type of additional technical information requested in these two instances by library staff fudged the issue. Many users do not come to the library prepared with a wealth of details. Indeed, they often arrive with only the vaguest of notions of what they want. Therefore, to ask users to provide detailed supporting information about their request may induce them to abandon their information search. Some users may get discouraged, since they have been told that there is a great deal of work still to be done, on their part, before anything can be found at the depository library.

Staff also tried to induce users "to accept more easily found information instead of the information actually needed" (Ross & Dewdney, 1998, p. 155). One proxy wrote as follows about a request for pricing and ordering information about a government publication.

> A somewhat odd experience occurred at one of the Academic Full Depositories. I have, or think I do, a very direct and clear way of speaking. I had mentioned to the . . . staff [member] that I wanted this specific ordering

information about this one book by this author, first name, last name. Despite a few more attempts on my part to underscore what I was asking (Jill Wherrett, *Aboriginal self-government*), the [library worker] instead seemed not to focus on what was asked but just what their collection actually held [and] gave [me] all the information on two completely different books.

Unfortunately, this was not an isolated occurrence. Another individual lamented that, "for the question about aerial photography . . . the librarian didn't even consider a government publication. She pulled out a pamphlet of a photography studio from her desk." The question about aerial photography proved especially vexing. Another proxy was less than pleased with a librarian who, after consulting "travel and photography books," suggested that existing aerial photographs of the general region, instead of the specific lake, would suffice. And, while the question concerning the Magdalen Islands specifically asked about House of Commons debates, one library staff person handed a proxy "five or six Transport Canada annual reports." These examples reveal that library staff often do what is most convenient for them, not what is most useful for users. The tendency to do the most convenient thing may be an indication that the staff member lacks in-depth knowledge about the government documents, or it may reveal an unwillingness to listen carefully to the patron's question.

Another common tactic involved telling the patron that the question was so difficult that an answer might never be found to it. Concerning the question about which piece of federal legislation dealt with the percentage of crown corporation motor vehicles having to use environment-friendly fuels, one proxy recalled that the librarian "proceeded to tell me that I may not be able to find the information in the library at all because knowing how many cars they (the government) own is like knowing how many pencils they buy a year. She had never heard of such an Act." Regarding the question about what percentage of Canadian-content sound recordings have French lyrics, another proxy was told that this question "would take a week of research" because "government documents were not indexed at all. He added that my question was not easy, especially since it was a 'statistical' question." In these two cases, the user is met not only with discouragement, but barely concealed exasperation on the part of staff that may cause him or her to feel that his or her question is ill-conceived or a time-waster. Surely this is not the proper attitude for reference staff to adopt. Instead, all questions should be treated in as respectful a manner as possible, keeping in mind that a user generally does not pose a question unless he or she has a genuine desire to locate an answer.

The final five strategies itemized by Ross and Dewdney (1998) were also reported by the proxies participating in the present study. Under the category of encouraging the user to abort the transaction voluntarily, one proxy reports how he "had to gather courage for these questions" because "some of [the reference staff] would roll their eyes and go (even if it's none of their bizzness [sic]) 'why do you care about that?'" Having experienced this reaction, he muses about "how is the general public supposed to feel about approaching these 'experts' in search of information they have a RIGHT to [capitalized in original]?" His concluding thoughts, although syntactically awkward, reveal a genuine concern for members of the public who may feel intimidated by dismissive reference staff: "I like to think I know better, that 1) they don't intend to intimidate or 2) if so they're crappy librarians—but does this console anyone else of reasonable intelligence and guts when approaching a gatekeeper? One who may not even be able to help them, or may mislead them further?"

If the librarian is a real gatekeeper, this proxy believes, she or he should not be intimidating, should start from the premise that the public has the right to government information, and should firmly believe that librarians have a duty to help patrons to find that information by being as knowledgeable as possible about all aspects of government services. In other words, librarians should do all in their power to avoid a situation whereby they "may not even be able to help" patrons or where they "may mislead" patrons.

Non-verbal gestures signifying the end of the reference interview were also used by library staff. One librarian "didn't look up at me once and continued rifling through date due slips. He retrieved the . . . report. I told him I was looking for something specific, he handed me the report and told me that [since] I was the one doing the research, I'd have to find it myself—never making eye contact!!" After receiving such service, what is a patron to think about the library? Instead of a polite and interested reference service interaction, the patron here is made to feel secondary to due date slips.

This was not an isolated instance. Another proxy reports how, after an initial attempt at locating sources, staff went back to reading at the reference desk.

> More specifically, no one spent more than five or ten minutes working on the question before telling me that the library was in fact not a full depository library and that I might have a better chance if I went to a full depository. It seemed pretty much a cop-out. It wasn't even that the libraries were busy or anything. They [the library staff] just went back to reading or doing whatever (i.e. not necessarily helping other patrons that were

waiting in line behind me). I wonder about the level of service I would have received had it been busy when I posed the question.

Still another proxy was not even accorded the courtesy of prompt service. In this case, the reference interview does not begin auspiciously: "The interesting thing was that some other . . . worker had gone to tell her that someone was at the reference desk waiting but I still ended up waiting and even when she came back from break she did not directly approach her desk where I was waiting. She kept chatting. She really didn't seem that concern[ed] that a patron was waiting for service." Patron frustration may ensue in a case such as this. The patron is left to wonder about the priorities of reference staff. And even though the proxy in this specific example did not walk away and waited patiently, some patrons may feel insulted that the library staff place a relatively low value on their time and information needs.

Much like the patron faced with the librarian checking due date slips, these patrons are made to feel as if they have intruded upon a more important activity. Staff give precedence to reading, chatting, or some other activity not directly related to helping patrons. Clearly, the reference desk is not serving its primary purpose. Will these patrons become regular and enthusiastic customers of the library? Or will the negative impression left by their initial encounter cause them to devalue the services potentially available at the library? After all, the reference desk at libraries is meant primarily to be a service environment designed to meet, as fully as possible, the needs of users when users are, in fact, present.

Under the category of giving up too easily or reaching an abrupt dead end without trying another possibly more fruitful approach, one proxy relates the following experience:

> While attempting to answer one of my questions (checking on current legislation), the librarian took a folder from behind the reference desk. She seemed to think that it would have the answer that I needed. It looked like something official that the staff had put together. When she opened it, there were 8 lines of text. She casually said something to the effect that it's not here. Pretty useless source if you ask me.

In a variation of this tactic, proxies also reported that staff claimed that the sought-after information is not to be found in a depository library, or does not even exist. While in the example about the eight lines of text in a folder, staff made at least a cursory attempt to locate the necessary data, in the following two cases no effort at all is made: "With the airphoto question, the librarian refused to believe I was looking in the right place and sent me away quickly. Same with the investments in Africa question—a gov[ernment]-doc[ument]s librarian at a[n] academic full deposit[ory] refused to believe that our government had ever published anything on this. 'Talk to an embassy' was the response."

From one perspective, the librarians here were being abruptly honest with the patron. To be sure, they were wrong about the fact that the Canadian federal government had never published anything about investment opportunities in Africa or did not have a department that provided aerial photographs, but they stood their ground and gave a direct answer. This was not the case in the following reference encounter—another example of Durrance's (1995) "disappearing librarian" and the final strategy itemized by Ross and Dewdney (1998): "On another occasion I asked a question and the librarian said she'd be right back. I watched her walk into the office behind the reference desk. She never returned. I waited about 10 minutes and decided to leave. I checked the office before I left but she had disappeared."

Hernon and Altman (1998) argue that libraries, in assessing the quality of the services they provide, should pay close attention to so-called "lost customers" and "never-gained customers (pp. 142–143)." From the point of view of reference service, lost customers can be defined as those who, as a result of being treated rudely, dismissively, or abruptly by reference personnel, have become frustrated and discouraged in their information quest. The bad experiences recounted here have the possibility of turning potential steady patrons into lost patrons for the depository library.

POSITIVE EXPERIENCES

When proxies talked about the good service they received, their comments centered on ways in which the behavior of reference staff contributed to finding the required answer. Taken together, these helpful behaviors can constitute a model for other government documents reference staff to follow. Dewdney and Ross (1994) provide a list of "staff behavior that helped" (p. 224) during reference interviews, and many of the points they list were also mentioned by proxies in the present study. The most useful actions undertaken by library workers were: displaying interest in the question; showing the patron exactly where to search, rather than just pointing in the general direction with vague instructions; refusing to become discouraged and showing willingness to investigate further; telling the patron to return if suitable information was not found; and following up to see whether the patron succeeded in the search. A strategy not mentioned by Dewdney and Ross (1994) that proxies in the present study commented upon repeatedly was collaborating with other staff members.

Genuine interest about the question on the part of staff was an essential precondition of successful reference interviews. One proxy wrote that "the people at [Library A] were extremely helpful and seemed to be very interested in helping us find the information. The librarians went to the point of finding the book and even the page that contained the information that we were after." Another proxy stated that the "staff at the public library were always eager to help, which made me feel more comfortable. . . . They were usually able to give me more information than I had asked for." In these two cases, interest or eagerness on the part of staff translates into service that could be characterized as above average. Here, proxies were led to specific sources ("the page that contained the information") or were offered a wealth of information (more "than I had asked for") instead of being given vague directions to browse an area of books or told that the question was particularly onerous. Expressing interest about a patron's question may be thought of as a sign of intellectual curiosity and willingness to be challenged to find a suitable answer. It may also be a sign of a willingness to learn new things, since finding the answer will likely entail a complex search strategy in both print and electronic sources. Finally, expressing interest may create a bond of empathy between staff person and patron, allowing the former to enter into the world of the latter, and thus making the search for information a joint enterprise.

Proxies were also impressed by library staff who did not merely point them towards a general area or give directions. One proxy commented on a librarian "who even took my friend downstairs to show him where the call number was and how to use the books." This type of service is in marked contrast to the proxy who felt that he had wasted his time going back and forth between different floors of the library: "The [reference] desk was closed, but I stood around with a few other people before someone in plain sight told us to go downstairs a floor for help. They then sent me upstairs again on my lonesome with a citation and a fuzzy idea of where the document was in the stacks." Staff should recognize that neither the physical layout of the library nor the arrangement of books and reports is necessarily understood by patrons. Patrons may find it daunting to traverse the intricacies of classification schemes without at least some initial guidance.

Proxies also appreciated staff members who were inventive, used multiple sources in an attempt to find answers, and followed up to see whether the patron was satisfied with the information. One proxy praised a librarian who, when "he couldn't find what I was looking for . . . would give me what related documents he had and suggest other research options." A proxy who visited a library during the weekend when reference service was being provided by paraprofessionals was struck by the level of knowledge displayed by staff: "The non-professional librarian (she told me she was not a professional 'expert' but had been trained to answer certain questions) helped me find the answer I was looking for but questioned whether I had all that I needed [about this question]. I did appreciate the fact that she mentioned that if I wanted more, I could come back during the week." In this instance, the paraprofessional provides high-quality service from three different perspectives. She gives as much help as she is able; she asks whether the found information is really sufficient to meet the user's requirements; and she suggests that further help may be received during the week when a professional government documents specialist will be on duty.

Another proxy had kind words to say about a staff person who used personal sources of information to track down an answer:

> Even when the staff had not been able to find the requested information in documents, they tried to find any other way to find out what I had asked for. When I asked for information about aerial photos, the staff person wasn't able to get prices. She then remembered that her husband had bought some aerial photos. She called him and asked him for a phone number for the prices.

Still another proxy lauded the librarian who "phoned me last week (for the 3rd time, and more than a week after I had first made my request by phone) with new information. She was in liaison with another government institution and was wondering if it was alright if she gave them my name and number so that they could contact me directly if they found the desired information." In this last example, the librarian has made it a special point to remember a particular question and to make subsidiary inquiries and searches even after the patron has left the library. Staff at this library seem to take reference questions very seriously, showing an uncommon interest in satisfying a patron's information need. A similar concern is evident in the following example:

> There are closed stacks for some materials . . . but the librarian expressed that it was not a problem for her to go and get as many of the books that I needed. I remember that for the first load I had waited awhile, but it was because she had looked in every book and noted where the section was

that I wanted. She was really the only one that did a follow-up to see if I had enough information.

In this example, it would have been quite easy for the librarian just to get the required items, and to leave the details to the patron. However, the librarian seems to have understood that finding material within government documents and reports is not a self-evident proposition. She therefore not only used her professional knowledge to assist the patron by finding specific sections and paragraphs, but also made a special effort to make subsequent inquiries about the usefulness of the found information.

A very useful helping behavior encountered by proxies was the willingness of a reference worker to collaborate with other library staff. One proxy recounted how "the one staff who I assumed was the head reference librarian enlisted the help of two other assistants, [and they spent] over 20 minutes [on my question]." Sometimes staff made an initial attempt on their own to locate the answer before calling upon other library workers.

> Only one [staff member] tried to look in more than one medium. The librarian took out a file folder of pamphlets, etc. of really dated stuff and had me look through it. Meanwhile, she went on the Internet to do a search of some government sites. She also tried looking at some pink sheets or booklet that listed government publications. Ultimately, she was not able to find the answer, although to her credit she did take down my name and number so that she could call me, and she wanted to talk to one of her colleagues about this one.

Here, at least three sources of information were used in an attempt to assist the patron. To her credit, the staff member does not give up after consulting one source. She could have easily dismissed the proxy after this search, but she persists by making use of the accumulated knowledge of her colleagues, and promises to get in touch with the proxy at a later date.

On other occasions, staff made an immediate determination that a colleague in another part of the library was more knowledgeable about a particular query. For example, the proxy who had received a referral to an out-of-service telephone number when asking about aerial photographs decided to ask the same question at another library. Unlike her first attempt, she was highly impressed because "the librarian called a colleague in the map library who proceeded to find the appropriate Web address and relay the costs over the phone." Another proxy provided a more detailed account of a number of collaborative efforts that resulted in a complete answer.

> I was impressed with the way they collaborated at [Library B]. The staff at [Library C] did the same thing. In one case, the librarian that I asked the question to turned and said to a colleague, I think you'll be able to handle this one better. They both stayed with me while I got my answer. The same sort of thing happened at another library. It seemed as if the librarians wanted to learn from each other.

Here, the librarian is not only willing to admit that he or she does not have specialized expertise in a particular area, but she or he is also aware of the subject expertise of colleagues. Pooling of knowledge is accepted as a positive development for the common good of the patron. In addition, this library has succeeded in creating an environment where learning is encouraged, where colleagues respect each other's knowledge and strengths. When a librarian who has learned from her colleague is able to apply that knowledge to solve a question on her own, the end result is better service for future patrons. Dixie Jones (1997) stresses that collegiality, often overlooked as a determinant of successful reference work, is a learned behavior that can be fostered by creating a management environment where staff "pull together to provide the best possible service" by not only being "aware of one another's strengths to capitalize on them," but also by trusting one another, learning from each other, and treating each other with respect and courtesy (p. 164).

In sum, reference workers who treat each patron request as vitally important seem to be the key to quality reference service. This respect may assume many forms, from consulting multiple sources, to asking other colleagues about the question, to suggesting other avenues of approach, to keeping an unresolved query in mind for weeks at a time, and to following up with a patron in order to determine whether success has been achieved. In other words, a strong sense of caring is required— caring that each and every patron who comes to the library with a request, no matter how trivial or complicated, be accorded the same amount of respect and time. The following account can stand as a symbol of such a service philosophy: "The librarian at [Library D] was quite impressive. In front of me in the line of people to see her were two small children; she gave them the necessary attention before helping me. I mention it simply because I respect the gesture. She then instructed me how to use the CD-ROM system." According to the proxy, "necessary attention" was paid. Each reference question, of course, demands a different amount of "necessary attention," but the important point here is that attention must be paid. Just as the reference worker in the above scenario did not cavalierly dismiss the two small children, reference staff, when faced with adult patrons asking complex questions, should not dismiss their queries with the type of careless, shoddy, and haphazard service described in the previous subsection: unmonitored referrals, telling patrons that the required information does not exist, and chatting with other workers while patrons struggle to find information on their own. For library workers answering government documents reference questions, paying "necessary attention" means displaying some of the characteristics described in this subsection: persistence, consultation with others, and initial, as well as continued, interest in the patron's information needs.

LACK OF SUBJECT KNOWLEDGE

In addition to comments about the positive and negative aspects of the way they were treated at government documents reference desks at depository libraries, another central theme emerging from the accounts submitted by proxies was the particular difficulty that library staff had in orienting themselves within the universe of Canadian government documents. One proxy wrote that "the librarians seemed completely shocked by the type of questions. . . . The public librarians seemed most distressed at the questions they received." In general, this proxy felt that when confronted with requests for government information, "the looks on the faces of the librarians were as vast [empty] and bleak as the harsh prairie that surrounded the city." This characterization is confirmed by the following evocative account.

> I think the thing that sticks in my mind about meeting various reference librarians is how they (majority) seemed so pleased to hear my question but then as soon as they learned that it involved government documents, physically, I saw their shoulders sink as if I put a ton of books on their back! Seriously, I heard a lot of "I am not very familiar with government documents" or "I really don't know that much about government documents." . . . I remember one librarian . . . seemed really uncomfortable with the question about the firearms and more uncomfortable that I followed her to whatever section she went to. I think that she would have preferred if I had waited at the desk. Her final response was just to look through piles and piles of debate reports.

To say the least, questions dealing with government documents are met with a fair degree of trepidation. The perception may be that such questions are very complex and may involve a significant investment of time. In addition, library staff may believe that they do not have the requisite knowledge about government information to direct patrons in the proper direction. Either they do not consider themselves to be specialists in the field, or they did not take specific government documents courses during their university training, or their library has not had training courses devoted to government information. Whatever the reason, staff feel their shoulders sag as if under a great weight, and their only recourse is to make the excuse that they are not familiar with government documents and hope that the patron is satisfied with such an acknowledgment. Given that staff are willing to admit their low skill level in government documents and given the fact that they feel "uncomfortable" in dealing with government questions on a daily basis, would it not be logical to expect that staff might try to learn more about the structure, function, and areas of responsibility of various government units on their own, absent a formal training program? Would it be so unreasonable to expect staff at libraries, on their own, to become familiar with, in broad general terms, the literature produced by government entities and the programs administered by various government departments? If staff took their responsibility to provide government information seriously, situations in which a proxy had to tell a staff person that "the *Canada Gazette* contained regulations, not debates in Parliament" might not occur.

If government documents reference staff had basic knowledge of government services, they might have avoided a number of situations in which they provided, in the eyes of proxies, woeful service. The question about aerial photography in particular revealed that library staff do not have a great deal of knowledge about the programs and services offered by the federal government. Most staff suggested that patrons call or visit a local photography studio instead of directing them to the specific federal agency dealing with aerial photography and mapping. Similarly, staff did not know that the Canadian government publishes material about investment opportunities in Africa. In addition, proxies commented more than once on the difficulty library workers had in finding statistical information about barley prices and federal job opportunities. However, if staff were aware of which government departments or agencies were responsible for these types of information, they likely would have a head start on locating the desired information. At the very least, they would not be making broad omnibus searches, but would, based on their knowledge of who does what in the federal government, be able to target more specifically the publications or Web site of the appropriate department or agency.

OVERALL IMPRESSIONS

It will come as no surprise that many proxies were scathing in their final assessments of the quality of service received when asking government documents reference questions. "I found that the staff at [Library F] were disappointingly dismal," wrote one proxy. Not only was she disappointed with the reference service, but a friend who accompanied her on one expedition bluntly stated that getting staff to provide any type of answer was "like kicking over an ant hill." This proxy concludes that, "almost invariably my questions were met with sighs, looks of panic, or rudeness clearly borne of stress."

It is interesting to note the emphasis on stress, especially in light of the comment by another proxy, who wrote that, "due to budget cuts, there have been significant reductions at [Library E] over the past few years. In spite of this, the librarians always find time to assist the public and do so in a professional manner with a friendly smile." Financial constraints at public and academic libraries in Canada have resulted in staff reductions, the replacement of professional librarians by paraprofessionals, and a concomitant increase in the workload of remaining workers. At the reference desk, where, in the past, there may have typically been two staff members present to assist the public, now only one is assigned. Alternatively, instead of the reference desk being open for eight hours per day, it may now be open only for four hours. In this scenario, if the number of reference questions asked per day remains constant, the rate of reference questions per hour doubles. Stress levels would naturally rise, and staff would be hard-pressed to provide an acceptable level of service. Still, many reference workers do indeed serve the public "in a professional manner with a friendly smile." In light of the often difficult economic circumstances in which libraries find themselves, this high level of service when faced with government documents reference questions speaks volumes about the commitment and care with which some library workers approach their daily tasks.

In general, however, proxies viewed government documents reference service at depository libraries as nothing less than abysmal. Whether low service levels were due to budget cutbacks or not, overall estimates of the help received at libraries are not flattering for library professionals and paraprofessionals. Consider the following appraisal.

> At first I was frankly appalled by the low or non-existent level of appropriate or adequate replies to the questions from the survey. I had feared that this might be some reflection on the Atlantic region in general; perhaps lower budgets and standards could be the cause behind such below

average performance. No one knew, or at best very infrequently, just exactly where a fact, text, [or] law was to be found. I was surprised at how often I was told to go elsewhere, ask at another library, or write away to an agency for the answers. If the staff had been overwhelmed or engaged in a myriad of tasks, it would have been more reasonable to be given such replies. Yet often, I was the only person around and the staff often reacted, if they had any reaction at all, to my presence as a gross inconvenience. I had thought that they would find my queries a challenge of some sort but obviously, they were not. It appears in talking to my fellow students that these dismal reactions are regrettably the rule and not the exception across the country. I hope I am not painting too negative a picture, the library personnel did not hiss as I walked toward them, they just were not, shall we say, overly welcoming on many occasions.

What is striking in this account is the proxy's feeling that he has been made to feel as if he were a "gross inconvenience." Library staff are lethargic and complacent, in his view, and do not wish to be challenged. They took the "easy way out" by sending him to other locations, but they themselves did not seem to be engaged in "a myriad of tasks." The picture that one gets of these depository libraries is troubling. What exactly do staff at the libraries visited by this proxy think their job is? For what purpose do they come to work every day? Are they aware of how their actions are perceived by members of the public, and of the possible affect of their complacency on how the library is perceived and valued within the community?

Perhaps the most eloquent statement about how poor library service translates into an attitude of great disappointment toward the profession of librarianship is given by a proxy who took her mother along on her trips to depository libraries.

> I can say that I was really disappointed and a bit embarrassed about the level of service that both my mother and I received while participating as proxies for the study. Very little in the level of customer service on the part of the librarians. . . . [In some libraries] I was completely lost in there. Very little help. I can tell you that if I, a library student, was lost, someone like my mother would be COMPLETELY lost [original emphasis]. I think that my mother would have been turned off of libraries for life if I had given the questions to her to pose. . . . This experience, particularly involving my mother, made me feel bad and depressed about the profession. My mother can't quite understand why I decided to go to library school. After all, I will probably be making less money and will presumably give up my secure job for a life of contract work and no pension. I started this thing excited about introducing my mom to "my new world" and chosen profession. After getting

very few complete answers to my questions and after receiving poor and indifferent service from librarians, my mother is still confused and not impressed with the profession. This experience has definitely not renewed her faith in my chosen profession. It's like if you brought your parents to a new restaurant that you had invested in as a partner or something. You brought them there so that they could be proud of you and see what you are getting involved in. Instead of beaming and being a really great experience for you and them, all three of you get treated rudely, maybe ignored, by the people working there, or maybe your other partners.

The proxy here sees herself through the eyes of her mother, and it is not a picture she enjoys. Initially enthused about showing her mother her "new world," this proxy ends up embarrassed and on the verge of bitterness. She wanted to be "proud" of her new profession and impress her mother with all the skills she was in the process of learning. Instead, she has to explain to her perplexed mother why exactly she made a choice to enter a profession where the norm is to ignore patrons or treat them rudely. The restaurant analogy is telling. Both libraries and restaurants depend on the good will of members of the public. Restaurants that provide poor service immediately feel the consequences on their bottom line. While the impact of poor service on the local library is less immediate, it can nonetheless be real since it is financed indirectly by tax dollars and, in the United States, directly by bond issues, or both. Taxpayers, through elected officials and single-issue referenda, have fundamental choices with respect to how their taxes are spent, and accumulated frustration about the utility of library service may impact detrimentally on library funding. A vicious circle may be one outcome. As funding declines, stress and workload increase, resulting in unhappy patrons, who opt to spend their tax dollars elsewhere.

RECOMMENDATIONS

Proxies did not just criticize or commend the service they received. They also had a number of useful recommendations to improve government documents reference service. One proxy was concerned that reference desks were not staffed by subject specialists, but by clerks who may or may not have adequate expertise about specific topics: "The woman went into the office part and happened upon the Gov Docs librarian who had an appropriate newsletter on her desk (and which wasn't even processed yet!) so that was good. . . . I just wish the Gov Docs librarian would work the desk sometimes!" The fact that the government documents specialist at this library was not providing reference service may indicate that she or he had been placed in an administrative role. Often, the best reference librarians are promoted to managerial positions, and their expertise is lost as less experienced staff replace them at the reference desk. The realm of government documents is sufficiently complex that libraries may wish to have subject specialists available at all times to help patrons. Absent the availability of qualified staff at certain times of the day and on certain days of the week, another idea is to have "a clearly-indicated notepad upon which one can write down a gov[ernment] doc[ument]s reference question, as well as the time/day when you require a response by." One proxy found this system to be particularly innovative and efficient, because "the reference staff promptly call you at home when they come on duty with an answer and leave the materials tagged at the reference desk for you when you can next make it to the library!"

Two other proxies commented upon the missed opportunities of intra-library cooperation, especially between selective depositories and full depositories. Such cooperation can take at least two forms. At its simplest level, it involves referring to another nearby full depository library.

> Another disappointing part of the study was the lack of cooperation between the libraries. I realize that each has priorities over whom they serve, however, to under-utilize the resources that are available is almost criminal. I would have preferred that the public librarians, if unable to answer the question or direct to a source, would be able to suggest the academic library.

On a more sophisticated level, cooperation might entail forging relationships that, on a regional basis, would involve "developing some sort of union catalogue to show selectives—and their patrons—what the (hopefully) nearby full depository has before sending them out the door without a clue." The advent of Web-based catalogues may facilitate the creation of such integrated holdings information. In addition, patrons would get a clear sense of the availability (or lack thereof) of material at other locations. Informed decisions about the next step in the search process could then be made.

A final set of recommendations concerns the role of the federal government in making information accessible to depository libraries. One proxy had blunt words of advice:

> In my humble estimation, if the government means to have libraries work as access nodes to info, they're going to have to 1) cut back on useless or superfluous deposit items for selective libraries (such as Hansards without

indexes!); 2) take what is saved to help improve their internet access and knowledge of online government resources; 3) improve access hours and product knowledge in full depositories.

The central theme in this comment is that the federal government has a responsibility to improve knowledge about government documents within the depository system. Government information, whether we like it or not, is a "product," and depository libraries that are responsible for disseminating this product should be as knowledgeable about it as retail establishments intent on selling their products. As the main supplier of information to depository distribution points, the Canadian federal government, through the Depository Services Program (DSP), has a vital role to play in educating library workers about government information. For instance, regularly scheduled training sessions could be conducted about various aspects of government services and publications, either in person or through remote electronic access. Such training would allow library staff to constantly update, broaden, and deepen their knowledge about government structures and functions, and processes. The ability of library staff to answer government documents questions completely and accurately could only improve.

CONCLUSION

Faced with the kind of dispirited service at depository libraries described here, some patrons may resolve never again to make use of depository libraries for government information. One proxy concludes that "[a]s for going back to the libraries to ask questions, we agree that both of us will never use the main branch of the public library for finding reference material." A second proxy states that while on two occasions she had good experiences at libraries because staff members were "helpful and nice, . . . the other times the librarians really did not want to deal with me and had the attitude that I should be able to find the information I was looking for on my own, or else I shouldn't be asking the question." Summarizing her experiences, she asserts that "it wasn't particularly enjoyable and I think that under normal circumstances, as in if I was really doing my own research, I would be hesitant to go back to that library and try to find other ways of getting information that I needed rather than asking the librarians for help." Still another proxy writes that "my overall impression of the service that I received at the libraries was not very useful" and that the staff "was not very interested in helping me actually find the stuff." At two libraries, members of the reference staff "didn't seem to care and actually looked at me like I was from outer space." As a result, the proxy vowed that "[i]n the future, I think I could handle finding information myself whether it be on the internet or the computer system at the library itself."

For all intents and purposes, these three individuals are what Hernon and Altman (1998) describe as "lost customers" of the library (pp. 143–143). Having experienced desultory service when attempting to locate government information, they now judge their own skills to be superior to those of trained reference personnel. The amount of foregone goodwill for the library in the community is immeasurable, since these patrons no doubt have friends, family, and work colleagues to whom they will relate their negative library experiences. As Web access from home and work becomes an accepted part of everyday life, individuals who have had bad experiences at libraries, or who may have heard about less than adequate service at libraries, may be tempted to bypass these institutions in favor of searching the Internet themselves for needed information. After all, if the service level at libraries consists of staff simply telling patrons to use the Web or pointing patrons vaguely towards book stacks, an individual may very well be forgiven for thinking that his or her skills are the equal of, if not superior to, library reference personnel. If members of the general public begin to perceive library staff as unable to deal competently and courteously with reference questions, important implications for librarianship as a profession arise. Librarians have constantly struggled to define themselves as highly skilled practitioners striving to provide prompt, accurate information service. Erosion, on the part of the general public, in the faith of librarians to continue to provide such service may be a precursor of a decline in the respect afforded to library workers and a concomitant decline in the willingness of administrators to view library staff as worthy of professional designation.

More specifically, members of the public may begin to question the role of depository libraries in providing adequate access to government information. They may begin to look elsewhere for needed information. As mentioned in Chapter 2, Beamish (1999) reports that many government departments in the United States have instituted programs whereby government officials accept questions, and provide answers, through e-mail. One proxy got to the crux of the matter by writing that her participation in this study "made me realize how ill-equipped librarians are to handle such questions. It will be even more interesting to see how information access is affected with the advent of the paraprofessional at the reference desk."

The implication is that reference service levels at depository libraries will decline even further, unless some kind of drastic action is taken. This action could take the form of extensive and periodic training programs stressing the vast array of government programs and services available to the general public. Depository libraries should no longer be content to act as warehouses of documents. Indeed, their warehouse function is fast becoming obsolete as the electronic data storage capabilities of the Web increase almost on a daily basis. Instead, depository libraries and their staff should strive to become as conversant as possible with the complex network of government information. However, becoming *conversant* does not mean having a "passing acquaintance with." Rather, it means having a sophisticated understanding of the intricacies and minutiae of government agencies, boards, departments, commissions, legislative entities, and executive branch bodies; it means knowing, in some detail, "who does what" in the federal apparatus. It means, for each reference staff member, always keeping one step ahead of the next reference question walking in the door. It means, when all is said and done, being confident that one's knowledge about government information is such that a patron will never become a "lost customer" for the depository library.

Chapter 4

Difficulty of Individual Questions

Chapter 2 dealt with the proxy-administered questions as a group. Attention is directed in this chapter to individual questions with a view to determining which were the easiest and which were the most difficult to answer. The individual characteristics of each question are examined with specific focus on the relative ease with which an answer to each one can be found using Web sources. Some of the accounts written by proxies about what happened when they asked a question are analyzed with a view to providing a glimpse into both positive and negative features of reference interviews. The average time spent by library staff in answering each question is compared with the average times that the student pre-testers took to locate answers to the same questions.

Figure 4-1 and Table 4-1 show the percentage of complete and partially complete answers to each of the 15 reference queries. Four questions—CRTC, Auditor-General, Rules, and Crime—were supplied with complete and partially complete answers at a rate of about 70 percent or more; three of these four are what Katz characterizes as document-retrieval questions. Nine questions had complete and partially complete answers at a rate of 30 percent or more; six of these nine—Auditor-General, Rules, Crime, Magdalen Islands, Fisheries, and Refugee—are also document-retrieval questions. Queries for which documents are to be retrieved appear to be easier to answer than data questions. This is a conclusion supported by an examination of the three questions—Books, Lyrics, and Fuels—that show complete and partially complete success rates of less than 20 percent.

Two of these questions, Books and Lyrics, clearly fall into the data-retrieval category. The former asks for a specific price; the latter asks for

Table 4-1
Types of Answers to Individual Questions

	Complete	Complete and Partially complete	Referrals	No/Incorrect
Auditor-General	66.7%	69.7%	15.2%	15.2%
Crime	66.7%	69.7%	0%	30.3%
Garbage	37.5%	43.8%	28.1%	28.1%
Barley	36.4%	45.5%	9.1%	45.5%
CRTC	36.4%	78.8%	3%	18.2%
Fisheries	34.4%	34.4%	12.5%	53.1%
Rules	33.3%	78.8%	0%	21.2%
Africa	18.8%	28.1%	31.3%	40.6%
Fuels	18.8%	18.8%	18.8%	62.5%
Firearms	18.1%	27.3%	12.1%	60.6%
Aerial photo	15.6%	25%	59.4%	15.6%
Lyrics	15.6%	18.8%	28.1%	53.1%
Magdalen Islands	15.2%	45.5%	9.1%	45.5%
Refugee	12.5%	34.4%	15.6%	50%
Book	12.1%	15.2%	60.6%	24.2%

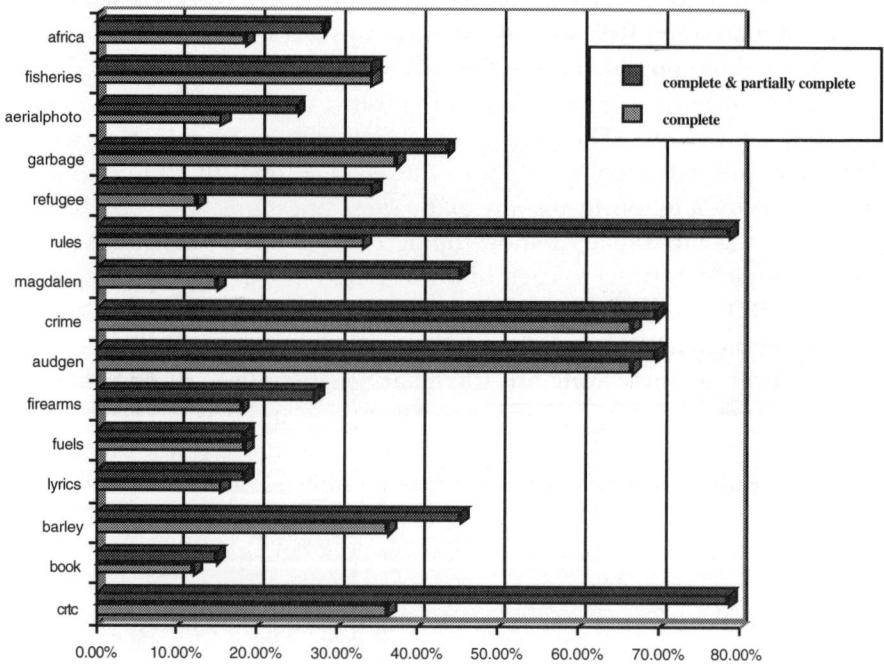

Figure 4-1 Responses Received by Individual Question

the percentage of French lyrics in Canadian-content sound recordings. The Fuels question was classified as a document-retrieval question because it asks specifically for the text of an act, though not by name. However, this question was deliberately written in such a way as not merely to ask, for instance, "Can I get a copy of the Alternative Fuels Act?," but it requested particular data about standards connected to unconventional fuels. The wording of this question therefore tests the hypothesis that "data questions are more difficult than documents questions" insofar as another question—that dealing with the Fisheries Prices Support Act—specifically mentions its act by name and is among those nine questions for which complete and partially complete answers were found the most. Since the Fuels question is among the three lowest for complete and partially complete answers, this lends additional credence to the fact that data questions are harder to answer than document questions, as discussed in Chapter 2 and shown in Figure 2-14.

Figure 4-2 displays the rank descending order of questions that were completely answered. Three clear groupings of questions emerge: those for which complete answers were provided at a rate of 60 percent, those for which complete answers were provided at a rate of between 20 percent and 40 percent, and those questions for which complete answers were provided less than 20 percent of the time. By a wide margin the Auditor-General and Crime questions were answered completely most frequently. Again, both of these are document questions.

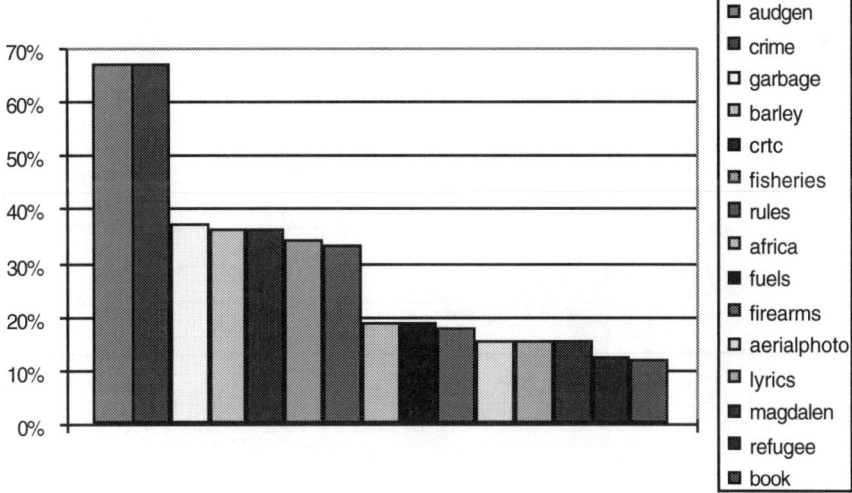

Figure 4-2 Rank Descending Order of Questions That Were Completely Answered

Another way to look at the individual questions is by dividing them into the following three categories: legislative-document questions, executive-document questions, and executive-data questions. There are five questions in the legislative-document category (Crime, Firearms, Rules, Magdalen Islands, Fuels), four in the executive-documents category (Africa, Fisheries, Refugee, Auditor-General), and six in the executive-data category (CRTC, Book, Barley, Lyrics, Garbage, Photo). Document-retrieval questions dealing with the legislative branch received complete answers 30.4 percent of the time, and complete and partially complete answers 48 percent of the time. Document-retrieval questions dealing with the executive branch received complete answers 33.1 percent of the time, and complete and partially complete answers 41.6 percent of the time. The figures for these first two categories are comparable. However, there is a drop in success rates for data-retrieval questions dealing with executive branch, making these questions the most difficult for library reference personnel to answer. Complete answers to these questions were received 25.6 percent of the time, while complete and partially complete answers were received 37.8 percent of the time.

Figure 4-3 displays the rank descending order of questions that received the most no or incorrect answers. While it might be expected that Figure 4-3 would be the exact reverse of Figure 4-2, this is not the case because the different rates of partially complete answers or referrals may impact on the rates of complete and no/incorrect answers. Five questions had no/incorrect rates of 50 percent or more; four questions had no/incorrect rates of between 30 percent and 50 percent; six questions had no/incorrect rates of less than 30 percent. The two most dif-

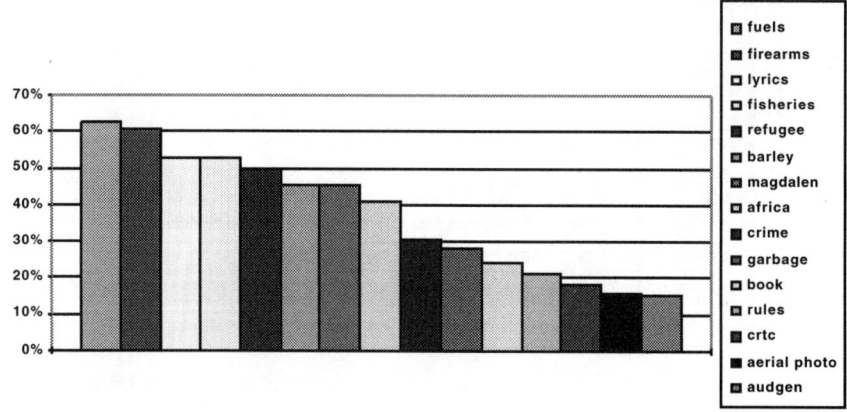

Figure 4-3 Rank Descending Order of Questions That Received Most No/Incorrect Answers

ficult questions were the Fuels and the Firearms questions. Both of these questions were also in the group that received complete answers less than 20 percent of the time. These consistent results make the Fuels and Firearms questions those which library personnel undeniably found the most difficult to answer. And, following the three-fold division among executive branch document-retrieval questions, legislative branch document-retrieval questions, and executive branch data-retrieval questions, the five legislative branch document retrieval questions, taken as a group, received no/wrong answers 44 percent of the time, while the four executive branch document-retrieval questions received no/wrong answers 35.8 percent of the time, and the six executive branch data-retrieval questions received no/wrong answers 30.8 percent of the time. Conversely, the six executive branch data-retrieval questions received the most referrals, 31.4 percent, while the four executive branch document-retrieval questions were referred 22.5 percent of the time and the five legislative branch document questions were referred the least, 8 percent of the time.

Table 4-2 compares the average time spent (in minutes) finding complete or partially complete answers by student pre-testers and library personnel in depository libraries. These averages do not include the time spent by library personnel when they gave referrals or provided no/incorrect answers. These averages are merely indications of tendencies.

Table 4-2
Average Time Spent (in Minutes) Finding Answers

Question	Student Pre-Testers	Library Personnel Who Found Complete and Partially Complete Answers
CRTC	2	9
Book	12.5	12
Barley	10	8
Lyrics	15.5	15
Fuels	5	10
Firearms	15	10.8
Auditor-General	3.5	6.7
Crime	10	12.3
Magdalen Islands	10	12.6
Rules	3.5	9.8
Refugee	12.5	11.5
Garbage	no answer	8.3
Photo	7.5	6.5
Fisheries	5.5	11.6
Africa	6.5	8

Given this caveat, on seven of the questions student pre-testers found complete or partially complete answers more than two minutes faster than library personnel. On six questions there was a two minute or less difference in the times spent finding such answers. For all intents and purposes, the time spent on these six questions should be considered as equivalent. On the other hand, library personnel were able to locate complete or partially complete answers significantly faster for two questions. Since both student pre-testers used Web-based resources to answer questions, this data suggest that library personnel might be more efficient at finding answers to government documents reference questions if they were better trained to use Web sources.

On average, the most time-consuming questions for library staff were legislative branch document-retrieval questions (11 minutes each). Questions dealing with executive branch data-retrieval documents and executive branch document-retrieval documents took about the same time (9.8 minutes and 9.5 minutes, respectively). For student pre-testers, the most time-consuming questions were executive branch data-retrieval questions (9.5 minutes), followed by legislative branch document-retrieval questions (8.7 minutes), and executive branch document-retrieval questions (7 minutes).

ANALYSIS OF INDIVIDUAL QUESTIONS

Question 1: Who are the Chair and other full-time members of the CRTC?

One reason for asking this question was to ascertain whether staff members would think to update information contained in a directory or realize that the information in the directory was inadequate for the question asked. In the three-month period previous to this study, well-publicized personnel changes had occurred within the CRTC. These updated

Table 4-3
Types of Answers Received by Type of Library for CRTC Question

	No/ Incorrect	Partially Complete	Referral	Complete	Grand Total
Academic full	2	3	0	2	7
Academic selective	1	1	0	0	2
Public full	0	1	0	2	3
Public selective	3	9	1	8	21
Grand Total	6	14	1	12	33

Difficulty of Individual Questions   107

changes would not appear in commonly used sources such as the *Canadian Almanac and Directory*, but would appear on the CRTC Web site, <http://www.crtc.gc.ca/ENG/BACKGRND/g2e.htm>, or in the *Corpus Administrative Index*. Credit for a partially complete answer was given to depository libraries whose staff used a single source such as the *Canadian Almanac*; credit for a complete answer was given for the ability to provide the most recent information.

One striking aspect of the answers received was that many library staff, especially at public selectives, did not have an up-to-date answer. Library staff who did update the answer turned to the Web. One model reference interview, in which multiple sources were used, started out with the staff member stating that "I think we can find the answer right here at the desk." The proxy was then put on hold for a short time. When the staff person came back, she said that she had checked the *Canadian Almanac*, but "it was not a good response and she would [therefore] look on the Web."

Question 2: I want to order a copy of *Aboriginal Self-Government* by Jill Wherrett, published in 1996. I'm sure it's a government document, and I specifically want to know how much it costs and any ordering instructions.

On the surface this is a difficult question, but a complete answer to this question could be easily found by searching the Depository Services Program Web site at the following address: <http://dsp-psd.pwgsc.gc.ca/search_form-e.html>. Here, a search engine is available that allows an author search to be performed. Three references to a book entitled *Aboriginal Self-Government* appear; two of these refer to books for which Wherrett is a co-author with Jane Allain. The book for which Wherrett is sole author is the book asked about in this question. Clicking on this title shows that the price of the book is $6.50.

Table 4-4
Types of Answers Received by Type of Library for Book Question

	No/ Incorrect	Partially Complete	Referral	Complete	Grand Total
Academic full	4	1	2	1	8
Academic selective	1	0	0	0	1
Public full	1	0	3	0	4
Public selective	2	0	15	3	20
Grand Total	8	1	20	4	33

A noteworthy aspect of this question is the high number of referrals made to various types of local bookstores, both chains and independents. In one case, only when one of the proxies responded by stating that she thought that chain bookstores did not usually carry government publications did a staff person suggest calling a government bookstore. Another proxy was told to check in *Books in Print*, and still another was told to look in the *Yellow Pages* to get the telephone number for a government bookstore. A number of full depositories had copies of this volume, and suggested that the patron come in to view the book, but these libraries could not provide the price. In a number of instances, library staff tried to talk the patron out of ordering a copy without trying to find out how to do the ordering. One proxy wrote that the staff person "just looked into [her] computer to see if they had it at the library [and] even when I told her I wanted to order it she kept saying to come in and look at their copy first and that I should just photocopy it because it is short." There was another case of how staff really did not listen to the proxy's question.

> For some reason, although I was very specific about wanting to order this book, giving the title and author (spelling the name) the staff on duty told me all she could find were two other books by the same author: *Aboriginal Peoples and . . . the Quebec Referendum* and *Indian Status and Band Membership Issues*, both written in 1996. I tried to make it clear, but she seemed not to understand my question.

In these two cases, staff try to substitute a solution which is easier for them, but which does not engage the patron's original question. Careful listening to the exact needs of patrons, as well a search strategy that goes beyond simply using the library OPAC, is vital for successful reference encounters.

Question 3: I'd like to know what the total payments were per bushel of designated barley for 1995–1996 in Canada. Specifically, I'm interested in the category "select two-row" of designated barley.

A complete answer for this question could be found in a number of locations, although, again, a relatively easy place to locate it is at the Web site of the Canadian Wheat Board, at <http://www.cwb.ca>. Once here, click under <u>Payments</u>. They are listed for specified years, and are given either in tonnes (metric tons) or in bushels. In print, the answer is available, in tonnes, from a publication entitled *Grain Trade of Canada*. The introduction to this book states how many bushels are in a tonne. On this question, an answer was judged to be complete if any price in tonnes was provided for a barley product.

Table 4-5
Types of Answers Received by Type of Library for Barley Question

	No/Incorrect	Partially Complete	Referral	Complete	Grand Total
Academic full	5	1	0	5	11
Academic selective	3	2	1	2	8
Public full	1	0	1	2	4
Public selective	6	0	1	3	10
Grand Total	15	3	3	12	33

Only two library staff members referred to the bushel/tonnes conversion available from print sources. In addition, only two staff members consulted the Canadian Wheat Board Web site. Just as many no/incorrect answers (15) were received to this question as the sum of complete (12) and partially complete answers (3). Many library staff did not want to get involved with such a question over the telephone, urging proxies to come to the library and look for themselves in statistical compilations of government data.

> My question was basically cut off. The librarian told me that it was not a straightforward question and that I should come into the library. Someone was on the reference desk between 9 and 5 and could show me several commodity books to check and a database that probably would give me the answer. When I persisted that I could not make it into the library and was willing to wait on the phone the librarian just said it would be much easier if I came into the library. The librarian was rather blunt and would not consider phoning me back with an answer.

Other staff members more or less conceded defeat by telling proxies "I am sorry, but I do not have any idea where to find that information; maybe you should try the Internet." It was a relatively rare occurrence that library staff made a concerted effort to check multiple sources. One particularly knowledgeable and conscientious staff member not only retrieved an answer from the Canadian Business and Current Affairs database (CBCA), but also provided a very specific Web address as well as a print document detailing raw materials prices for 1995–1996.

Question 4: I'd like to know how many new Canadian-content sound recordings (albums, tapes, CDs) released during 1990–1994 have French lyrics?

Answers to this question could be found using Statistics Canada sources, either print or electronic. In print, a publication entitled *Sound*

Table 4-6
Types of Answers Received by Type of Library for Lyrics Question

	No/ Incorrect	Partially Complete	Referral	Complete	Grand Total
Academic full	2	0	3	2	7
Academic selective	2	0	0	1	3
Public full	4	0	0	1	5
Public selective	9	1	6	1	17
Grand Total	17	1	9	5	32

Recordings (#87-202) as well as *Canada's Cultural Heritage and Identity: A Statistical Perspective* could be used to locate the required information. The Statistics Canada Web site <http://www.statcan.ca> also contained the answer. Here, choose the subsection Canadian Statistics, then People, then Culture, Leisure, then Profile of the Sound Recording Industry.

On six of the 12 occasions when this question was asked at a full depository, proxies received an incorrect answer or no answer. More than half of the answers (17) to this question were no/incorrect. Many library staff members were unwilling even to attempt answering this question. The following type of reference encounter was not untypical.

> I did not receive an answer—the librarian I spoke to rather curtly explained to me that this was *not* the type of question they answered over the phone, and would take "hours of research" to answer, if it could be answered at all, which she doubted. She then suggested that I come to the library in person, and try to find the answer myself.

Here, the librarians adopts one of Ross and Dewdney's (1998) classic negative closure strategies, warning the user that the difficulty and obscurity of the question made finding an answer almost impossible.

According to a proxy researcher, another reference person "refused to have anything to do with the question. He said that they do not answer such questions." Another proxy wrote that the reply she received was "not a very helpful answer! The librarian said he had no idea. I asked if he knew of any place I could check, again he said he had no idea, he said the library had books on music, but that was about it and then he said 'Good day.'" Still another proxy was transferred between a university library and the media center, each suggesting that the other location would be able to help. Clearly exasperated, another reference staff person referred a proxy to a local record store.

Difficulty of Individual Questions   111

Question 5: I'd like to get the text of the act that requires crown corporations to power their motor vehicles with fuels that do not harm the environment. How many of their vehicles have to use these non-conventional fuels in fiscal 1998?

This question attempted to test whether library personnel were aware of the search engine available at the Web site of the Justice Department. The question did not specifically ask for a statute by name in order that the search engine facilities might be used. Full texts of Canadian laws are available at <http://canada.justice.gc.ca>. Click the search icon. Then enter the following search string in the query box: "motor vehicle*" and "crown corporation*" and "fuel*." All these terms were specifically stated in the text of the question. The very first hit is the Alternative Fuels Act, in which the complete answer about how many vehicles owned by crown corporations must be powered by non-conventional fuels can be found. The answer is also available in print from the *Statutes of Canada 1995*.

Again, more than half the responses received (20) were judged to fall in the no/incorrect category. Some reference staff were not happy that proxies "did not know the specific act name and number," and thus stated that "they would be unable to locate the text without a very long search." Another proxy was first directed to the text of an 1985 law, but when she asked for something more recent, the staff person was not able to find anything "because he couldn't find it by subject, he needed the number of the law, and if I knew the number of the law I could call back and he could help me." A similar attitude was conveyed by the staff member who told a proxy that "I am unable to answer your question. It would take a lot of digging and research to find the stats and the act itself. Go to the Law Library, where the acts are, or go to the Web to the Canadian governmental site yourself." Another proxy wrote that "the librarian

Table 4-7
Types of Answers Received by Type of Library for Fuels Question

	No/ Incorrect	Partially Complete	Referral	Complete	Grand Total
Academic full	8	0	2	4	14
Academic selective	2	0	1	0	3
Public full	2	0	0	1	3
Public selective	8	0	3	1	12
Grand Total	20	0	6	6	32

started to look through an index of statutes and said, "There are two or three places where that information could be, but I am not going to do your research for you."

A number of reference personnel provided good starting points for further research towards a complete answer. One library suggested an Internet search using the terms "Hansard" and "environment." Another library suggested visiting the Parliamentary Web page and typing in the search term "transportation." A third library used multiple sources, observing that the information could be in one of three acts: Energy Efficiency Act, Motor Vehicles Fuel Consumption Act, or the Canadian Environmental Protection Act. This library also gave the related information that one third of the House of Commons fleet changed to natural gas and that Transport Canada's fleet has been reduced by 178 vehicles since 1991.

Question 6: There was a Parliamentary sub-committee on the draft regulations on firearms that submitted a report to the House of Commons in 1997. I'd like to see a copy of this report.

This question tested whether library staff members could find committee reports. A relatively simple way to locate this report was through Web-based resources. Go to the main Parliamentary home page at <http://www.parl.gc.ca/36/main-e.htm>. Click on the heading entitled Site Map. From there, scroll down to the sub-section labelled Committees. Pick the committees for the House of Commons, then select Reports. Then scroll through the various committees until you reach the Standing Committee on Justice and Legal Affairs. The final report is available at <http://www.parl.gc.ca/36/1/parlbus/commbus/house/juri/reports/jurirp04-e.htm>. One surprising finding here was that some library staff members went immediately to CBCA—the Canadian

Table 4-8
Types of Answers Received by Type of Library for Firearms Question

	No/ Incorrect	Partially Complete	Referral	Complete	Grand Total
Academic full	5	1	0	6	12
Academic selective	8	0	1	0	9
Public full	1	1	0	0	2
Public selective	6	1	3	0	10
Grand Total	20	3	4	6	33

Business and Current Affairs database. Another worrisome finding was the performance of full depository libraries—on six of the 14 occasions that this question was asked at full depositories, no answer or an incorrect answer was provided.

Many of the reference encounters described by proxies were disappointing. On numerous occasions staff members considered that their work was done after entering a few keywords into the OPAC terminal. One proxy wrote that, "after a quick online search under 'firearms,' I was told to do a search in another local library but that unless I had more specific details about the report, such as a bill number/name or more details about the regulations, they could not help me." Another proxy was told that "the code number of the document" was necessary to find the report, "but [the staff member] did not suggest how I could find the code number."

Other proxies were directed to incorrect information sources for a variety of reasons. One library worker found a number of sources for American regulations for firearms, but could not get the Canadian governments database to work. In frustration, she sent the proxy to the House of Commons debates without any further explanation. Another proxy was also directed toward Hansard, the record of the House of Commons debates. The proxy recounts how, "without explaining what it was or how to use it, she handed it over and suggested I look through it, at the same time ending the interview." Another proxy was first told to go to a section of the library where statutes and other law documents were kept. Finding nobody on duty there to assist her, the proxy returned to the original staff member, and repeated that she was looking for a subcommittee report, not a law. Thinking that "this would be a good place to find reference made to a report submitted to the government," the staff person then recommended a current affairs database of magazine and newspaper articles. Unfortunately, no further help was provided, and the proxy spent "about 30 minutes looking for a reference but could find nothing."

Some library staff did indeed locate documents dealing with the general subject matter of the question, but these documents were invariably not what was required. After a staff member conducted a search using the terms "firearm" and "parliament," one proxy was presented with three documents about gun control, which various lobby groups had presented to the Standing Committee on Justice in 1995. Another librarian searched under "firearms" and "Canada." The proxy was then told "to look through all of the files that matched the search. If it had "GO" beside it, it would be a government document." Unfortunately, the latest committee report was from 1990, and when the proxy asked for help in finding it, the staff person "acted as though she could not be bothered with this." Eventually the report was located, but the proxy noted that the librarian "didn't ask if I needed any more help in finding more info."

Question 7: I'd like to know if the Auditor-General said something in the 1992 annual report about forest management practices of natives, specifically about the good job done by the Stuart Trembleur Lake Band.

This was one of the two questions for which the greatest number of complete answers was received. Many libraries had print copies of the 1992 Auditor-General's report, and library staff showed patrons how to use it, and even indicated the exact chapter where the desired information could be found. The answer is also available electronically at the Web site of the Auditor-General: <http://www.oag-bvg.gc.ca/oag-bvg/rep92/1992e/html/menu_e.html>. The answer is in Chapter 15, subsection 60, where the Stuart Trembleur Band is praised for sound forest investment and management.

As shown in Table 4-9, very few no/incorrect answers were received to this question. When proxies did not get an answer to this question, they were told that the report was not physically available at the library. One proxy was told that the report was not even available on the Web. Another proxy had to work hard to get the answer, as the following account shows.

> Having clearly indicated to the librarian that I was interested in the Auditor-General's report for 1992 (twice), she went to a card index located behind the counter and came back with two drawers of cards. One contained publications on forestry management, the other, native materials. Standing bewildered, I asked why she could not get me the annual report that I

Table 4-9
Types of Answers Received by Type of Library for Audgen Question

	No/ Incorrect	Partially Complete	Referral	Complete	Grand Total
Academic full	2	0	0	7	9
Academic selective	0	0	0	4	4
Public full	1	0	0	2	3
Public selective	2	1	5	9	17
Grand Total	5	1	5	22	33

wanted and which was supposed to contain the information. Finally, she made a phone call and had someone bring the report upstairs, but made no further effort to help with the reference question, nor did she ask any follow-up question.

Again, this is an instance of a staff person not paying attention to what a patron wants. She focuses on the words "forest management practices of natives" in the question, to the exclusion of other pertinent information. In this case, the proxy reminds the staff person to get back on track, taking responsibility for what, after all, is her own question. Staff may get carried away in trying to answer queries, and the experience of this proxy is a good reminder that patrons should not let themselves be taken in directions that they may not necessarily want to be led. Sometimes patrons who know exactly what information they want can contribute to the success of their quest by reiterating, rephrasing, or reformulating their questions.

Question 8: I'd like to see a bill that was introduced into the House of Commons this past fall. It has to do with the profits convicted criminals might make if they were to publish books about their crimes.

As with the previous question, 22 complete answers were received for this one. A caveat, however, must be attached to these impressive results. Even though the question specified that the bill was introduced in the fall of 1997, an answer was coded as being complete if the library staff member located any of the three versions of the bill introduced in the past three years. This private member's bill, entitled An Act to Amend the Criminal Code and the Copyright Act (profit from authorship respecting a crime), received a great deal of media coverage during the autumn months of 1997. It can be found through the Parliamentary Web page of the federal government. Within the 36th Parliament, choose the

Table 4-10
Types of Answers Received by Type of Library for Crime Question

	No/ Incorrect	Partially Complete	Referral	Complete	Grand Total
Academic full	3	1	0	7	11
Academic selective	2	0	0	5	7
Public full	1	0	0	3	4
Public selective	4	0	0	7	11
Grand Total	10	1	0	22	33

sub-section headed <u>Private Members' Bills</u>, then scroll down to the appropriate bill, numbered C-220. The final address is <http://www.parl.gc.ca/cgi-bin/36/pb_prb.pl?e>. When using this Web service, a bill number is not required. Some library staff members, however, told patrons that bill numbers were required to locate the required information. Other librarians unsuccessfully made use of such Internet search engines as Infoseek by typing in keywords "crime" and "profits."

On the whole, depository staff adopted a number of useful and praiseworthy reference interview and search strategies to answer this question. For example, collaborating with colleagues turned out to be very beneficial. One proxy recounts how a staff person "started to look on the Web for the answer [when] two other librarians arrived and asked if she needed help." A second proxy also made a point of mentioning the benefits of collaboration between staff upon witnessing an individual more experienced in government publications come to the aid of a less experienced person. Another proxy related how, at a particular moment in the search, the first librarian "was puzzled and asked a colleague. The next librarian led me to the Private Members' Bills section and we found a copy of the bill."

The use of multiple sources also turned out to be useful. One successful search began with the librarian looking at a number of bills in print, but then discovering that there was no index. "He then looked in the House of Commons debates, looked at one of the publications, and he said he was not sure how to proceed." Instead of giving up at this point, he tried again, this time accessing the Parliamentary Web page, where, after about three minutes of exploring, he located the required bill. Another proxy recounts how a staff person stopped briefly to think about the question, then went to a current affairs database, searched on key words, found a mention of the bill and its number in a news story, then used the mentioned number to locate the bill in the government documents area of the collection.

Question 9: I'm doing a class project about the Magdalen Islands, and there was talk about closing the marine radio station there. I'd like to know if anything was said in the House of Commons about this topic in the last year, and if anything has been decided about its fate.

This question deals with Hansard, the official record of debates in the House of Commons. While the subject matter of the question might seem esoteric, the question is intended to test ability to identify and use Hansard. The basis of this question would be no different were a question to be asked about what, for instance, any other politician said about any political issue. Go to the House of Commons debates sections of the Parliamentary Home Page at <http://www.parl. gc.ca/36/1/ parlbus/chambus/house/debates/indexe/homepage.html>. An alphabetical index of subjects and the names of members is located here. Since information about the Magdalen Islands is required, scroll down to the M's. Click on the M, then scroll down until the subject heading Magdalen Islands is reached. Click on any of three documents until relevant information is found. The answer is that the federal government is "not closing the station but rather it will be operated from Rivière-au-Renard." A decision is still pending about whether to relocate workers from Cap-aux-Meules.

As shown in Table 4-11, very few complete answers were received to this question. Many library staff consulted the compendium publication *Ottawa Letter*. Many others simply took patrons over to the print issues of Hansard, for which no indexes were available, and suggested that they look through the accumulated issues themselves. One proxy in particular was less than pleased at the inability of staff to explain how Hansard works:

> The librarian walked patron to this title on the shelves. No explanation on the use of this source was provided. When patron re-approached the librarian, he was told to "check the volume for this past year." No mention of indexes or easier methods of access were provided. Patron became frustrated and left the library without receiving an answer to his question (only a vague citation).

Another proxy told how "the librarian led me to a web terminal, and went to Hansard, then said, 'I don't really know much about how this works. Why don't you try searching it on your own?' She then left to assist another patron, without asking if I knew anything about it, either!"

Table 4-11
Types of Answers Received by Type of Library for Magdalen Question

	No/ Incorrect	Partially Complete	Referral	Complete	Grand Total
Academic full	4	4	0	2	10
Academic selective	2	1	0	2	5
Public full	2	4	0	0	6
Public selective	7	1	3	1	12
Grand Total	15	10	3	5	33

Another staff person was only able to find "some articles on the Internet on the Magdalen Islands [which were otherwise unrelated to this question]. She said that without an exact date or number she could not find it." Two proxies reported that staff were aware of the electronic version of Hansard, but that they were not aware that debates were arranged according to Parliamentary session. Thus, in checking under the Magdalen Islands, they told these proxies, incorrectly, that nothing had been said about marine radio stations.

Despite such unsuccessful efforts, several proxies commented on the inventiveness of staff in trying to locate information about this question. One librarian, noting how the closure of isolated lighthouses and navigation aids had been a big news story in certain parts of Atlantic Canada and British Columbia, thought to check a current affairs database for possible newspaper or magazine articles about the Magdalen Islands closure. She was successful in finding two stories about the marine radio station. Another librarian tried five different sources, including print and electronic versions of Hansard, the Canadian News Index CD-ROM, the Canadian Legislative Index, and the House of Commons order papers and notices.

Question 10: I'd like to know the complete set of rules that govern Question Period in the House of Commons.

The answer to this question can, again, be found from the main Parliamentary page. Go to <http://www.parl.gc.ca>. Choose <u>Reference Material</u> from the available subjects on this first page. Then scroll down to <u>Reference Works—Procedural</u>. The correct answer is contained in the *Standing Orders of the House of Commons*. In addition, a print version of the *Standing Orders* exists. One interesting aspect about this question is that only two library staff members chose to use a Web-based source. While 11 depository libraries answered this question completely, those whose

Table 4-12
Types of Answers Received by Type of Library for Rules Question

	No/ Incorrect	Partially Complete	Referral	Complete	Grand Total
Academic full	0	4	0	1	5
Academic selective	0	0	0	1	1
Public full	1	3	0	2	6
Public selective	6	8	0	7	21
Grand Total	7	15	0	11	33

answers were recorded as partially complete showed patrons either the *Précis of Procedure* or a general work about the functioning of Parliament.

Of more concern is that a number of library staff members showed patrons reference works dealing with procedures in the Congress of the United States. When questions were being developed, this question was thought to be one of the easiest, since it only involves directing the patron to the *Standing Orders*. It is disquieting, therefore, to find that two thirds of the library staff approached for this question failed to identify this major reference tool. Staff simply do not seem to have the requisite knowledge about this tool, as the following account demonstrates.

> She first looked in some reference books about Parliament and took me to the Government documents area. She found the Statutes of Canada volumes and told me to look under Parliamentary Procedures. She came back with a couple of reference books. Then she took me over to the Pamphlets and Clippings filing cabinets and under House of Commons we found a book with a little explanation of Question Period. There was also a fact sheet on Question Period explaining traditions and procedures that was printed in 1989. I went back to Government documents after that but I could not find anything in the reference books on Question Period.

Evident here is the amount of time staff lose by not being cognizant of readily available sources. This proxy indicated that the staff member spent 20 minutes trying to help—a period of time that could have been spent helping others. Rather than being considered time away from front-line service, formal training and self-training leading to a detailed knowledge of sources should be thought of as a means to help patrons not only more effectively, but also more efficiently. Consider also the following case. While the amount of collaboration exhibited here is to be commended, the proxy notes that it took 45 minutes for her to get an answer. The first librarian gave the proxy a vertical file about the House of Commons, which did not prove useful. A second librarian then attempts to find the information on the Web, but "unable to find it quickly, she asked a third librarian who suggested checking the printed sources in the reference section."

Question 11: I want to know if there is any official document about the possibility of immigrating to Canada as a refugee claimant because of persecution based on gender.

The results received for this question are an indication of the difficulty government documents reference staff experience when dealing with what appears to them to be a judicial question. Fully half of the

Table 4-13
Types of Answers Received by Type of Library for Refugee Question

	No/ Incorrect	Partially Complete	Referral	Complete	Grand Total
Academic full	3	0	1	3	7
Academic selective	4	0	1	1	6
Public full	2	1	1	0	4
Public selective	7	6	2	0	15
Grand Total	16	7	5	4	32

responses fall into the no/incorrect category, while only four of the answers were categorized as being complete. This is especially disturbing, given the potential importance of the subject matter of the question to a patron. One common location to find the answer in print is as an appendix attached to a report by Margaret Young entitled *Gender-Related Refugee Claims* (1994), published by the Laws and Government Division of the Library of Parliament. The required information is also accessible through the Web site of the Immigration and Refugee Board of Canada, which is available at <http://www.cisr.gc.ca>. From the home page of this site, choose the subject heading Legal References. The very first screen of this hyperlink contains a section entitled Chairperson's Guidelines—Women Refugee Claimants Fearing Gender-Related Persecution.

Some library staff members consulted only ready-reference sources such as the *Canada Yearbook*, which obviously did not contain the needed answer. Others directed proxies to dated and very cursory informational leaflets about immigrating to Canada. For instance, one such leaflet, *Sponsoring Refugees: Facts for Canadian Groups or Organizations*, was from 1986. Other proxies were directed to the *Self-Counsel* series on immigration. Still others were shown the Immigration Act and left to examine it for themselves. Two proxies who took the time to look into these sources came away with the impression that, "as far as I can understand claiming refugee status because of persecution based on gender is not one of the five ways you can claim refugee status. The five categories are persecution based on race, political opinion, religion, nationality and membership in a particular social group." Another proxy added that she thought that "war or revolution" was another claimable category, but not gender. Still another proxy pored over the wording of the Immigration Act with the staff person, who concluded from its wording that "no document concerning gender discrimination exists." Another staff member suggested the *1997 Annotated Immigration Act of Canada*, but, after briefly glancing through it and warning the proxy that she was not a lawyer, observed that "no actual sections answered this specific question." Despite these failed efforts, a librarian at a small public selective depository had no trouble locating the answer, directing the proxy to the *Annual Immigration Plan* for 1998, which "discusses the 'Women at Risk' program, the reasons for it and the criteria governing it, as well as the fact that there is no ceiling as to how many applicants can be accepted under it."

Question 12: Someone I know is looking for work hauling garbage. Would there be any specific opportunities to put in bids for contracts in this field with the federal government?

Like the question dealing with the Magdalen Islands, the subject matter of this question may at first appear to be obscure. However, a patron could ask for bidding opportunities connected with any field of endeavor, and the answer could be found in the same location. This is the type of practical question that may be of great financial importance to certain patrons. Probably the best print source is the weekly or bi-weekly *Government Business Opportunities,* although there is no index in this publication. An electronic source is the Public Works Canada Web site at <http://contractscanada.gc.ca/en/index.html>. Then go to Database of Current Government Bidding Opportunities at <http://contractscanada.gc.ca/en/tender-e.htm>. This is the MERX system at <http://www.merx.cebra.com>. Type in "garbage" under Opportunity Search. This system was monitored throughout the time period for this study; there were many contracts for hauling garbage available.

A substantial number of library staff members gave only the vaguest possible answers to this question. Some referred the proxy to "government offices that dealt with this field"; others told the proxy "to go and

Table 4-14
Types of Answers Received by Type of Library for Garbage Question

	No/ Incorrect	Partially Complete	Referral	Complete	Grand Total
Academic full	0	0	1	4	5
Academic selective	4	0	0	1	5
Public full	2	0	0	2	4
Public selective	3	2	8	5	18
Grand Total	9	2	9	12	32

see the minister who deals with garbage disposal"; still others referred the proxy to local municipal authorities. One staff person told a proxy that "unless a contract was published in the newspapers, the library had no information of this sort." The proxy then "specifically asked if there is a federal government contracts bulletin or source where such contracts are listed, and was told no." Another proxy was directed to a book entitled, *Selling to Government: A Guide to Government in Canada.* It sounded promising at first, but it was published in 1989 and likely would not be of much use in December 1997.

A number of proxies also complained about reference librarians who merely told them to search the Web without any further help or instruction. "I was provided with a government online directory and pointed to a terminal," writes one proxy. "The librarian gave no indication of where to begin [and] no assistance was offered in using the computer. An experienced Internet user may be able to find the answer without great difficulty, but the average patron would not likely have found it." Another proxy, after being given minimal instructions on how to get to the Canada government Web site ("pick government, then Canada, then federal"), was told to "just pick through the different subjects." Help of this sort is almost no help at all. The reference personnel in these two cases seem more interested in processing the patron through the system than with offering real assistance.

Contrast the experiences of the two above proxies with the professional approach of the librarian in one of the Prairie Provinces who "led me to an on-line terminal, and went to a government documents link off the library's own home page. From here we went to a search engine which searched all Canadian gov docs, and attempted a search using the terms 'contracts' and 'bidding.' We found several sites that looked helpful," including the <http://www.merx.cebra.com> site. Another librarian not only offered the print source *Government Business Opportunities,* but also suggested that the proxy phone Public Works Canada for more detailed information about tenders specifically in the local area.

Question 13: My mother's birthday is coming soon, and I want to order a color enlargement of an aerial photograph of the lake where my parents have their summer house as her present. Could I have a price list for the enlargements, and information about what I need to do to order such a photograph?

One reason that this question was selected for inclusion in the study was that it tests the knowledge of library personnel about government

Table 4-15
Types of Answers Received by Type of Library for Photo Question

	No/ Incorrect	Partially Complete	Referral	Complete	Grand Total
Academic full	0	0	7	0	7
Academic selective	0	0	2	1	3
Public full	1	1	2	1	5
Public selective	4	2	8	3	17
Grand Total	5	3	19	5	32

services without specifically mentioning that aerial mapping and aerial photography can be provided by the federal government. The most complete source is available on the Web. Go to the Geomatics Canada site at <http://www.geocan.nrcan.gc.ca>. Then, under Thematic Mapping, there is a link to the National Air Photo Library (NAPL) at <http://airphotos.NRCan.gc.ca/main.html>. This site is searchable by key words; choose prices, enlargement, or ordering. Price lists for enlargements can be found at <http://airphotos.NRCan.gc.ca/prices.html>. Many provinces also have departments that provide aerial photography. In addition, by using the Yahoo Canada directory Web site, available at <http://www.yahoo.ca>, the National Air Photo Library is the first returned hit if the search term "aerial photo" is entered.

One significant aspect of this question is the large number of referrals to local photography shops. To be sure, some local photographers would be able to direct patrons to the proper government agency; nevertheless, the inability of some library personnel to identify a government service is cause for concern. For instance, one proxy wrote that "the librarian showed me a number of travel books and photographic picture books of the local area. She said that she didn't know of such a price list [and] told me to consult the local photographer." Another proxy was informed that catalogues of aerial pictures were available, but that the latest ones dated from 1985. Still another proxy was told that she could "consult aerial photographs in the library's map collection and have enlarged copies made on the library's photocopiers." To obtain a color copy, the proxy was directed to a professional copying business, but at the same time the staff member "wasn't sure if the photos could leave the library. She really wasn't very helpful." Another staff person was aware that aerial photographs were available, but only of areas within the jurisdiction of the local city hall. Any color enlargements would again have to be done at a local photocopying shop.

Contrast these unsuccessful reference interviews with the following simple yet efficacious procedure of a staff person in a public selective depository in Ontario. "The librarian thought for a moment, turned around and took the *Guide to Federal Programs and Services* off a shelf, opened it, and referred me to two sections" and two phone numbers, one of which was to the NAPL. Here, the staff person's strong sense that aerial photography is a service provided by the federal government leads to a brief, professional transaction from which it is likely most patrons would emerge with a positive image of library reference staff.

Question 14: Can you help me find any regulations or enabling statutes associated with the Fisheries Prices Support Act?

Unlike Question 5, above, this question specifically mentions a statute by name. But answers to both questions may be located in the same place, namely, the Justice Canada Web site available at <http://canada.justice.gc.ca>. From this site, choose Laws, then Text Versions of Statutes and Associated Regulations for Download. Statutes, and the regulations that pertain to them, are listed in alphabetical order. Click on the letter F, and then scroll down to the Fisheries Prices Support Act. There are three entries for regulations: Canned Mackerel Support Order, Frozen and Cured Herring Price Support Order, and the Small and Extra Small Heavy Salted Dried Cod Price Support Order. These regulations were last updated in 1994.

More than half the answers received fell into the category no/incorrect. Some staff members at full depositories only used the 1985 version of *Revised Statutes of Canada*, which by itself would not answer the question. But staff who did provide a correct answer to this question displayed a vast knowledge of the intricacies of finding government material. For example, one proxy was much impressed as she was, first, given a print

Table 4-16
Types of Answers Received by Type of Library for Fisheries Question

	No/ Incorrect	Partially Complete	Referral	Complete	Grand Total
Academic full	5	0	1	4	10
Academic selective	3	0	0	1	4
Public full	0	0	0	2	2
Public selective	9	0	3	4	16
Grand Total	17	0	4	11	32

Difficulty of Individual Questions   125

copy of the required act from the updated version of *Statutes of Canada* (to April 30, 1993) and, second, was "led through the government web site, consolidated statutes and regulations listing all applicable information current as of December 31, 1996." Some library personnel employed the *Canada Gazette Part II: Consolidated Index of Statutory Instruments*, updated to September 1997, to locate the list of the regulations. Another proxy was handed an extensive pathfinder about locating government regulations and then told to return to the desk if any problems were encountered. Another library staff member spent slightly more than an hour with a patron in a successful attempt to track down these regulations. Finally, one particularly thorough staff member, in addition to finding the required regulations, thought to check the *Canada Statute Citator* to see whether this act had been cited in any court cases. Laws cited in litigation could very well be interpreted from a new perspective, and the body of precedent attached to a law could give it new scope and meaning.

Question 15: Does any government department put out any newsletters or bulletins about business opportunities in Africa? If so, I'd like a copy of the latest one.

This question tests the ability of library personnel to find periodicals published by the government. Again, this is the type of question that may have immediate practical consequences for some patrons. The answer could readily be found using the Web site of the Department of Foreign Affairs and International Trade at <http://www.dfait-maeci.gc.ca>. From here, the library staff member has a number of equally valuable options. After glancing at the main page, the following sub-headings could be accessed: News Releases, Statements, and Publications, under the section The Department; Market Information, under the section

Table 4-17
Types of Answers Received by Type of Library for Africa Question

	No/ Incorrect	Partially Complete	Referral	Complete	Grand Total
Academic full	1	0	1	2	4
Academic selective	3	1	0	0	4
Public full	1	0	2	1	4
Public selective	8	2	7	3	20
Grand Total	13	3	10	6	32

Trade; Africa & Middle East, under the section The World. Under News Releases, Statements, and Publications, go to the section labelled Publications; then choose Trade. Under this heading, one can find a publication called *Africa & Middle East Bulletin*, which briefly summarizes the potential that African countries have for Canadian businesses. Clicking on Market Information leads to a page entitled Market Reports: Information by Region and Sector. Choose the African sector; this leads to an alphabetical listing of countries. Choosing a country leads to detailed information about trade, exploration, and export opportunities. Although some information is password protected, any Canadian citizen is issued a password after completing a basic informational form. Under The World heading, choosing Africa leads to a cornucopia of business information about this region. For instance, there is a publication entitled *The African Development Bank Group: A Guide to Business Opportunities for Canadians*.

Only six complete answers were provided to this question, while 13 no/incorrect answers and 10 referrals were registered. Some library personnel suggested calling relevant African embassies in Ottawa. Others gave out publications listing overseas jobs, most of which were in Asia or South America. One staff member suggested writing to UNICEF; another thought that the Canadian International Development Agency (CIDA) or the United Nations would be the appropriate place to make inquiries. Still another staff person suggested that the proxy consult an Ethiopian newspaper carried by the library.

Some staff thought that pointing vaguely to a stack area or Internet terminals would magically cause an answer to appear. After typing in the keywords "Africa" and "business" into an online catalogue, one reference worker told the proxy to browse the shelves for relevant books or reports: "Just skim the titles until you find what you need." When another proxy asked this question, the staff member "walked into the stacks and cut off my question." Not giving up, this proxy "repeated the question in full and the staff member pointed to various provincial and federal materials. I repeated the question again and was told to come back or leave a message for the director of the library." Here, the librarian uses a two-pronged "negative closure" strategy. First, she signals "non-verbally that the transaction is over by... turning away" and then encourages the user to give up by implying that question is so difficult that only the director of the library can deal with it (Ross & Dewdney, 1998, p. 156).

Despite repeated assertions by the proxy that newsletters or bulletins were wanted, another staff member focused exclusively on finding statistical information. She directed the proxy to the *Statistics Canada* catalogue for 1997 and told her to check under the listing "Canadian international trading patterns" and "Imports; merchandise trade." When the proxy again repeated that she wanted newsletters and bulletins, the staff person "suggested that I search the government web site and pointed toward the terminal." Ross and Dewdney (1998) identified this reference coping strategy as one where staff members try "to get the user to accept more easily found information instead of the information actually needed" (pp. 155–156).

However, knowledgeable staff can make all the difference between success and failure in finding information. Good reference personnel can even make a tough question appear easy and straightforward. At a public selective depository library in Atlantic Canada, the proxy gave the following account of a five-minute interaction with staff.

> The librarian first consulted the directory called *Your Guide to Canada's Federal, Provincial and Territorial Government*. The librarian then indicated I would want to read through the section heading of Department of Foreign Affairs and International Trade. Within this section she noted the Africa and Middle East Bureau . . . and gave me [a] telephone number as a contact; the second contact she pointed out was Africa and Middle East Business Development Section. I was also directed to the section in the Reference department covering books on Canada and International Trade. The librarian showed me the newsletter entitled *CanadExport* that covered various sources such as an International Business Opportunity Centre located in Ottawa. This centre provided a list of tenders out for an electrical project in Africa.

Not only were multiple options presented to this proxy, but the librarian stayed with her and pointed out subsections and relevant numbers contained in these publications. In effect, the librarian took the time to make sure that the proxy would not get lost when using the sources. The librarian did not just merely give the book to the proxy and expect her to be able to locate the necessary information. In addition, the entire process took five minutes—an efficient use of library resources. But the high-level of competence displayed by the librarian was likely possible only because she had been extensively trained in government documents. The time devoted to training of course takes away from the time these individuals can devote to front-line reference provision, but, if the example provided here is any indication, well-trained personnel will more than compensate by giving quick, efficient, and highly accurate service in the future. Regular and ongoing training of reference personnel is therefore a cost-effective way to allocate resources.

Chapter 5

What Happens When Libraries Make Referrals?

Faced with a question to which the answer is not known or for which the resources of the library are inadequate, library reference personnel often make referrals, whether to other sections of their own library, to other library workers within the library, to other libraries, or to other external institutions and individuals. Patricia Gebhard (1997), for example, writes that "[t]he best strategy for some requests is to make a referral" (p. 32). Patrick Wilson (1983) contends that, especially in academic settings, patrons only want, need, and expect correct referrals to appropriate sources. Yet, despite repeated calls for research about what happens when reference staff make referrals, there has been no systematic examination about what happens after the initial referral has been made. Do patrons receive satisfactory answers to their queries, or do the referrals turn out to be less than adequate? Knowing what happens after a referral has been made has implications for the delivery of high-quality reference service and for the development of reference service policy. For instance, the Management of Reference Services Committee (1994) of the Reference and Services Division (RASD) of the American Library Association (ALA) urges libraries to adopt policy statements explaining both "the guidelines to be used by library personnel when referring patrons to other libraries" and "the guidelines that apply to library patrons being referred to other libraries" (p. 168). If front-line reference staff and management are under the impression that making

---

Many of the referral calls to various government institutions and libraries discussed in this chapter were made by Moya K. Mason, my research assistant for this project. Accordingly, the pronoun "we" is used throughout the text of this chapter.

a referral satisfies the needs of patrons, the use of referrals may become an acceptable response at the reference desk, especially in light of the increased number of paraprofessionals providing reference service.

BACKGROUND

There is some dispute, first, as to what constitutes a referral in the library realm and, second, as to the reason referrals are made. George Hawley (1987), after surveying the definitions offered by a number of dictionaries, proposes that referral is simply "an act by library employees of responding to individuals' needs by directing these individuals to another person, or to a place under the control of another person, for the fulfillment of those needs" (p.137). Based on interviews with public and academic reference librarians, he suggests that the principles of equity and efficiency are the major variables involved in any decision taken by staff to make a referral. Efficiency comes into play because the referral should be made to a location able to fulfill an individual's information needs "without unnecessary loss of these individuals energy, time, money, or materials" (p. 28). For him, "equity asks what users, outside resources, personal contacts, coworkers, the director, and the individual librarian owe and are owed [while] efficiency accentuates equity by asking what limitations must be imposed on what is owed due to the scarcity of resources" (p. 110). Under this theory, what people receive "should be proportional to what they contribute to the interaction or to the system." This "contribution rule" has two components. Contributions may either be "economic," that is, related to the "cost of the work done measured in time or money . . . or social, related either to status in the community or to positive interpersonal qualities, such as friendliness or attractiveness" (p. 137). Hawley argues that inter-library relationships are a key factor in deciding whether to make a referral. Library staff "seemed to avoid asking significantly more favors than they received from another library, except in a few cases in which the other library was felt to be obligated to assist outsiders or at least encouraged use by outsiders" (p. 139). He notes, too, that the frequency of referrals increases as the amount of perceived preparation that the user has done before asking a question decreases. Finally, he observes that "librarians at times provide service based on the importance of the requester" (pp. 91–92, 139).

Thomas Childers (1980), however, suggests that there are two types of referrals. The first type is called "steering," where a patron is merely provided directions to another resource and which entails no further action by library staff. The second type is termed "referring," which involves an attempt, on the part of staff, to make contact with the party to whom the referral is made (p. 928). Childers (1979) elsewhere defines this second expanded concept of referral as taking proactive steps to "make contact with an outside resource by making an appointment, calling an agency, etc." (p. 2036) or as "[f]acilitating the link between a person with a need and the resource or resources outside the library which can meet the need" (Childers, 1984, p. 1). The notion of proactive behavior on the part of library staff is connected with Information and Referral (I&R) work in public libraries, defined as building community networks between and among various governmental departments and non-profit organizations working in the broad fields of health and social services in order to direct people who might not ordinarily use libraries to the most appropriate agency.

Ross and Dewdney (1998) make a similar distinction. According to them, referrals can be either unmonitored or verified. An unmonitored referral is defined as "a strategy of negative closure" the main purpose of which is "to get rid of the user, not to maximize the chance that the user will find a helpful answer" (p. 161). When giving an unmonitored referral, "the librarian doesn't know enough about the real question or about the match between information need and recommended source(s) to have any reasonable confidence that a user who follows the advice will find an acceptable answer" (p. 154). A verified referral, on the other hand, is one "in which the reference staff has verified that the recommended source will actually be of some use in answering the question" (p. 161). As noted in Chapter 3, Ross and Dewdney believe that unmonitored referrals are typically made so that staff can process users through the system as quickly as possible. "Increasingly harried as fewer people do more work and face longer line-ups of users," librarians "win" the reference game "when the transaction is completed and [they] can move on to the next question" (p. 154). While such strategies of "negative closure" allow staff to deal with more information requests, users are frustrated at the quality of service they receive.

How often do libraries make referrals? Marcia Myers (1980) found that 27.6 percent of reference questions generated referrals. Of these referrals, slightly more than half were internal referrals within the originating library, just over 30 percent were to other libraries, and just under 10 percent were made to external agencies such as the post office or a travel agency (p. 138). McClure and Hernon (1983), in their study of government documents reference questions in the Northeast and Southwest of the United States, found that 17.4 percent of the questions were referred (59 out of 340). The three most popular places to which referrals were made were: government agencies, a librarian in the same library, and a larger regional depository library (pp. 89–103). Further examination of their data led them to conclude that referrals were not given in a systematic fashion. Referrals did not, as a rule, follow a reference interview where the librarian was unable to provide an answer. Moreover, the chance of a referral did not increase with an increase in the duration of the reference interview (Hernon & McClure, 1982, p. 157). Based on these studies, libraries make referrals for about 20 percent of reference questions.

While these studies have been important in gauging the extent of referrals in libraries, very few studies have considered the effectiveness of referrals through an examination of what actually happens when the referral is carried to its conclusion. Childers (1980) unobtrusively asked 20 different questions a total of 1,110 times at 57 public libraries in one New York county, finding that referrals were made 179 times to nonlibrary locations. He further reported that about 66 percent of the non-library referrals turned out to be "correct" or "mostly correct" (p. 926). Hernon and McClure (1982) argue that "research related to the referral process is critically needed if libraries are to compete effectively with the myriad information providers in our society today," especially given that the role of the librarian as a "switching station to direct the patron to appropriate information . . . is also likely to take on increased importance [in] the current climate of cooperation and resource sharing among various types of library and nonlibrary agencies" (p.162). Marjorie Murfin (1995a) also calls for more "in-depth investigation" of the number and effectiveness of referrals (p. 14).

PURPOSE

The purpose of this chapter is to judge the usefulness of referrals made by library staff. In Chapter 2, data showed that 98 out of 488 questions (20.1%) were referred to various governmental and non-governmental institutions. Academic full depositories made referrals 18 times; academic selectives did so six times; and public full depositories did so nine times. By far, public selectives made referrals the most frequently—65 times (66.3%). Based on the written reports of proxies, all referrals fell into the category of non-verified referrals, as defined by Ross and Dewdney (1998). Twenty-two of these referrals were to exclusively French-language sources, while 76 were to English-language or bilingual sources.[1] Half the referrals (49) were to government departments or agencies that were not libraries. Proxies were referred to governmental or legislative libraries seven times; to other non-governmental libraries, usually at a university, 28 times; and

14 times to external non-governmental agencies or establishments that were not libraries. This chapter looks at all referrals made to English-language or bilingual sources.

Telephone calls were made by the author and a research assistant to all 76 English-language locations to which proxies were initially referred. Although the researchers were based in City X, since the proxy had initially asked the question at a depository library in City Y or City Z and had received a referral, for example, to a local government office in City Y or City Z, the researchers telephoned the number in City Y or City Z rather than the equivalent office in City X. If a subsequent referral was made by the initial referral location to another location, another telephone call was made to the secondary referral location. This process was continued until no more referrals were made. Information provided by any of the referrals was recorded manually on sheets of paper during and immediately after the telephone calls. Calls were not taped.

RESULTS

Table 5-1 summarizes what happened when initial referrals were followed to their conclusion. Thirty-one of the 76 referrals led to a complete answer (40.8%). About two-thirds of these successful referrals were the result of chaining telephone calls; that is, the initial referral given by the depository library provided another telephone number as a secondary referral, and so on. Conversely, 23 referrals elicited no information whatsoever: the answering party either said that she or he had no idea about the particular question, or stated that the wrong department had been called (30.3%). No further referral was given in these 23 cases. Nineteen referrals resulted in a partial, though incomplete answer (25%). Referral callers were told to come into the library once (1.3%), and in another two instances, referral callers were told that the information sought was available, but that it could only be provided on a fee basis (2.6%).

Of the original 15 questions, only two were not referred. Both of these were legislative branch questions: one dealt with the text of a bill about the proceeds of crime introduced in the Canadian Parliament; the other concerned rules about Parliamentary procedure. Thirteen questions were referred, including all 10 legislative branch questions.[2] The greatest number of referrals was given to the questions about the costs and procedures for ordering aerial photographs and a government-published book.

To give greater insight into what patrons face when library staff make referrals, the referrals for each question are discussed in greater detail

Table 5-1
Resolution of External Referrals by Question

Question (# keyed to Table 2-5)	Number of referrals	Received complete answer	Told to visit a particular institution in person	Received partial answer with no further referral	Told that information is priced	No attempt at answer or no idea, and no further referral
Aerial photograph (13)	14	8	0	5	0	1
Book by Jill Wherrett (2)	14	2	0	6	0	6
Business opportunities in Africa (15)	9	4	0	2	0	2
Percentage of Canadian-content French lyrics (4)	9	2	0	1	1	5
Job contracts for hauling garbage (12)	8	2	0	0	0	6
Non-conventional fuels (5)	6	3	0	1	0	2
Sub-committee report on firearms (6)	4	4	0	0	0	0
Auditor-General's report (7)	3	3	0	0	0	0
Fisheries regulations (14)	3	3	0	0	0	0
Refugees and gender persecution (11)	3	0	0	3	0	0
Marine radio station on the Magdalen Islands (9)	2	0	1	0	0	1
Price of barley to farmers (3)	1	0	0	0	1	0
Totals	76	31	1	19	2	23

in separate sections below. To be sure, the original questions from which the referral was derived were government documents reference questions, and so the findings here may not be generalizable to other types of questions. Government documents questions are generally acknowledged to be among the most difficult faced by reference staff. Hawley (1987), for example, notes that the one area in which librarians were "noticeably weak in their knowledge of outside resources" was the type of materials contained in government depository systems (pp. 61–62). Still, library staff may get a sense of the frustration and success levels experienced by users who are told to pursue their inquiries at locations other than the one at which they first presented their question.

Aerial Photography

Eight out of 14 referrals ultimately received complete answers to this question (57.1%). Seven of these referrals (4 successful, 3 unsuccessful) were to various municipal, provincial, or federal government agencies; three were to university libraries or departments (2 successful, 1 unsuccessful); and four were to private photography studios (2 successful, 2 unsuccessful). The correct answer is available from the National Air Photo Library (NAPL), a division of Geomatics Canada, Natural Resources Canada. Prices for enlargements depend on size and format; for example, a 40 × 60-inch color enlargement is $180 CDN.

A typical referral experience involved one or two calls to a provincial or federal government department prior to be being directed to the NAPL. In total, this happened four times. For example, an initial referral to a local Geological Survey of Canada office or to the Remote Sensing Office was referred to Natural Resources Canada, the department of which NAPL is a part. On the other hand, two initial referrals to local or municipal government departments did not lead to any further useful information, nor was any pertinent information gained from a local governmental bookstore.

Another initial call to a university library also led subsequently to the NAPL, while an initial referral to a university geology department led to the home phone number of a faculty member who "often has aerial photographs," which in turn led to the NAPL. A third referral to a university depository library led to a subsequent unsuccessful referral to the local archives, where someone bluntly stated that he/she did not know anything about aerial photography. Two photography stores were able to provide direct information about the NAPL, while two others had absolutely no idea.

Book by Jill Wherrett

Only two out of 14 referrals ultimately received complete answers to this question (14.3%). A complete answer to this question could be easily found by searching the Depository Services Program (DSP) Web site. Here, a search engine is available where a search by author can be performed.

Three references to a book entitled *Aboriginal Self-Government* appear. Two of these refer to books for which Wherrett is co-author with Jane Allain; the third is by Wherrett alone. Its original price was $6.50.

Seven of the referrals for this question (1 successful, 6 unsuccessful) were to government bookstores, publishers, or departments; three were to local bookstores (1 successful, 2 unsuccessful); two were to university or college bookstores (both unsuccessful); and two were to university libraries (both unsuccessful). One referral call to a university library was particularly disappointing. The library had the book, but when asked about the price and where it might be ordered, the staff person asked "where I was from [and] before I could answer, she said I must be from the United States and did not understand that a library does not sell books, but rather, lends them. In a very demeaning fashion she . . . explain[ed] about library cards, how they worked, and how I could get one."

Bookstores, whether private or based at universities, typically checked microfiche indexes provided by the government, but, according to the clerks in these stores, the microfiche did not list authors' names and so the exact book could not be located. At one of these stores we were told to call "one of the Indian groups around Canada, since they would probably know where to get a copy or photocopy." Another store informed us that we needed a catalogue number to find and order the book.

Business Opportunities in Africa

Out of nine referrals, four were eventually successful (44.4%). These four led to the Department of Foreign Affairs and International Trade (DFAIT) by way of either the Canadian International Development Agency or the toll-free omnibus federal government information line, Reference Canada (RC). At DFAIT, the names of two individuals working in the Africa and Middle East Development Division, which is responsible for 25 countries in Africa, were provided. Upon contacting these people, we received complete information about the Canadian Win Exports System, a database used by Canadian trade commissioners abroad to promote a company's products to foreign buyers. Information was also given about DFAIT's Market Research Centre, which produces numerous industry sectorial studies to help Canadian exporters. Finally, we were put on the mailing list for the newsletter *CanadExport*, which surveys international export opportunities, including Africa.

The complete information gained in the above four calls was offset by five referrals which either provided no useful information or, at best, partial information. An official at the Federal Development Bank stated that there were no bulletins or newsletters about business opportunities in Africa. During a referral call to Industry Canada, we were told that they only deal with issues inside Canada. The same referring librarian that had urged us to call Industry Canada also told us to call "External Affairs," a department that no longer exists, but whose current equivalent is DFAIT. But, unlike the four positive experiences with DFAIT staff above, this time we were told that only a 1994 country profile of one country was available. Another reference worker told us to call a provincial Ministry of Public Works and Government Services, where no one knew anything about business opportunities in Africa.

On two occasions library staff curtly made referrals to foreign embassies, convinced that the Canadian federal government did not publish any information on the topic. The consulates and high commissions of the two foreign countries did indeed send us a wealth of information, but it was of a general nature lacking specific details about the current business climate. For example, we received a copy of the Ghana Investment Promotion Centre Act (1994) and the trade regulations pertaining to the Imports and Exports Act (1980). While such publications have an intrinsic interest, they would likely not be of much practical use for businesspeople unless they already had made initial business contacts.

Job Contracts for Hauling Garbage

Only two out of the eight referrals for this question received complete answers (25%), even though complete information could be obtained from the Web site of Public Works Canada or, in print, from the weekly or bi-weekly *Government Business Opportunities*. On one occasion, we were referred to a local employment center, which in turn referred us to the Reference Canada (RC) information line, which referred us to a procurement center, where someone promised to send brochures and instructions about how to make bids for government contracts.

On a second occasion, we were initially referred to a provincial legislative library. There, the librarian found a publication dealing with government bids and contracts from 1994, which listed an obsolete 800 phone number as well as a regular toll number. After calling the latter number and being transferred twice, we finally were put on a mailing list for an information kit and free government-sponsored seminars about how to make bids.

Six referrals were not as productive as the previous two. One of these referrals was to RC, which resulted in the name of an official who, despite being called three times and having messages left on his voice mail, never returned our calls. Another referral was made to both Environment Canada and Industry Canada. At the former location, the official to whom we talked thought we were "completely crazy," while at the latter location, we were passed along to an administrative assistant who told us "not here you can't," and then hung up. A third referral was, again, made to Environment Canada. Again, the person to whom we spoke had absolutely no idea about our question. A fourth referral was to the sanitation department of a municipal city hall, where we were bluntly told that we had called the wrong place. A fifth referral was made to the Business Services Center of the federal Department of Industry, Science, and Technology—a department that is no longer in existence because of successive administrative rearrangement. A sixth referral told us to look in the local phone book for the "Provincial government building downtown." Noting the lack of specificity of this location, we asked "for the [telephone] number for inquiries for the provincial government and [were] told that there was no such listing."

Percentage of Canadian-Content French Lyrics

Only two referrals out of nine led to a complete answer (22.2%). When we first called the university library, we spoke to a librarian "who said to call her tomorrow because she had no idea what to do." The next day we called again, "and she was so happy that I returned her call and excitedly told me that it was a lot easier than she had anticipated—she said some of the questions you expect to be really hard, often are the easiest." Using two Statistics Canada publications entitled *Sound Recordings* and *Canada's Cultural Heritage and Identity: A Statistical Perspective,* this librarian found the exact number of Canadian-content sound recordings with French lyrics for each of the years in question. The second successful referral began with the National Library of Canada, where we were transferred from the general reference desk to the music division, and then to the head of the music division. Although this individual could not himself provide the information, he gave us phone numbers for the Canadian Recording Industry Association (CRIA) and its Québec counterpart. We phoned CRIA, where we were told that the needed information was available under the Cultural Statistics heading of the Statistics Canada Web site.

The relative ease with which a complete answer was received during the above referrals was not to be repeated on the seven other occasions that this question was referred (5 times to government departments, once each to a for-profit establishment and a university library). Three times we were referred to the Canadian Radio and Television-Telecommunications Commission (CRTC). On all three occasions, no one knew the answer, nor could they provide any further ideas. The following experience gives an indication of the difficulty patrons may experience when contacting government officials.

> I called the CRTC directly and was told that I was being directed to Canadian Content. The man who answered told me that he dealt only with television, but knew (since he was francophone) that French music was on the rise and that it was very dynamic. He talked with me a little more about his job and actually ran through his career with the CRTC from 1979 onwards. I find that many government workers seem lonely and like to talk for awhile when someone calls for information. Did not refer me because he did not know who would have that kind of statistic.

Another referral was made to an agency called Statistics Canada. Here we were told that getting an answer to this question "might be a possibility . . . but I would have to submit a research requisition to begin the process. It could turn out to be an expensive proposition, I was told." Given the fact that the required information was located in free print sources by the university librarian mentioned above, the answer received from Statistics Canada is dismaying. Still another failed government referral was to a local Canadian Broadcasting Corporation (CBC) radio station. The person who answered here quickly said "no idea" and hung up. A referral to a local store selling tapes and CDs also met with no success; we were told that we were a "prank caller." A referral to another university library elicited much the same response: "They had no idea why I would be asking *them* for the information. Had no idea where one would find it either."

Non-conventional Fuels

Three out of the six referrals were successful (50%) for this question. Two of these were straightforward: an initial referral to Reference Canada (RC) led to the Natural Resources Publication line, where a clerk promised to send us a number of free publications detailing what percentage of government vehicles must use non-conventional fuels by what date.

The path leading to the third successful referral was more serpentine. A library staff person initially provided us with two referral possibilities: one to the local office of Public Works and Services and a second to Statistics

Canada. Upon calling the former location, someone informed us that we "should go to the library for that kind of information." When we told this individual that we were referred by the library, "he still thought it was the best place to go." Upon calling Statistics Canada, we were immediately referred to Natural Resources in Ottawa, who referred us to a specific individual in Energy, who referred us to yet another individual, who was always out-of-town. However, someone in this last person's office "finally took pity . . . and is sending me a copy of the [appropriate] act."

Three referrals were unsuccessful. In the first of these, a staff person at a university law library asked us to repeat our question, laughed, said he had no idea, and hung up. In the second, we were referred to a university science library, where staff also had no idea about the question. Finally, we were referred to both the federal general information line (RC) and a provincial equivalent. RC referred us to a specific individual at the Crown Corporations Division of the Treasury Board, but this person never returned our call. We then tried the provincial inquiry line, who suggested the Vehicle Management Center in the provincial capital, who suggested the Crown Corporation Secretariat, who suggested the Ministry of the Environment. No answer was forthcoming from any of these locations.

Auditor-General's Report, Sub-committee Report on Firearms, and Fisheries Regulations

All three referrals concerning the Auditor-General's report led to complete answers. Two of these referrals were to provincial legislative libraries, and one was to the office of the Auditor-General (AG) in Ottawa. A staff person at AG sent us a copy of the report, while the librarians at the two provincial legislature libraries had the required report on CD-ROM and were able to find the appropriate sections through keyword searches.

With respect to the four referrals about the sub-committee report on firearms, one referral led to a university law librarian, who found the report and put it aside for us to examine the next day. Another referral was to the main publishing arm of the federal government publisher, where a clerk informed us that the report could be ordered for a small fee. The third successful referral for this question ultimately led to the office of a local Member of Parliament, where a staff member promised to send us a copy of the sub-committee report. He explained that the office just happened to have copies on hand, since it was currently a much-discussed topic. The fourth successful referral was to a provincial legislative library.

All three referrals about fisheries regulations were to university libraries, and, again, all referrals were successful. Staff cheerfully and promptly gave the address of the federal Web site where both laws and attendant regulations could be located, or looked up the regulations in print sources.

Refugees and Gender Persecution

None of the referrals for this question was successful, although one common location to find the answer in print is as an appendix attached to a report by Margaret Young entitled *Gender-related Refugee Claims* (1994), published by the Laws & Government Division of the Library of Parliament. The required information is also accessible through the Web site of the Immigration and Refugee Board of Canada.

Two unsuccessful referrals were to "the federal government dealing with immigration," where, on one occasion, we were told that "there was nothing on paper, no documents or laws, but [the staff person] remembered a case where a woman was given refugee status because of abuse she was suffering at the hands of her husband [but] when she got back with her husband, she lost her citizenship possibilities." Another referral was to a university library, where the librarian stated that "she remembered hearing that one woman had entered Canada on those grounds, and figured that a good place to start was to search a newspaper or magazine database, because she was not sure if that policy had been made into a law and doubted that they would have a hard copy in the government documents section at this point."

Marine Radio Station on the Magdalen Islands and Price of Barley

The three referrals for these two questions were unsuccessful. One referral about the Magdalen Islands was to a local Member of Parliament, whose office did not return repeated calls. Another referral for this same question was to a university library, where we were told to come in during a very restricted span of hours if we wanted to get in touch with a person who might be able to help. For the question about the price of barley, we were referred to Statistics Canada, who told us that "they would have to charge ... anywhere from $40 to $100 to do the research for this question." Again, the tendency to offer priced information is dismaying, given that the required information is available for free at the Web site of the Canadian Wheat Board, where payments are listed for specified years, and are given either in tonnes or in bushels. In print, the answer is available from a publication entitled *Grain Trade of Canada*.

DISCUSSION

Based on the findings of this study, library staff who make non-verified and unmonitored referrals to external sources when trying to answer government documents reference questions should be aware that patrons will achieve success only about 40.8 percent of the time. The most difficult questions for the parties to whom the original question was referred were those that required statistical or administrative data of some kind (e.g., percentage of Canadian-content French lyrics, price of barley, the price of a book), while the questions that frequently received complete answers were those that had to do with designated reports or laws (e.g., Auditor-General, sub-committee report on firearms, fisheries regulations). Library staff did not refer two questions: the text of a bill about profits convicted criminals might make if they were to publish books about their crimes, and parliamentary procedure. Based on the above two sentences, the questions that present the least number of problems for both library staff and external entries to which referrals were made are, broadly, those that ask for the text of a bill, law, regulation, or report.

From one perspective, this is not surprising, given that such documents are indexed, listed, or catalogued somewhere, whether on a library OPAC, or on a government database, checklist or repertoire. Questions asking for specific data that is likely not indexed or catalogued are much more difficult. This is one reason why library staff should become much more cognizant of the workings of, and services offered by, specific government departments or agencies. The more that reference personnel know about who does what within the government, the more likely they will be available to identify quickly and accurately the source of any requested information. Given that public selective depositories made about 66 percent of the referrals, staff at these libraries should pay particular attention to mastering the intricacies of government departments and their services. After all, each question could be answered using readily accessible government Web sites—a circumstance that has the effect of making every selective depository library into a full depository library.

Library staff should also recognize that officials in specific government departments or agencies are often not even themselves aware of the information that their department possesses. Our calls were frequently met with suggestions to get in contact with individuals in other government departments, most of whom did not have toll-free numbers. In addition, many government officials did not return calls despite messages left on their voice-mail services. When library staff make referrals, they should keep in mind that many patrons may not be willing to invest the time, energy, and money to make numerous calls in order to track down an answer to a question. Hawley's (1987) suggestion that referrals be made so as to avoid "unnecessary loss" of patrons' energy, time, and money should be kept in mind (p. 28). Furthermore, patrons may be faced with a situation where, during one of their numerous calls to entities outside the library, they may be told that "you should go to the library for that information." An answer such as this may prove frustrating and annoying to the patron, given that the library was the originating locus for the subsequent series of referral calls. Library reference staff who are well-trained and well-versed in the mandates, areas of responsibility, and typical outputs of various government departments and agencies and who are expert and up-to-date in knowing the content of government Web sites can obviate, for the patron, an often fruitless quest for information involving multiple transfers between departments or unreturned voice-mail messages by directly providing the needed information.

Accordingly, Ian Douglas's (1988) characterization of referrals to an external agency or sources as the "third mode of failure" in reference service should be taken seriously. While a referral *per se* does not have to be a problem because patrons may indeed get the information they need from a referral, Douglas observes that it is the uncertainty of them doing so that is problematic. If librarians are going to be referring patrons, they should know in advance if the outcome will be positive. This may mean phoning ahead of time to ensure success. Another way to reduce needless referrals is to actually reduce the total number given by identifying areas of service that are inadequate (including lack of proper tools to answer certain types of questions), as well as by providing staff with additional training so that they are more aware of the sources at their disposal.

Certainly, it may be argued that none of the questions discussed in this chapter should have been referred out of the library or, alternatively, that they were referred to places where they should never have been sent. Nonetheless, these referrals were made, and they were made to the places discussed here. An individual receiving a referral does not know whether that referral is appropriate or inappropriate. The patron merely knows that a referral was given by a reference staff member, and if, as a patron, he or she is interested in following up the original question, he or she will attempt to contact the referral location. Judgments about the appropriateness or inappropriateness of referrals are moot, since the patron typically trusts the library to make a good-faith effort to provide the highest quality of information possible. If the patron receives a referral, then the patron likely believes that the referral represents valuable information.

RECOMMENDATIONS AND CONCLUSION

This chapter has shown that unmonitored referrals lead to complete answers in a haphazard fashion. Occasionally, patrons do end up speaking with someone who is committed to locating the needed answer and who has expertise about the subject matter, but just as often, if not more so, patrons referred to external sources by library staff end up no further ahead in their information quest than when they made their initial request. The distinction made, on the one hand, by Childers (1984) between "steering" and "referring," and, on the other hand, by Ross and Dewdney (1998) between unmonitored and verified referrals seems appropriate. Staff members who steer patrons toward external sources may only be hoping that someone else will be able to provide an answer to a reference question. Based on the results of the present study, such hope is fulfilled only 40.8 percent of the time.

One way to improve the act of referrals is to adopt the approach suggested by Gebhard (1997), who urges that librarians "verify the success of referrals ahead of time" by calling the location to which the patron is being sent. Although her advice is meant to apply specifically to students in an academic library environment, calling ahead is a worthwhile suggestion since the librarian "can explain" the particular information need of the individual, thus determining whether help will be forthcoming at that location. Moreover, calling ahead "can keep referring librarians from feeling that they have sent [patrons] on a wild goose chase" (p. 41).

External referrals function as poor substitutes for a good-faith effort by reference staff to help patrons with their questions. Tygett, Lawson, and Weessies (1996), after conducting an unobtrusive proxy-driven evaluation of reference service based on customer perception followed by focus groups, found that Wilson's (1983) suggestion that patrons only expected referrals "was not upheld [because] students... wanted instruction on how to find materials by themselves" (p. 274). Reference service policies that either encourage, do not discourage, or are neutral about the practice of external unmonitored referrals should be revisited. Consideration should be given to adopting specific policies about the process of verifying referrals ahead of time, and to making patrons aware that the only type of referral that will be made is a verified referral. In addition, a mechanism to ensure feedback about the efficacy of referrals by patrons may prove useful to library reference staff (Gebhard, 1997, p. 45; Gers & Seward, 1989, pp. 33–34). For example, in addition to the referring librarian giving the patron a form to present at the referral location, as recommended by Patricia Gebhard, Art Anthony, and Gary Peete (1978), patrons could be given forms to fill out about how they were treated at the referral location and whether their information need was met. Data from these patron evaluation forms could be compiled and the conclusions used to create a flow chart for referral decisions based on the perceived utility of certain referral locations.

The implementation of practices taken from the I&R model, in which detailed searchable databases or cross-referenced lists containing the names of appropriate and up-to-date contact persons competent to provide help in specific areas are maintained and then matched with clients who have particular needs in specific social, welfare, or health sectors, should also be given serious thought. As Childers (1984) observes, the I&R model suffers from "relatively obscurity" because, first, most I&R services are "aimed at deprived persons, or persons in trouble of one sort or another," and, second, because "few I&R services have been developed that can respond to the 'average' person who is *not* in trouble, who *does not* have a grievous problem, but who *does* have a need—a question about how get something, do something, or find something" (original emphasis, p. 3). Libraries interested in improving their referral service for "average" users with average information needs may find many useful ideas in the I&R model.

Perhaps none of these solutions can work adequately if reference staff are not aware of the range of resources available in their immediate geographical or online Web environment. Kathleen Dunn and Myra White (1991) describe an innovative project undertaken in California whose starting premise was that "better informed librarians would provide better service by making appropriate referrals." The project's aim was to help reference staff, both professional and paraprofessional, in five libraries "become more aware of the collections and services of . . . surrounding libraries . . . and local resources [so as] to make meaningful referrals" (p. 363). Accordingly, each participating library developed a complete package of orientation tours, training, and internships for the staff of the other libraries of the informal consortium. One noteworthy feature of the training component was a plan to have a "representative group of . . . librarians . . . work reciprocally in the reference areas of the five libraries [in order to] learn the reference collection in depth" (p. 364). Although the parameters of this plan were reduced due to staffing considerations, the broad outlines and assumptions of this initiative deserve a careful look. Detailed knowledge of resources contained in other collections is here judged to be imperative for high-quality reference service. This principle is even more important in the evolving world of digital and virtual libraries insofar as library staff should now have a responsibility to be aware of a vast array of online resources. While some library administrators may argue that constant and rigorous attention to training detracts from the time available for front-line reference service to patrons, Ross and Dewdney (1998) suggest that many patrons dissatisfied with their initial service encounter will begin the process anew with a different reference worker, thereby duplicating staff effort and resulting in an "inefficient use of resources" (pp. 160–161). Training may therefore be considered a cost-saving measure.

Patrons who initially visit the reference departments of libraries in search of specific information, but who are then quickly directed or referred elsewhere, may eventually conclude that they may forego the services of the library altogether. Future research needs to be done about how patrons feel when they are referred externally and when their information need is not met by the institution or person to whom the referral was made. What do these patrons feel about the library and staff person who gave them an unmonitored referral? Do these individuals become, in the words of Hernon and Altman (1998), "lost customers" of the library (pp. 142–143)?

NOTES

1. Bilingual referrals were those made to various federal government departments and agencies in Ottawa, the capital of Canada. Since Canada is a bilingual nation, federal government services in the Ottawa-Hull capital region are available to citizens in both official languages, English and French.

2. Only 12 questions appear as being referred in Table 5-1. The reason is that one referral to a French-language source was made for the question about the CRTC (the first question in Table 2-5).

Chapter 6

Newspapers and the Reference Desk

Given that newspapers are an important source of daily information about a wide variety of topics, the question arises as to whether reference librarians should be reading newspapers on a daily basis, or at least glancing at the headlines to get a sense of the state of their country and the world. At one time, the answer was an unequivocal yes. Frank Keller Walter, in an address to the graduating class of the Wisconsin Library School in 1925, urged librarians to not only promote reading among the public, but also to realize that "[i]n self defense the librarian [too] must read if she wishes to succeed." More specifically, to keep up with the pace of world events, he recommended that, "[o]ne often must get out of the current to see the progress of the stream and to notice that it is the stream and not the banks which moves." Continuing his analogy, he suggested that, because "[i]nformation is the real water of life to the mind," it is "most often in books, in magazines and newspapers that one can get the best perspective of social progress in the limited periods of . . . leisure [available to the librarian] (pp.31–32)."

James Wyer, in his 1930 *Reference Work*, urged librarians to "[f]aithfully read at least one local newspaper" and to "[k]eep somewhat in touch with affairs of state and nation as well as city . . . through a metropolitan daily or an able review" (pp. 120–121). Margaret Hutchins, in her 1944 *Introduction To Reference Services*, was adamant about the central role that newspapers play in the provision of superior reference service. She

---

Many of the telephone calls to public libraries discussed in this chapter were made by Moya K. Mason, my research assistant for this project. Accordingly, the pronoun "we" is used throughout the text of this chapter.

noted, first, that "a very large proportion of the reference work in practically all types and sizes of libraries is accomplished by means of periodicals and newspapers" (p. 103). Accordingly, newspapers and periodicals are "indispensable" because they "supply the most up-to-date information on all subjects" (p. 103). Nevertheless, questions about current events often pose real problems for reference staff because the librarian is either "ignorant of the particular sources of information" or is "at fault in failing to keep himself [or herself] informed on current affairs and technical subjects... (p. 69). Hutchins thus urges librarians to constantly read newspapers and periodicals.

> A reference librarian seen scanning newspapers and periodicals is not passing his [or her] hours in a light and frivolous manner. He [or she] is producing in his [or her] own mind rolls of films of page setups so that when a question comes on a topic on which he [or she] recalls having seen something recently, he [or she] remembers how it looked on the page and how the publication felt in his [or her] hands and what publication it is that has those characteristics, and so he [or she] can say, "Oh, yes, I saw that in *Survey* yesterday." (p. 70)

To say the least, Hutchins emphasizes the necessity for reference librarians to be well-informed and able to orient themselves, with a minimum of difficulty, in relation to current topics of importance. Moreover, the page layout and unique identity of each newspaper or periodical becomes a rich mnemonic device. The newspaper or magazine is not only useful for its content, but also as a self-referential and efficacious way of ordering and classifying that content.

The focus on reading newspapers as an important part of reference service was still alive in the early 1960s. Katherine Harris (1963) addressed this topic in a special issue of the *Journal of Education for Librarianship* devoted to trying to determine the "most basic needs and present shortcomings in reference training" (p. 175). Summarizing an emerging consensus and following the admonitions of Mary Poole (1960), she wrote that one of seven key areas identified as requiring further attention was "[t]he need to be alert to what is going on in the world and to keep informed by reading newspapers and periodicals as well as books." The rationale given for this was that "if you know authors, languages, sports, music, mathematics, food and wines, coins, paintings, someday someone ... will be grateful to you for an answer" (Harris, 1963, p. 184; Poole, 1960, pp. 1522). Clearly, reading newspapers or periodicals—repositories of diverse information where the reader is as likely to learn about sports as about music—was considered to be an avenue towards expanding a librarian's generalist knowledge, to ensuring a state of alertness and confident familiarity with national and world events. The corollary was that such generalist knowledge could be useful at some undetermined date in the future, when the librarian would be called upon, following Hutchins' metaphor, to unroll the stocks of accumulated film in her mind and locate a necessary fact.

There is a decreasing emphasis, after 1963, on the role of newspapers in the provision of general reference service, particularly in public libraries. One reason for this may be the fact that reading newspapers for their intellectual content may have been mistakenly conflated with clipping and filing newspapers and periodicals. This latter activity, as William Katz (1969) makes clear in the first edition of his *Introduction to Reference Work: Reference Services*, was something that was felt to be undesirable for reference staff, since it was overloading them with ancillary functions that could be performed by others (pp. 19–20). Relying mostly on the 1961 report *Reference Service in American Public Libraries Serving Populations of 10,000 or More* published by the University of Illinois, Katz points out that some 75 percent of large public libraries clip newspapers and magazines, and, as a result, the "average reference librarian today is definitely other than either a generalist or subject specialist" (p. 19). Katz's central point was that a reference librarian should be concentrating on other tasks, such as actively helping users with their questions. If this confusion and blending of tasks did indeed occur, then it is easy to understand the almost complete disappearance of reading newspapers as a systematically recommended activity for reference librarians.

Nonetheless, sporadic mention of the value of newspapers in reference work does exist. For example, it was mentioned by the 1986 *Self-Assessment Guide for Reference*, published by the Continuing Library Education Network and Exchange Roundtable of the American Library Association (ALA). A multiple-choice quiz consisting of seven questions appears under the section heading "Knowledge of the Community." Two of the questions deal either directly or indirectly with newspapers. In one question, library workers are asked what is the best way "to keep up with current information about the community served." The correct answer is "read the local news section of the newspaper" (p. 6). In a second question, the library worker is asked whether ordering additional résumé and vocational material for the library was the right thing to do upon learning that "the major industry in the community was planning to employ fewer people." Here, the correct answer was that this action was indeed desirable, not because such materials "could be expected to increase circulation statistics," but because "it anticipated the needs of the community"

(p. 7). And, while this second question does not explicitly mention newspapers, it is reasonable to assume that one source for the information that the community's major industry was in the midst of downsizing came from the local paper. Accordingly, what is common to both these questions in the *Self-Assessment Guide for Reference* is the need for library personnel to anticipate the needs of the community. One good way to do so is to peruse newspapers regularly. Newspapers and periodicals are also lauded for their ability to provide the most up-to-date information. Rochelle Yates (1987) emphasizes the importance of continuous updating for all types of information, particularly government information, urging librarians to "scan several periodicals and newspapers for important changes and record various events or data on information cards or factsheets" (p. 40). This is especially necessary, she observes, for telephone reference work, where speed and convenience of sources is a primary consideration. Another exception is Charles D'Aniello (1980), who emphasizes the importance of "cultural literacy" for reference librarianship, and suggests that one way that public service librarians can acquire a generalized cultural vocabulary is to "regularly read newspapers and newsmagazines as well as such critical book reviews as *The New York Review of Books* and *The New York Times Book Review*" (p. 374). Moreover, he explicitly makes the connection between cultural literacy and the ability of librarians "to interpret queries and offer detailed advice and answers." Nonetheless, his article concentrates on the utility of librarians being familiar with E.D. Hirsch's 1987 book *Cultural Literacy: What Every American Needs to Know.* Yet, the content of newspapers is rich beyond belief, and provides a constant updating of cultural, social, political, economic, and historical information.

To be sure, an objection to the need for public library staff to spend time looking at stories in newspapers and periodicals at the dawn of the 21st century is the existence of electronic databases such as ProQuest and Lexis/Nexis. In addition, the amount of valuable and easily accessible information available on Web-based documentation increases daily. Many questions asked at the reference desk may be quickly answered by searching the Web or proprietary databases with one or more keywords, the application of simple Boolean logic, and the use of a few well-chosen proximity operators and restrictions.

Yet, a general knowledge of current issues and emerging trends is an integral part of good library service because it allows for the anticipation of information needs. Collection development librarians, for instance, want to know the release dates of major films based on books and the title of the latest novel recommended by Oprah Winfrey because, in this way, they can anticipate increased demand for these titles in their libraries by ordering additional copies. John Charles and Shelley Mosley (1997) suggest various ways to forge a collection development department that will be impervious to outsourcing. One of their main recommendations is that librarians must keep up with current issues and trends so as to better anticipate demand (p. 30). In the same way, current news stories stimulate reader interest in finding out more about the subject under discussion. This is one of the reasons that the online bookseller Amazon.com instituted a sponsorship arrangement with the Web page of a nightly network news program on which it advertises, through hyperlinks, books dealing with the topics of key news stories reported that day. Librarians who understand the relationship between current topics and increased demand for books about such topics are taking an important step in serving the needs of their community.

THE GROWTH OF ENVIRONMENTAL SCANNING

Perhaps surprisingly, the best example of the value of anticipating user needs by tracking current news stories through newspapers and periodicals comes from the business world (Choo and Auster, 1993). Here, the concept is called "environmental scanning." As explained by James Newsome and Claire McInerney (1980), numerous corporations and nonprofit organizations have established scanning teams to identify and analyze contemporary events and trends that may be of use in their work. There are three levels of scanning. The first level is defined as "the passive scanning that we all do in order to keep abreast of what is happening in the world." The second level involves "scanning the environment actively" and creating "broad categories to help sort out the glut of information discovered." Some of these categories may be: political/governmental, social, economic, and technological. The third level is concerned with requests "in a directed way" for information on a specific topic (pp. 285–293).

There are a number of things to notice in this scanning model. The first two levels of scanning are non-directed; that is, no specific request for any of the gathered pieces of information is ever made. Yet, it is often this type of information that proves most valuable for an organization in the long term. In addition, the most successful scanning programs are described as concentrating on newspapers and periodicals. Recommended reading consists of the *The New York Times, The Washington Post, The Wall Street Journal,* the *Utne Reader, American Demographics,* and even *Seventeen.* Finally, only at the third scanning level does a search of electronic databases come into play because only at this level is there a request for a specific piece of information. Corporations and non-profit organizations that have instituted scanning programs are thus implicitly recognizing the existence of what J. F. Cove and B. C. Walsh (1987) have called "serendipity browsing" (p. 185), a process which, by its very nature, does not depend on the sheer size and power of databases. Nonetheless, it is an essential component of a larger information-awareness culture within an organization. The gathered information serves not only as a potential repository of immediate answers to specific questions, but also as a resource that may provide a contextual starting point for a process that eventually leads to a required answer.

Chun Wei Choo (1994), after extensively examining the information scanning practices of chief executive officers in the Canadian telecommunications sector, found that, although these high-level managers "use printed sources to perform general, wide-area viewing of the external environment before they home in on particular issues of concern," they nevertheless require filtering and evaluating services to translate this external environmental information "into terms that are meaningful internally"(p. 37). Choo therefore saw a new or expanded role for special librarians in corporations, since they could institute "[a] more systematic approach to information gathering and organization" that would have the added benefit of "avoid[ing] information gaps that may result from simply relying on personal memory or serendipitous encounters to supply information about environmental change" (p. 38).

A perfect example of what Choo had in mind is provided by Leigh Buchanan (1999), who reports on the central role played by the special librarian at Highsmith, Inc., a leading mail-order supplier of book displays, audio/video tools, and educational software for schools and libraries. The CEO of this company has specifically mandated that the special librarian, Lisa Guedea Carreño, be in charge of "searching for nascent trends, provocative contradictions, and most important, *connections* that could eventually reshape his business [original emphasis]" (p. 43). To accomplish this, she sifts through "stacks of articles on subjects ranging from juvenile crime to semiotics to the anatomy of dragonflies" in order to ensure that the company never becomes short-sighted and possesses a vision of what the future might resemble. In essence, Carreño seeks to identify, assemble, and analyze far-flung societal developments for Highsmith, Inc. Her project, called "Life, the Universe, and Everything," involves spending "20 percent of her time scanning newspapers, magazines, on-line databases, and web sites . . . and her antennae are always up for interesting tidbits from television, radio, advertising, or casual conversation" (p. 54). The significant point here is that Carreño never knows what she is looking for or what she will find. Instead, she has to be alert to a wide variety of issues, themes, social trends, and occurrences, and her perusal of media sources has to be sufficiently detailed so that she can reject material as well as flag it as potentially valuable. As a result, she becomes a walking, well-informed resource for everyone in the company, not just those who have assigned her specific tasks and searches.

What can public library reference staff, including government documents specialists, learn from the concept of environmental scanning? Again, the central issue is anticipation of user needs. Just as companies have implemented scanning strategies to serve their goals of developing new products and strategies to increase profits, librarians who wish to make their reference area a centre of proactive excellence should seriously consider staffing it with personnel who, in addition to their electronic- and print-source searching skills, have a broad base of knowledge about current topics and emerging trends. This knowledge can only add to the informational options and assets available to the general public.

Intriguing from this point of view is an observation made by Alasdair Kemp (1979), who, in a book devoted to explaining the function and purpose of current awareness services, recommends that public libraries follow in the footsteps of special and academic libraries by instituting current awareness services for the benefit of a wide variety of community groups, ranging from politicians to local horticultural clubs. Public libraries, he writes, "seem to be losing (indeed in some cases more finally to have lost) an excellent opportunity of publicity for themselves, as well as the chance to reach a larger and more various clientele and potential clientele, not just in industry and commerce, but quite generally" by not offering this type of service (pp. 21–22). Kemp's argument is that, were public libraries to offer what amounts to an environmental scanning service for targeted groups, they would be viewed as providing an indispensable service—one that would be at the top of any priorities list when it comes to governmental funding. Ultimately, libraries are responsible to the taxpayers—stakeholders—of their funding communities in much the same way as corporations are responsible to their shareholders. In a sense, then, the environmental scanning movement of the 1990s is not so very far removed from Hutchins' 1944 appraisal of the importance of regular reading of newspapers and periodicals for librarians. Common to both concepts is the desire to provide added-value services to the shareholders, or stakeholders, of an organization, whether it be for-profit or non-profit.

BACKGROUND TO THE STUDY

The primary purpose of this chapter is to examine whether library reference staff are cognizant of popular media sources such as newspapers as a potential source of ready reference information. A second purpose is to gauge the quality of telephone reference service in public libraries in Canada. Third, it aims to explore what happens when library staff members make referrals. Telephone reference service was chosen as the unit of analysis for two reasons. First, libraries are promoting telephone reference services as an integral part of their community service. As Brian Quinn (1995) reports, in the 1980s the ALA used the slogan "Call your library" in a national advertising campaign, and the New York City Public Library System handed out wallet-size cards with the message "Call the library for fast facts." Second, telephone reference service is generally characterized by a need for speed. Quinn identifies speed as one of the four essential qualities in telephone reference service because, among other reasons, callers do not like to be kept waiting (p. 40). If a library staff member is in the practice of glancing at newspapers or periodicals on a regular basis, she or he will likely remember seeing or reading a story about a particular topic and will be able to retrieve the relevant item in a relatively short period of time. Moreover, Daniel Smith (1993) notes that the three components in developing a sound collection development policy for telephone reference are relevancy, accessibility, and timeliness (pp. 64–67). Newspapers and periodicals fit all three criteria.

Although telephone reference has always been an significant component of reference work, the 1990s in particular have been marked by an increased attention to improving the quality of telephone reference service. For example, the Orange County Library System in Florida separated reference service offered to walk-in patrons from reference service provided to phone clients by implementing a program called Quest Line (Tour, 1997, p. 256). Located in a non-public area, Quest Line is staffed by 12 full-time librarians who have access to "approximately 270 titles located on a special carousel with five rotating shelves" and who work at nine computerized workstations equipped with the Internet, CD-ROMs, and an in-house database (p. 257). Over 140,000 queries were received in 1996, and some 75 percent of these were answered during the patron's initial call. Questions that cannot be answered with the resources available to the Quest Line department are "electronically transmitted and printed out for the appropriate subject department's librarian to answer" (p. 256). Answers are then later forwarded to patrons either by voice messages or fax services.

What types of questions are asked through telephone reference service? Frank Allan and Rita Smith (1993) report that only about 33 to 35 percent of calls could be classified as reference questions, with the remainder being informational and directional in nature (library hours, library policy, CD-ROM signups, etc.). However, a study of after-hours telephone reference service in Maryland by Deborah Duke (1994) reports that approximately 95 percent of the questions could be considered as ready reference. Success rates also vary. A series of early unobtrusive studies examining telephone reference service found that the rate of correct answers, both in public and academic libraries, hovered between 50 and 57 percent (Bundy, Bridgman & Keltie, 1982; Childers, 1970; Crowley, 1968; Myers & Jirjees, 1983). Beth Paskoff (1991), in a study of telephone reference service in academic health sciences and hospital libraries, reported that completely accurate responses were received 63 percent of the time, and that partially complete responses that were nevertheless not inaccurate were received 78 percent of the time. Duke (1994) noted a success rate of 84 percent in answering telephone reference queries, although this figure is based on self-evaluation by library personnel.

METHODOLOGY

Over a six-month period extending from late February 1998 to early August of that year, 11 news stories that appeared in various sections of *The Globe and Mail*, Canada's national newspaper and paper of record, were selected. Five of these questions (identified as [G] below) were government reference questions, four questions (identified as [NG] below) were unambiguously not government reference questions, and the remaining two questions (identified as [G-NG] below) sought information of the type that very well could have been within the purview of government departments, but in reality was not. As discussed in Chapter 2, many library reference personnel were unaware of recent government initiatives or changes despite the existence of reports about them in the popular press. If they had been aware of such initiatives, the success rate in answering proxy questions would likely have been much higher. This chapter therefore starts from curiosity about the general level of attention paid to the content of newspapers. In addition, Crowley's (1968) study focussed on current affairs questions, in large part because they required only short answers of a factual nature.

Within one week of the appearance of each story, a research assistant telephoned the central branches of the public libraries in the 20 most populous census metropolitan areas in the English-speaking provinces of Canada, as identified by Statistics Canada, with a reference question based on each of the 11 news stories. The largest public libraries in Canada were selected in order that "best-case" results might be achieved, since large public libraries provide telephone reference service to a greater extent than smaller libraries. The research assistant was provided with copies of the stories from which the questions were drawn, and was asked to become familiar with the general themes of the story so that she would be able to provide, if necessary, further details and a likely rationale for her information need to a library staff member. This follows the practice of Childers (1970), who recommended that proxies be encouraged to sound as natural as possible so that their information need would seem real (pp. 40, 125–126). There are two large public libraries in Toronto, and thus a total of 21 public libraries was called 11 times each. In sum, 231 questions were asked unobtrusively. Responses received from library personnel were recorded manually during and immediately after each telephone conversation, and then transcribed. Conversations were not taped. Libraries were not identified by name or location in the final transcription of results to preserve anonymity. All 21 libraries had subscriptions to *The Globe and Mail*.

Stories were selected based on a combination of prominence within the newspaper and their susceptibility to forming a factual telephone ready-reference question. Taken as a whole, the questions covered a broad range of subjects. Prominence was defined in the following ways. A selected story appeared either on the first two pages of the entire newspaper, the front page of any of the major sections, the op-ed page, or it was reprinted/matched from *The New York Times*. This last criteria was included on the assumption that a reprinted story from the paper of record in the United States was likely to be a major story of particular interest.

The 11 questions are listed below. Bibliographical information about the news story follows each question.

- Do you know where I could find a copy of the official CIA report about the Bay of Pigs? (C.I.A. bares own bungling in '61 report on Bay of Pigs. [1998, February 22.] *The New York Times*, A1, A6; Secret report blames CIA for Bay of Pigs fiasco. [1998, February 23.] *The Globe and Mail*, A11.) [G]
- Can you give me some information about whether the musical work *Symphony No. 3* by the British composer Sir Edward Elgar has ever been finished? (A change of heart brings a new Elgar Work. [1998, March 12.] *The New York*

Times, B1, B9; Pomp and circumstance. [1998, March 14.] *The Globe and Mail,* C17.) [NG]

- Can you tell me the name of the architect for the National Museum of the American Indian in Washington, D.C.? (Museum of the Indian drops its designer. [1998, April 4.] *The New York Times,* A13, A15; Cardinal ignores dismissal notice. [1998, April 7.] *The Globe and Mail,* C1, C2.) [G]

- Could you provide me with any kind of list of all the plants that are endangered globally? (One in every 8 plant species is imperiled, a survey finds. [1998, April 9.] *The New York Times,* A1, A22; Plant species threat cited. [1998, April 9.] *The Globe and Mail,* A15.) [G]

- Has there ever been a credit union owned by blacks in Canada? If so, could you provide me with some details? (A community loses its line of credit. [1998, May 1.] *The Globe and Mail,* A2.) [NG]

- Do you know of any publication that provides a list of abandoned communities (towns, villages, outports) in Newfoundland? (What's lost and what's in danger. [1998, May 4.] *The Globe and Mail,* A13 [op-ed page].) [G-NG]

- Are there any statistics available on how many children have been using Ritalin in Québec in the last few years? (Ritalin raises alarm in Québec. [1998, May 27.] *The Globe and Mail,* A1, A5.) [G-NG]

- Are you aware of any studies that link how well CEOs of companies play golf with how well their companies perform on the stock market? (Duffers need not apply. [1998, May 31.] *The New York Times,* Section 3, p. 1+; Study links golf to great returns. [1998, June 2.] *The Globe and Mail,* B12.) [NG]

- Can you give me some information about the first person to circumnavigate the world solo? (A hero except back home. [1998, July 17.] *The Globe and Mail,* A2; Canada's own ancient mariner. [1998, July 18.] *The Globe and Mail,* D16 [front page of weekend book section].) [NG]

- Could you give me some information as to whether it is legal to sell the manganese-based gasoline octane booster MMT in Canada? (Threat of NAFTA case kills Canada's MMT ban. [1998, July 20.] *The Globe and Mail,* A1, A5; Gas war: The fall and rise of MMT. [1998, July 24.] *The Globe and Mail,* A1, A5.) [G]

- I'd like some information about the approximate number of native artifacts that have to be returned by Canadian museums under the terms of the Nisga'a treaty with the federal government and British Columbia. (A time for giving back. [1998, August 1.] *The Globe and Mail,* C1, C8.) [G]

RESULTS

As summarized in Table 6-1, forty-five correct answers were received to the 231 telephone questions. This is a success rate of 19.5 percent. Referrals

Table 6-1
Summary of Most Common Responses by Question

Question	Type of question	Correct answers	Referrals to external sources	Come in/do own research, usually with suggestion	No idea/no further attempt to help	Outdated or wrong answer
CIA and Bay of Pigs	G	1	13	0	6	1
Elgar Symphony	NG	0	2	6	0	13
Architect	G	5	3	9	3	1
Endangered plants	G	5	7	6	3	0
African-Canadian (black) credit unions	NG	4	3	10	4	0
Abandoned Newfoundland communities	G-NG	0	6	6	9	0
Ritalin statistics for Québec	G-NG	2	4	15	0	0
Golf and CEOs	NG	7	1	9	4	0
Sailing solo around the world	NG	0	4	15	2	0
Gasoline additive MMT	G	10	6	3	2	0
Native artifacts in Nisga'sa treaty	G	11	8	1	1	0
Total		45	57	80	34	15

to external sources, such as university libraries or government agencies, were made at a rate of 24.7 percent (57 times). Patrons were asked to come into the library and perform their own research 34.6 percent of the time (80 times). In this category, an initial source internal to the library was suggested about two thirds of the time; the remainder of the time patrons were simply told to visit the library. Library staff members provided no help at all *or* checked only their own library OPAC holdings and did not offer any further help 14.7 percent of the time (34 cases). Incorrect or outdated answers were given at a rate of 6.5 percent (15 cases). The five questions identified as specifically government document reference questions were answered correctly at a rate 30.5 percent (32 out of 105 cases), while the six questions that were not government document reference questions were answered correctly at a rate of 10.4 percent (13 out of 126 cases).

Forty of the 57 referrals (70.2%) were followed to some form of resolution. At least one referral was followed for 10 of the 11 questions. Of these 40 referrals, 24 eventually led to a correct answer (60%), while 16 referrals did not do so (40%). Successful referrals were: CIA and Bay of Pigs (seven); native artifacts (five); gasoline additive MMT (five); architect of National Museum of American Indian (three); black credit unions (two); abandoned Newfoundland communities (one); and sailing solo around the world (one). Unsuccessful referrals were: endangered plant species (seven); abandoned Newfoundland communities (four); Ritalin statistics (three); sailing solo around the world (one); and golf and CEOs (one). If, based on these findings, satisfactory referrals are apportioned to the count of correct answers on a 60 percent basis (that is, 34 theoretically successful referrals out of 57 total referrals), library reference staff provided correct answers *or* initiated a chain of events that led to a correct answer 79 times (45 + 34). From this perspective the rate of correct responses was 34.2 percent. Responses received to each question are discussed in greater detail below.

The CIA Report about the Bay of Pigs

The release by the Central Intelligence Agency (CIA) of its own report on the 1961 Bay of Pigs misadventure was a major news story in both the United States and Canada in the latter part of February 1998. Both *The New York Times* and *The Globe and Mail* carried lengthy stories about this report, officially entitled *The Inspector General's Survey of the Cuban Operation*. The final paragraphs of each story noted that it was released under the U.S. Freedom of Information Act to the National Security Archive, which collects and publishes declassified government documents. Both news stories also provided the Web address of the CIA report, and *The New York Times* carried extracts. A correct answer to this reference question was defined as one that mentioned the Web address or referred to the media coverage of the report.

The most common responses received to this question were referrals to university libraries or to the CIA itself. Each type of referral occurred five times. Two library staff members suggested calling the American embassy, while another said that such information could only be accessed through a special petition made under the Freedom of Information Act. Another staff person suggested taking a trip to a border city in the United States, because "someone in that city is bound to help you."

Referrals made to the CIA and the American embassy were followed up. Both these referrals turned out to be useful, since staff members were able to identify the location of the requested document. Personnel in the Media and Cultural Affairs Department of the American embassy recommended the CIA Web site and provided the correct Web address. An individual in the Public Affairs Department of the CIA also stated that the report was available on their Web site.

More troubling were the responses received from library personnel who had no idea about the question. Six libraries fell into this category. Some were plainly rude, and treated the request as a far-fetched joke. Others did not even bother to check their holdings, replying immediately that they could not help. One reference staff member sarcastically mentioned that Canadian libraries are not to be confused with American government depository libraries, and implied that this question was a waste of time. Another reference staff member said she was "flabbergasted" by the question, and was "certain" that such a report was unavailable.

Another library staff member, while providing the address of CIA director George Tenet in Washington, was rather condescending in his approach, explaining that "big shot George would have a secretary who opened his mail [and that this person] would probably pass [the] request on to a more suitable person." During another call, the reference person consulted with a colleague, and both were heard to be laughing in the background about this "weird" request. The person taking the call then returned and suggested calling the CIA. Although a firm conclusion cannot be made about these two calls, the general impression left by these two telephone interviews was that the reference person was providing the CIA address as an attempt to humor the patron and complete the call as quickly as possible. They were not treating the information request seriously, and likely were not offering the CIA phone number in good faith.

When all is said and done, this was a question about the location of an official government document that had received wide media coverage. Indeed, the one library staff member who was able to provide information about the report had seen a story about it on the television show *Hard Copy*. Public library reference staff who are not paying attention to current news may therefore be providing a level of service that is not as good as it could be.

Elgar Symphony

Sir Edward Elgar, upon his death, left behind him unfinished fragments of his Third Symphony with the injunction that these "rough drafts" be burned, or at the very least, never be tinkered with. However, the contemporary British composer Anthony Payne persuaded Elgar's descendants to let him attempt to finish the symphony. The reason for the decision to go against Elgar's wishes was that the unfinished musical sketches had been published in 1936, and would consequently pass into the public domain in 2004 after copyright expiration. Thus, anyone could try to complete the symphony. Family members were thus more willing to entrust the sketches to a scholar with a wide musical background and proven dedication to Elgar. In February 1998 the BBC Symphony performed what was referred to in the program as the *Elgar/Payne Symphony No. 3* to almost universal critical acclaim. Again, the news about Elgar's now-finished masterpiece was given extensive press coverage.

The most common step taken by library reference staff when faced with the question about the finished or unfinished state of Elgar's symphony was to consult either the *New Grove Dictionary of Composers* or the *Oxford Dictionary of Music*. Reference staff members in 12 libraries chose this approach, while another library worker used a biography of Elgar. Accordingly, the answer provided by all 13 libraries was that the symphony was unfinished and existed only in sketches. Clearly, this answer was incorrect. Here, then, is a situation where accessible ready reference tools are outdated. Both Hutchins (1944) and Yates (1987) stressed the importance for library staff to institute policies about updating information. One method that may help reference personnel to provide the most up-to-date information to patrons is to scan newspapers on a regular basis, keeping an eye out for facts that may supersede information contained in standard reference tools.

Architect of the National Museum of the American Indian

At the beginning of April 1998, the Smithsonian announced a controversial change in the design team for the National Museum of the American Indian. The contract of Douglas Cardinal, a prominent Canadian architect of Blackfoot ancestry, and his collaborators GBQC Architects of Philadelphia, was terminated because of delays and disagreements over the delivery of working and technical drawings. Smithsonian officials emphasized that they were more than pleased with Cardinal's conception and vision for the museum, but that if they hoped to complete the project on time and within their tight budget, which was wholly dependant on Congressional appropriations, the architectural team had to be replaced. The Smithsonian hired another set of architects—James Stewart Polshek and Partners as well as Tobey and Davis—to conduct a "peer review" of the project. Reports were rampant that Polshek's appointment was a precursor to his taking over the project. Cardinal was given until the end of April 1998 to appeal his dismissal, and it was apparent that he intended to mount a strong challenge to remain as the architect of the National Museum of the American Indian. Native groups, both in Canada and the United States, gave Cardinal unequivocal support, asserting that the Smithsonian's action was tantamount to "letting someone [else] finish your painting." Since Cardinal is Canadian and designed the much-praised Museum of Civilization in Hull, Québec, the story received wide coverage in Canada.

A correct answer to this question was defined as one which took into account the existence of a controversy connected with the identity of the architect. Five library reference staff provided correct answers; they identified Cardinal as the original architect but also stated that he had just been fired and that another architectural team was now assigned to the project. One library identified Cardinal after a quick search, but did not mention any controversy about the National Museum of the American Indian. By far the most frequent response to this question was to urge the caller to come into the library and look at books or magazine and periodical indexes. Three libraries offered no help whatsoever, and one of these stated that they could not be expected to help because they were not "architectural specialists."

Three referrals were made. One was to the Smithsonian, another was to the tourist bureau in Washington, D. C., and a final referral suggested that "any architect in town" would know the answer. These referrals were followed up. The name of an architectural firm was selected at random from the *Yellow Pages* directory of a major city in Canada. The company's advertisements stated that it had been in business for over 40 years. While the individual who answered did not know the answer to the question, he suggested using the *Yellow Pages* directory on the Internet by selecting Washington as the required city and the National Museum of the American Indian as the required business or institution.

The Tourist Bureau of Washington was also contacted. Since the library worker who made this referral did not provide a phone number, the first step was to call long-distance directory assistance. Unfortunately, the provided number turned out to be the Tourist Bureau in Chicago. But the Chicago office did give the correct number of the Washington Convention and Visitors Association, who recommended calling the Smithsonian and gave a number for its Public Information Line. Here, we were told to call the Smithsonian Office of Public Programs, who in turn directed us to call the Public Affairs Department at the National Museum of the American Indian. Here, finally, a very polite individual informed us that the design architect was indeed Douglas Cardinal, but that he and GBQC of Philadelphia had been terminated as working architects. Although all three referrals eventually would lead to a correct answer, the number of steps needed to reach this answer might prove daunting, not to mention expensive, from the standpoint of long-distance charges, to some individuals.

Endangered Plants

In April 1998, the World Conservation Union released a list of nearly 34,000 plants species endangered globally. The result of more than 20 years of work by botanists and biologists around the world, the so-called Red List contains more than 750 pages of plant names divided into five categories. Endangered plants make up some 12.5 percent of the world's known species of plants, and the United States harbors 29 percent of all these imperiled species. Front-page coverage of the report's release in *The New York Times* and a same-day reprint in *The Globe and Mail* meant that this story would receive broad coverage in other media outlets across North America. *The Globe and Mail* also printed the Web address of the World Conservation Union.

Five library reference staff provided the correct answer, defined as telling the patron the existence of the Red List. Three specifically mentioned *The Globe and Mail* report, while another one had heard about it on *ABC World News Tonight*. Six libraries urged the patron to come into the library and conduct research, although some in this category doubted that anything could be found on such a broad topic. Three reference personnel simply had no idea, and seven libraries made referrals to various government departments or environmental action groups. Two referrals were made to the general Reference Canada (RC) information line, two more were made to Environment Canada, another was to Agricultural Canada, yet another was to "any government department," and a final referral was to the Canadian Wildlife Federation (CWF).

Again, we followed these referrals. The CWF informed us that no such list was available for plants endangered on a worldwide basis, but that they could provide a list of endangered animals in Canada. They also suggested calling the World Wildlife Fund at a toll-free number. We followed their advice, and were informed, again, that no such list existed, and they offered to send us a brochure listing all endangered fish, animal, bird, and plant species in Canada. Some weeks later we received the publication *List of Canadian Wildlife at Risk: Your Guide to Protecting the Web of Life*. The following categories of at-risk Canadian plants were contained in the brochure: 2 extirpated (found elsewhere, but no longer in

Canada), 33 endangered, 37 threatened, 38 vulnerable, and 22 in a recovery plan.

We also followed up the referrals to federal government agencies. The RC information line gave us the number for the local Environmental Conservation Branch of the Canadian Wildlife Service, and assured us that this office was open during regular business hours. Repeated calls to this number were made, but we only received voice-mail messages stating that no one was in the office at this time. Messages to return our calls were left, but no answer was received. We called RC back, explained the above situation, and were then given a number for the Environment Enforcement Coordinator. This number, however, proved to be the number for a local home cleaning service. We again called RC, and this time they gave us a toll-free number for Environment Canada in the National Capital Region of Ottawa-Hull. The first person we spoke to here informed us that there was no such international list, but that he could provide us with a list of plants and animals that cannot be imported into, or exported from, Canada. After repeating our request about plant species, he transferred us to another individual. This person, who was on the Committee on the Status of Endangered Species and Wildlife in Canada (COSEWIC), informed us, predictably, that an international list of threatened plant species did not exist, but that there was a list specifically for Canada. This list contained 32 vascular plants and one lichen species. Names of these plants were available at their Web site. Since we were unsuccessful in the above instances, we tried again by phoning an alternate number given to us by RC, this time in Toronto. Yet again we were told that Environment Canada had no such list, but that perhaps Agricultural Canada could help. We were consequently transferred to the Pest Management Service, but this turned out to be a department of Health Canada rather than Agricultural Canada. They did not have any knowledge about endangered plant species.

Unlike the referrals for the CIA Bay of Pigs report and the name of the architect for the National Museum of the American Indian, referrals for this question did not eventually lead to a satisfactory resolution of the initial information need. A referral by library reference personnel to the RC information line may seem like a simple solution when faced with what appear to be government documents reference questions, but the experiences described above suggest that many difficulties lie ahead for individuals who attempt to retrieve information from official Canadian government sources about information that is not specifically produced by the Canadian government. In this case about endangered plant species, library personnel who had paid attention to the news about the publication of the Red List could have obviated many of the frustrations connected with a very general and broad referral.

Credit Unions Owned by Blacks

At the beginning of May 1998, *The Globe and Mail* reported the liquidation of the only black-owned financial institution in Canada. The George Washington Carver Credit Union was founded in 1950 by Moses Coady in East Preston, Nova Scotia, a rural municipality just outside Dartmouth. It was an institution that was entirely run by volunteers. Unable to increase its deposit base beyond $300,000, it could not offer such services as checking accounts, automated teller machines, or large business loans. Loan losses in the early 1990s resulted in growing debts, and the credit union was forced to close.

Four library reference desks provided the correct answer to this question, and three of these mentioned that they had read something about this in a recent newspaper or periodical account. Another four libraries had absolutely no idea, and offered no further suggestions. Nine libraries recommended that the patron come in and consult such diverse sources as magazine and periodical indexes, CD-ROM databases, the entries under "credit unions" or "blacks" in *The Canadian Encyclopedia*, general history books about the black experience in Canada, or "to try looking in a history of credit unions if there is such a thing—we don't have anything like that in our database." Three referrals were made, two of which were subsequent to a library staff person checking the *Directory of Associations in Canada* under the heading "credit unions." In both instances the name and number of a specific person at the Credit Union Institute of Canada who might know the answer was provided. We called this person, and were indeed provided not only with the name of the black credit union in question, but also the name and number of the outgoing chief executive officer, in case more information was required. One lesson here may be that the more specific the referral, the greater the chance of acquiring needed information.

Abandoned Communities in Newfoundland

A popular daily feature on the op-ed page of *The Globe and Mail* is a column devoted to less well-known aspects of life in various Canadian provinces. In early May 1998, this column contained an account of efforts in Newfoundland to take stock of the villages, outports, and towns that have had to be abandoned for reasons of unsustainability, mostly connected with the vicissitudes of the fishing industry and governmental resettlement policies aimed at economic diversification. In the past five years, interest in rural Newfoundland life has shown a marked increase across North America, the result, in part, of the success of such best-selling novels as E. Annie Proulx's *The Shipping News* and Howard Norman's *The Bird Artist*. In Canada, of course, Newfoundland constantly appears in the news, whether because of the recent discovery of massive nickel deposits at Voisey's Bay, the offshore oil reserves at Hibernia, or the stubborn refusal of fishers to abandon their traditional way of life despite the troubled state of the East Coast cod stocks. The book detailing abandoned communities in Newfoundland, by Tor Fosnaes, is called *Where Once They Stood: A Gazetteer of Abandonment,* and lists some 340 locations.

No library was able to provide a correct answer. By far the most common response by library workers was that they simply had no idea about the question. This occurred nine times, and on four of these occasions, reference staff told the patron to call back when a part of the title of the book or the author's name was known. Six libraries recommended that the patron visit the library, and three of these made mention of a specific book or encyclopedia title. Six referrals were made. Two of these were to university libraries, two were to the Newfoundland government information line, and two were to major bookstores.

We followed up all these referrals. A correct answer to the question was received from Centre for Newfoundland Studies (CNS). CNS staff also provided a mailing address through which the book could be ordered. Our experiences with the Newfoundland government information line were less rewarding, despite the fact that everyone we talked with was more than pleasant and willing to help. We were initially transferred to the Department of Economics and Statistics, then to Municipal Affairs, then to the local government subdivision of Finance and General Operations, where we were informed that the government only has figures on the current number of incorporated communities. Based on the experiences here and with the question on endangered plants, referrals to federal or provincial government agencies may not be the most suitable types of referrals for library staff to make in those instances when there is not absolute certainty that the data being sought is in fact generated by a specific government agency. It is therefore incumbent upon library reference personnel to be very familiar with what type of information federal and provincial governments do and do not provide. Otherwise, the result may be many unsuccessful telephone transfers between various government departments or dead ends.

We also consulted the Web page of one of the largest bookstores in

Canada. Although *Where Once They Stood: A Gazetteer of Abandonment* is available through this outlet, a person attempting to find this book through keyword or subject searches would be unable to do so. The reason is that at the time we tried to locate the book, the word "Newfoundland" was not associated with it in the description field. Thus, while a search under the term "abandon*" would theoretically find this text, there would be no way to tell that it was indeed about Newfoundland, since there is no indication in the title about the book's pertinence to that Canadian province. To be sure, as this Web site evolves, description fields will be added to all available books, and these fields will no doubt be indexed. When that occurs, an answer to the reference question asked here would be readily available through the Web site of this bookstore. This circumstance raises the troubling issue of the relevancy of the public library in an era in which online bookstores, with their massive catalogues, are proliferating. If patrons begin to discover that many of the questions and problems that they would have traditionally gone to a library to find answers for can now be solved through online facilities, the image of the public library as a valuable taxpayer-funded institution may become tarnished and its role in the community may be increasingly precarious. Accordingly, one way to maintain, or enhance, the image of the public library might be to make a strong commitment to providing superior value-added reference service. This would mean a group of highly trained staff who, collectively, is extremely comfortable with all types of print and electronic reference tools and who pays attention to daily developments in electronic and print information sources.

Ritalin use in Québec

This story appeared on the front page of *The Globe and Mail* in late May 1998, although it had been reported in late January 1998 by some Montréal newspapers. It detailed new statistics about an alarming increase in the usage of Ritalin by elementary school children in Québec. According to a study performed by International Medical Statistics (IMS), based in Montréal, and Pierre Paradis, a professor of education at the University of Québec at Rimouski, the number of children using Ritalin soared by about 380 percent since 1990, reaching a figure of 179,000 in 1997. The article in *The Globe and Mail* generated controversy, with many articles in the local Montréal press disputing the statistics and methodology of the Paradis report. Here, a correct answer was defined as making reference to any newspaper report about Ritalin and Québec.

Two libraries supplied a correct answer, while 15 others suggested visiting the library and making use of magazine and periodical indexes, current affairs databases, or consumer medical databases. Two referrals were made to university libraries, and a further two referrals were made to a provincial learning disabilities association and the Canadian Medical Association (CMA). We followed these last two referrals. The provincial learning disabilities association could not provide any information. We also called the CMA, where we were told that they were "not the best place to look for this [kind of information]" and instead directed to contact either the Canadian Pharmaceutical Association (CPA) or Statistics Canada. Upon contacting Statistics Canada, we were told that they did not collect such information, but also recommended the CPA as a likely source. The CPA, however, informed us that its mandate does not include collecting statistics, and directed us to get in touch with IMS Canada in Montréal. At IMS, we were immediately transferred to the account management department, where we were told that they did indeed have the required Ritalin statistics, but that, since they were a for-profit health data company, the information would cost "a few hundred dollars minimum." Although the four referrals for this question did not lead to a satisfactory conclusion, a majority of library staff members readily identified newspapers or periodicals (listed in indexes or on CD-ROM databases) as the most plausible source for information about this question, even though they themselves had not read about it in the press. Library reference staff are therefore aware that much statistical data may be obtained from newspapers and periodicals.

Golf and CEOs

A light-hearted story examining the relationship between golf scores of chief executive officers (CEOs) of major companies and the success of their companies appeared both in *The New York Times* and *The Globe and Mail* in late May and early June 1998. Its conclusion was that CEOs who are better golfers, as measured by their golf handicaps, deliver above-average returns to shareholders, as measured by the performance of the company's stock over a three-year period. A correct answer in this case was defined as knowing that such a study had been recently performed.

This is the type of story that, especially at the beginning of the summer golf season, would receive broad diffusion over the radio and television. Seven libraries provided a correct answer to this question, and some were specifically able to cite *The Globe and Mail*, a report in their local paper, or a television network broadcast. All seven knew that a study of this kind had been recently conducted, and recommended current newspapers or periodicals as a source. Four libraries could not give any answer at all. Among this group was one reference staff member who, in exasperation with the question, stated that "if you want to know such things, you should probably be reading the papers." Eight libraries recommended visiting the library, but unlike previous questions where an initial source was suggested, six of these eight libraries did not give the patron any starting point. Indeed, two libraries stated that the question was a difficult one that would require much research that could only be done in person. Two libraries made referrals. The first was to either a golf store or a golf organization, and the second was to "any golf site" on the Internet. Neither the referral to the golf store nor to the golf organization, which we defined as the headquarters of the Royal Canadian Golf Association (RCGA), was fruitful. The RCGA representative said that he would have no idea where to begin with such a question.

Sailing Solo Around the World

Two stories in *The Globe and Mail* on two consecutive days in mid-July of 1998 discussed the exploits of Joshua Slocum, a Canadian who was the first person to circumnavigate the world alone. The first report was a human-interest story appearing as part of the popular Compass series of reports on page 2, and the second report was the lead review, on the weekend Books page, of a biography of Slocum, entitled *Alone at Sea: The Adventures of Joshua Slocum.*

No library was able to provide the correct answer. Two reference staff said that they had no idea, and offered no further help. Fourteen library workers recommended coming into the library to conduct research, and mentioned history books, microfiche, and old newspapers as the most likely sources of information. One library in this category had a local archives, and so the library staff member was sure that something about this question could be found there. Three referrals were made to university professors or university libraries, and one vague referral was made to "a provincial library on the East Coast." One reference staff member recommended trying the Internet. We followed two of these referrals by phoning the history department of a major Canadian university and by contacting the legislative library in a province on the East Coast of Canada. Staff at the legislative library were unwilling to help with this question. At the university history department, we were referred to a specialist in naval history who very graciously told us that he would look into the matter. About five weeks later, the naval historian called and informed us about Joshua Slocum and recommended a number of biographies about his exploits.

Gasoline Additive MMT

During the summer months of 1998, the gasoline additive MMT was the subject of ongoing, sometimes bitter, controversy in Canada. The government of Canada had banned imports of, and interprovincial trade in, MMT for environmental reasons, but an American-based manufacturer, Ethyl Corporation of Richmond, Virginia, was threatening to sue the government under the provisions of the North American Free Trade Agreement (NAFTA). Faced with a legal opinion that it was likely to lose the court challenge, the federal government dropped its ban on MMT and paid $10 million to Ethyl Corporation for legal costs and lost profits, despite the existence of new evidence that MMT could cause nervous-system damage and attention deficit disorder in children. Car companies severely criticized the government's decision, claiming that MMT had a detrimental impact on emission controls. Numerous front page stories in *The Globe and Mail* about this controversy during the last few weeks of July 1998 attest to the importance of this story for Canadians.

The correct answer to this question was given 10 times by library reference personnel, who often cited reports in *The Globe and Mail* as their source. Only two libraries had no idea about the question, while another three urged the patron to visit the library and conduct research. Six referrals were made: one to a gas station, one to a university chemistry department, two to the Reference Canada (RC) information line, and a further two to Environment Canada. RC also made a reference to Environment Canada. After calling two separate numbers at Environment Canada, we were transferred to the Commercial Chemicals Department, where we were informed that the person who could answer this question would return our call soon. And, in fact, we were called back the next day with a complete history of the legal status of MMT in Canada. In addition, the referral to a gas station turned out to be successful. We looked in the *Yellow Pages* and found a toll-free number for the customer service department of the largest service-station retailer in Canada. The representative with whom we spoke remembered that she had recently been given an FAQ (list of frequently asked questions) about MMT. Upon finding this FAQ, she was able to provide us with as much information about MMT as we wanted, including summaries of scientific studies about its benefits and drawbacks.

Native Artifacts

Another major story in Canada during the summer months of 1998 was the signing, after protracted and often acrimonious negotiations, of the Nisga'a treaty between natives in British Columbia, on the one hand, and the federal government in Ottawa and the provincial government of British Columbia, on the other. While the main points of the treaty deal with financial compensation and ancestral land claims, another provision requires that two Canadian museums, the Royal British Columbia Museum in Victoria and the Museum of Civilization in Ottawa-Hull, return some 250 artifacts belonging to the Nisga'a people of British Columbia. This provision addresses the issue of repatriation of sacred objects to their rightful owners—an issue of growing importance to native peoples in the United States as well as Canada. The front page of the weekend Arts section of *The Globe and Mail* was devoted to the repatriation clauses of the Nisga'a treaty, and the story also included relevant Web site addresses. A correct answer was defined as knowing that native artifacts had to be returned under the terms of the treaty.

This question generated the greatest number of correct answers via telephone from library reference staff. Eleven correct answers were received, and many of these made specific mention of the report in *The Globe and Mail*. There were eight referrals, five of which were either to the Reference Canada information line, the Department of Indian Affairs, or to the Museum of Civilization. One library worker had no idea about the question, and another reference staff member recommended a visit to the library for further research. We followed the five specifically named referrals above. After transfers between various government departments, very complete information about the exact number of native artifacts was received from the Chief of Ethnology of the Museum of Civilization as well as from the Indian and Inuit Arts Center, by way of the Historical Research Center of the Department of Indian Affairs. In particular, the Chief of Ethnology not only took the time to return our call from Vancouver, where she was travelling to attend a meeting, but also explained in some detail the difference between artifacts that had to be returned, as per Schedule L1, and those for which a shared custodial arrangement had been forged, as per Schedule L2.

DISCUSSION

Unobtrusive studies are often criticized for the artificiality of the questions asked. But, as Melissa Gross (1995) points out, librarians have long recognized the existence of the "imposed query," as distinct from the self-generated question (p. 236). Imposed queries occur when a question is asked, negotiated, and "transacted outside the purview of the person originating it" (p. 237). Gross (1998) observes that there are numerous instances when imposed queries are asked: school assignments, company projects, and immigrant children sent on missions by their non-English speaking parents (pp. 290–299). Thus, on the one hand, Gross acknowledges the existence of these types of queries. On the other hand, she suggests that their existence can help to explain low reference success rates because imposed queries are "subject to various degrees of mutation as they are transferred, transacted, and returned to the [original] imposer" (Gross, 1995, p. 242). Service evaluation, she believes, has been conducted "on the assumption that questions are self-generated"—a situation where there is no agent between the original imposer of the question and the reference librarian to muddle matters (Gross, 1998, p. 291). The existence of the interposing agent therefore makes the job of the reference librarian that much more difficult, resulting in lower success rates. Perhaps unintentionally, Gross establishes the legitimacy of unobtrusive research on reference service performance by admitting the existence of imposed queries. And, although she believes that these types of questions are complex and given to misinterpretation at each of the various stages of development through which each question goes before it is answered, she does not account for short, fact-based questions that could be asked either by members of the public or by trained proxies who are prepared for question negotiation by having a plausible rationale for the question that they are asking.

Accordingly, unobtrusive tests can give valuable insights into the quality of library service. Basing their work, in part, on recent management studies that examine ways to improve quality, Hernon and Altman (1998) provide a broad framework for measuring library service quality with the concept of loyalty ratios. This concept allows managers to assess "such important things as the length and strength of customer relationships as measured by the frequency and intensity of library use" (p. 150). Loyalty, furthermore, is influenced by customer requirements, one of which is accuracy. Accuracy has a way of increasing customer loyalty and generating a positive reputation in the community. Libraries are not exempt from this principle. "If libraries fail to retain, maintain, and expand the customer base, they are likely to be in trouble. Getting and keeping customers is what it is all about, and the platitudes about service, education, or imparting of knowledge will not change the need for customers"(p. 178).

Reference service success rates on fact-based questions, far from being an unrepresentative measure with little validity, are an important component of ensuring the continued vitality of the library. Patrons who receive poor service during one reference interview situation may think twice about making use of reference service, or any other service, at that same library in the future. Making a mental note about the poor quality of service received on a prior occasion, they may turn elsewhere to resolve their information need. As Hernon and Altman (1998) note in a different context, librarians have begun to complain that "students prefer inferior material in electronic format to better material in the form of hard copy" (p. 148). It is not inconceivable that potential users of a public library, dissatisfied with the service they have received in the past at their library, will attempt to make use of the vast resources of the Web on their own from their homes, even if this results in information that is inferior or incomplete.[1]

CONCLUSION

The primary purpose of this chapter was to examine whether library staff are paying attention to daily information sources such as newspapers or magazines. Questions dealing with current topics of importance, as reported in a major newspaper, were unobtrusively asked of reference desk personnel by telephone. Questions requiring a short, fact-based answer were selected. There was no way to determine whether the person on duty at the reference desk was a librarian or a paraprofessional. Reference staff provided accurate answers during the initial call or during a call-back at a rate of 19.5 percent. A further 24.7 percent of questions was referred to an external source, and of these referrals, 60 percent led eventually to correct answers. Consequently, library reference staff either provided correct answers themselves or initiated a chain of events that led to a correct answer at a rate of 34.2 percent. Patrons were told to visit the library 34.6 percent of the time. No matter which way success rates were measured, library reference staff performed at a level substantially below the findings in other unobtrusive reference studies.

Only two reference questions were answered correctly a rate close to or above 50 percent. These questions concerned the gas additive MMT and the Nisga'a treaty. The common feature of these questions was that both dealt with topics which had not only been in the news for a prolonged period of time, but also were prominently featured on the front pages of newspapers. The fact that about 50 percent of library reference staff were able to answer these two questions is an indication that at least some library workers realize the importance of keeping up with current news, at least those stories which are given extremely prominent coverage, as part of the array of their tasks. However, numerous other types of plausible reference questions could be answered quickly and efficiently by library reference workers were they to devote time and energy to a regular and complete perusal of daily information sources such as newspapers and periodicals. And, while the study was not meant to yield an overall appraisal of the quality of telephone reference service in Canada, it does give an indication of the general knowledge and current awareness level of personnel at public libraries who are responsible for fielding questions from members of the general public.

The relatively low level of current affairs knowledge among library workers, as manifested by their inability to expeditiously answer the questions posed in this study, may be explained by at least three reasons. First, newspapers and periodicals may not be recommended as valuable sources of information and reference tools in reference courses at schools of library and information science in Canada. Based on the findings presented in this chapter, teachers of reference courses at library schools may wish to reconsider this lacuna when they prepare syllabi in the future. Second, the habit of reading newspapers and periodicals as part of being a well- and broadly educated individual may be outmoded. Felicity Barringer (1998) reports that paid newspaper circulation in the United States during 1997–1998 declined by 11 percent from a 1984 peak of 63.3 million readers. Numerous reasons have been advanced for this decline: time pressures, increased diversity of entertainment choices, the rise of more immediately available news through 24-hour news broadcast channels, and the explosion of Web-based news sources. From one perspective, if members of the public are reading fewer newspapers and periodicals than in the past, this should be reason enough for professional librarians to become more familiar with these information sources. Third, Harris and Marshall (1998) have noted that budgetary constraints have forced many academic libraries to replace professional library reference staff with paraprofessionals. Hernon and Altman (1998) also recognize this phenomena, and specifically link it to poor service quality: "Despite a rather low percentage of accuracy in answering questions, many libraries, both academic and public, on the grounds of economy, regularly staff reference desks, especially on evenings and weekends, with students and library assistants" (p. 177). Paraprofessionals working at reference desks may be even less cognizant of the value of current news information sources than professional librarians. In addition, it may often be the case that the most experienced reference librarians are promoted into management positions that take them away from front-line public service work. Library administrators may wish to structure work arrangements and schedules in such a way that experienced personnel who have management responsibilities remain directly involved with the delivery of public service functions such as reference work. Another solution, implemented by Texas A & M University, is to establish standards and "baseline competencies for the humanities, science, and the social sciences" that have to be met by any reference personnel before they are allowed to work without supervision (Hernon & Altman, 1998, p. 177). Worthy of consideration too is a rigorous certification and a regular re-certification process for librarians, along the lines of what an increasing number of state governments are demanding for elementary and high-school teachers (Archibold, 1998, pp. 22–25, 30–31).

Another finding of this chapter is that referrals are successful at a rate of 60 percent (24 out of 40 questions). In Chapter 5, where another set of referrals was studied in greater detail, the success rate was 40.8 percent (31 out of 76). When these findings are added, the overall referral success rate is 47.4 percent (55 out of 116). However, this figure was only achieved because many expensive long-distance telephone calls during regular business hours were made to far-flung locales. In this regard, library personnel should keep two things in mind. If statistics are kept about reference completion rates, referrals should not automatically be counted as a satisfactory conclusion to a reference inquiry. Based on the findings of this chapter, referrals lead to correct answers only about 50 percent of the time, and library statistics that do not take this into consideration may not give an accurate picture about the proficiency of reference service. Second, many patrons may not be able to afford long-distance calls to locate a specific piece of information, and so the referral success rate may be even lower than the figures indicated here. Library reference personnel may wish to consider all local possibilities before making a referral that involves the expenditure of money by the patron.

Patrons have many reasons for making a telephone reference inquiry rather than making a physical visit to the library or sending an e-mail inquiry. Certainly, many patrons could come into the library, but there are just as many patrons who are unable to do so. They may be strapped for time, or they may be unable to get to the library because of physical constraints or the lack of transportation. (In addition, many potential library users cannot afford their own computer.) In these instances, a reference staff member who suggests that a patron come into the library to look for an answer may not be offering a real alternative. In the study reported here, 36.4 percent of telephone reference inquiries ended in the patron being told to visit the library. In light of this, Canadian public libraries may wish to consider instituting a telephone reference system of the kind described by Tour (1997), where visiting the library to get an answer is not a requirement.

Public libraries that provide accurate telephone reference service to current events questions at a rate of either 19.5 percent (not counting referrals) or 34.2 percent (counting successful referrals) may not be offering the public real value for its tax dollar. In the current value-added economic environment, library reference staff should challenge themselves to make a strong commitment to an ongoing self-education program, a component of which should be maintaining a high level of current awareness about significant issues of the day. Otherwise, there is a danger that public library reference work, long known for its service and care ethic, will be seen as expendable and replaceable by what Ronald Heckart (1998) broadly describes as "machine help" (pp. 250–259) and which, as outlined by John Richardson (1998), is already available in the form of a Web-based decision support system for ready-reference questions (pp. 29–37). And, although Richardson positions this system, called Question Master, as a tool that would "free up the valuable time of reference librarians so that it could be spent answering the more demanding research-type questions" (p. 30), it is not hard to see that Web-based intelligent technology of this type can just as easily be used from the home as from the library. This is a circumstance that does not augur well for the continued vitality of the public library as an indispensable community information source staffed by knowledgeable, service-oriented, and caring library professionals who take pride in their abilities and work.

NOTE

1. Another promising idea for putting a true value on reference service is described in David W. Harless and Frank R. Allen, "Using the Contingent Valuation Method to Measure Patron Benefits of Reference Desk Service in an Academic Library" (*College & Research Libraries* 60 [January 1999]: 56–69). And even though this article specifically applies to academic libraries, it may also be useful for public libraries. Harless and Allen suggest that the concept of use value must be supplemented by trying to quantify the value of reference services "to potential users who place value on the option of seeking assistance in the event they desire such services" (p. 67). In addition, it is necessary to ask not just actual users of reference services, but random members of the entire community served, whether or not they have used reference services at the library in the past.

Chapter 7

Conclusion and Recommendations

When all is said and done, the 26 reference questions discussed in the previous chapters were not difficult. A passing acquaintance with current news sources as well as Canadian government Web sites would have given any library reference staff member the necessary tools to direct patrons to required information. In addition to the low levels of accuracy, proxies also were not very impressed with the service ethic displayed by reference personnel. As described in Chapter 3, many reference staff members simply did not care whether the patron located the sought-after information, often using unmonitored referrals as a means to process the patron quickly through the system.

STRUCTURAL REASONS FOR REFERENCE FAILURE

Are there reasons for reference failure, and can anything be done? There has been no end of explanations, and a plethora of solutions has been advanced to improve reference service. One popular explanation is that management, not librarians, is to blame for low service levels. Jennifer Younger (1991) suggests that W. Edwards Deming, the developer of the Total Quality Management (TQM) system, was correct in his assessment that some 94 percent of the blame for low quality levels in products or services can be attributed to production processes, which are under the control of management. According to Younger, the situation in libraries is no different. Rao Aluri (1993) concurs, noting that the missing piece in any discussion of reference service is "a systems view of the reference process, and the recognition that library managers, who have management responsibility for the reference system, are equally, if not more, accountable for the quality of the reference process" (p. 221). Aluri cites a range of factors that contribute to success or failure in the reference transaction: the physical environment of the reference area; the depth and accessibility of the reference collection; the totality of demands on the reference librarian; level of, and access to, technology; staffing resources; expectations of management; and existing policies, practices, and philosophies. The librarian, with his or her level of education, subject specialty, experience, competence, and willingness, is only one factor among many, and it would therefore not be appropriate to lay all blame for reference failure on a single cause. In other words, underlying systemic problems need to be addressed before any individual finger pointing takes place. Indeed, Aluri maintains that "library administrators hold primary responsibility for the system. It is management's policies and procedures, its departmental organizations, its rewards and punishment systems, and its three-pronged performance evaluation in academic libraries (library service, community service, and research) under which reference librarians labor" (p. 224). Is it fair, then, to lay all the blame on reference librarians and punish them, especially when administration often takes the best reference librarians off the desk to do committee work and special projects, and refuse to provide the funds for training and continuing education, while they push for publication? Aluri, clearly, believes that it is not.

STRUCTURAL SOLUTIONS

Accordingly, systemic problems demand systemic solutions. Terry Mackey and Kitty Mackey (1992) advocate adopting Deming's 14-point TQM plan for libraries. Of particular importance for libraries are: driving out fear of making mistakes; breaking down the barriers between and among staff and departments; eliminating slogans, exhortations, and targets for the workforce; eliminating numerical quotas; removing barriers that rob people of pride in their work; and encouraging education and self-improvement. Janet Dagenais Brown (1994), also relying on the theories of Deming and Swedish airline magnate Jan Carlzon, urges library staff to focus on the "moment of truth," defined as the moment of contact between customer and employee. "Reference librarians will encounter many of these moments of truth during each shift at the reference desk. How well these moments are managed will determine how satisfied our customers are with our service" (p. 213). If these "moments of truth" are not properly handled, library users may feel frustrated and leave with negative feelings about the librarian and the library itself. They certainly will not be eager to come back again too quickly.

Four strategies are suggested for understanding this moment better: implementing a problem log, creating a suggestion box, using the Wisconsin-Ohio Reference Evaluation Program, and starting a reference department quality circle.

Virginia Massey-Burzio (1992) notes that because "traditional reference service is best at providing information to questions that take only a few minutes to answer, the more in-depth or difficult questions are necessarily handled too briefly and superficially" (p. 277). Thus, traditional modes of reference service underutilize the skills of professional librarians and underserve many patrons. She therefore suggests a two-tiered approach to reference service, with library professionals working from private and quiet "research consultation offices" and dealing only with those queries referred to them by front-line paraprofessional staff (p. 279). Beth Shapiro (1987) calls for a three-tiered model: information desk, general reference desk, and specialized reference desk. Both of these proposals build on Durrance (1982), who argued that differentiated service would raise the expectations of both librarians and patrons, since the environment surrounding traditional reference service triggers mixed signals in patrons because they are never sure if their inquiry is being directed at a professional or a paraprofessional. Currently, patrons have low expectations when it comes to the skill of librarians, and librarians themselves find it hard not to become burned out with a succession of directional and routine questions. In a tiered system, the level of expectation is increased as patrons are referred to a professional research librarian who is better able to use his or her skill and problem-solving techniques. By letting patrons know what they are capable of doing, librarians would be better able to gain their respect. As Massey-Burzio (1992) observed, "[T]he reference interaction can be problematic because, although reference users seek information or advice in a situation that sociologists would define as a professional encounter, the setting itself seems to suggest a different interaction—one more like a quick, commercial encounter with a bank teller or department store clerk" (p. 278). Because librarians seem to equate availability of service with quality service, there needs to be a realization that this mentality only results in poor reference performance and an undermining of their own value as professionals. Tiered service may not only increase the ability of librarians to deal accurately and knowledgeably with reference questions, but it may also contribute to establishing a more professional role for working librarians, with a concomitant increase in job satisfaction.

William Whitson (1995) also believes that the days of the undifferentiated reference service model are numbered. He advances a number of reasons: the high cost of having professional staff answering all questions, some of which could be handled by support staff; lack of control, in the sense that no matter how busy the desk gets, librarians are expected to answer all inquiries with accuracy and in a timely manner, which causes stress; inflexibility in utilization of staff, meaning that by using less qualified staff members, the quality of service will be negatively affected; and lack of accountability because "there is no mechanism for varying the level of priority by type of question, or clientele, except by issuing guidelines to reference staff and relying on them to implement the guidelines as best they can [and] there is no way to allocate more or less staffing support to a particular kind of service—to budget resources in a precise way" (p. 104). Undifferentiated service also reinforces unrealistic expectations on the part of the patrons, since they believe that no matter the inquiry, the person at the desk will be able to answer it very quickly. If he or she cannot, which is often the case with questions requiring in-depth research, the patron considers the staff member deficient. Finally, like Massey-Burzio, Whitson believes that it conveys the wrong image of librarians, because many patrons do not see professional librarians as anything more than service clerks behind a desk, much as they see circulation staff. Instead, a differentiated service model, comprised of five service areas, should be implemented. These areas are: directions and general information, technical assistance, "information look-up" for clients, research consultation, and library instruction. As a result, librarian and staff roles are clarified for users. Services become clearer to clients, and there is less pressure on staff, which results in a greater effectiveness of each service.

BEYOND STRUCTURAL REASONS FOR REFERENCE FAILURE

Missing from the analysis of Durrance, Massey-Burzio, Whitson, and Aluri, however, is any concerted emphasis on improving the knowledge level of individual librarians and other reference staff. To be sure, Durrance mentioned the concept of "raising expectations," but then linked it to structural change within the physical environment of the library. Yet structural change is only as good as the individual components making up the structure. Expectations of patrons about the service they will receive can be raised if patrons begin to understand that library reference personnel have an extraordinary breadth and depth of knowledge about a variety of subjects. McClure and Hernon (1983) found that "the individual library staff member is the single most significant factor affecting the quality of reference service for government documents" (p. 111).

Certainly, McClure and Hernon's concept of the "individual library staff member" is multi-faceted, including behavioral traits as well as knowledge levels. An important article by Dewdney and Ross (1994) summarizes significant helping behaviors that patrons have remarked upon and that would tend to cause them to return to the same reference worker with another question. Carole Larson and Laura Dickson (1994) focus on the development of behavioral performance standards for the reference desk. They suggest that reference staff meet as a group to develop a picture of what constitutes ideal service. Each librarian records at least one key behavior he or she believes to be indicative of optimum service. Typical behaviors identified as important include: displaying a manner that invites users to ask questions, conducting both a reference interview and a follow-up discussion, being aware and knowledgeable about library policies, exhibiting teamwork, and being knowledgeable about the reference collection and tools. With the identification of these key areas, the next step is to prescribe a series of behaviors for each area, such as "uses eye contact" and "smiles while asking a patron if she or he needs help."

IMPROVEMENT OF STAFF KNOWLEDGE LEVELS

Comparatively less attention has been given to the need for library staff to improve their general and subject knowledge levels. Training, of course, is mentioned, but this typically involves short courses or seminars about technological innovations. For instance, Shapiro (1987) recommends ongoing staff training, when reference staff, on a regular weekly basis, are provided "with current information on new resources available within their own units and on resources available elsewhere in the library so that proper referrals can be made" (p. 76). Numerous libraries have implemented variations on this model. While important, such training cannot substitute for a commitment on the part of staff to deepen their knowledge of specific subject areas through a concerted program of study and exploration. In short, staff have a responsibility to themselves and to the library to read something on a daily basis. As Walter, Wyer, and Hutchins observed in the 1920s, 1930s and 1940s, newspapers are almost a necessity for high-quality reference work. But reading should not stop with current news sources. Rather, individual articles in newspapers and magazines should be the starting point for a more in-depth exploration of interesting and relevant topics.

In a sense, Jerry Campbell (1992) recognizes the importance of knowledge acquisition by referring to librarians as "knowledge cartographers," professionals who are "aware of all new sources of information and establish access links between them and users" (pp. 32–33). Howard Harris (1996) points approvingly to the theories of Peter Senge, who advocates both "team learning" and "personal mastery," which begins with a personal commitment to lifelong learning, the first step in becoming "the best person possible" and the cornerstone of building a "learning organization." Darlene Weingand (1994) concurs, stating that "continuing professional education is no longer an option; it is vital to professional health, [since] . . . the quality of information service is based in large part on the competence of personnel. When competence is maintained—or improved—the quality of service will be correspondingly affected" (p. 174). As librarians "map" knowledge in the 21st century, they are, for all intents and purposes, doing what Hutchins told librarians to do in the 1940s: read, remember where you read it by producing "rolls of films of page setups" in the mind, and then read some more.

An example of a very practical approach to knowledge acquisition that would be highly useful at a reference desk is provided by Mary Seng (1978). She describes a massive data collection project extending over three years that collected and categorized 18,738 reference questions asked at the business library of a large American university. Questions were categorized according to whether they were directional, informational, or general. The general reference questions were those that were "answered through the use of information resources," while informational questions dealt with information resources and their use (p. 22). Particularly noteworthy about this project was the fact that, under the "general" heading, staff also categorized specific types of questions. One outcome of this system was the discovery that certain types of statistical questions and certain types of questions about business mergers appeared repeatedly. Having noticed these patterns, staff could make a special effort to locate the necessary sources, thus anticipating future reference questions. Staff time would be saved, and patrons would be assured of finding the correct answer. As Seng observes, "reference librarians should be able to improve the efficiency and effectiveness of their services by establishing their own database of reference questions by noting each reference question asked for a six-month period and tabulating the results" (p. 28). With this database in hand, areas in which staff training and knowledge need to be improved can be readily pinpointed. In addition, reference staff are alerted to new categories of users with specific needs in particular areas as well as the growing importance of emerging disciplines or cross-disciplines. One of the virtues of this system is that it can be applied in any library, public or academic, and in any library sub-area, such as government documents. Staff could then track the most popular questions and be prepared to answer them quickly, thus giving them more time to answer unique and uncommon questions.

METHODS OF IMPROVING THE KNOWLEDGE LEVELS OF REFERENCE STAFF

As librarians and library staff struggle with ways to improve service not only at government documents reference desks, but at reference desks in general, intriguing questions about how to encourage continuous knowledge acquisition are being raised. Chapters 2 and 6 briefly suggested the possibility of initial certification and re-certification for librarians, based on the growing trend of states to require public school teachers, at regular intervals, to pass tests designed to show competency in core and specialized subject areas (Archibold, 1998). Just as Texas A&M University established standards and baseline competencies for the humanities, science, and the social sciences that have to be met by reference personnel before they are allowed to work without supervision, public libraries could also implement appropriate baseline competencies for their staff. Reference staff could be tested on a broad array of topics reflective of the range of subject matter a reasonably well-informed and well-read individual could be expected to possess. One idea might be to slot librarians and other reference staff into three basic categories—beginner, general, and master—with appropriate gradations in each category. Every two years each staff member would have to pass an all-purpose test about reference sources and general world knowledge in order to retain his or her current ranking. In order to move up one gradation or one category, extra tests on more specialized topics would have to be passed. In this way, rhetoric about continuous learning and knowledge acquisition would not be a mere platitude, but would assume concrete meaning.

PERFORMANCE-BASED COMPENSATION

Another possibility is that libraries could move toward performance-based (also called results-based or success-based) compensation—a concept that has, to a certain extent, taken root in the business world. For instance, as Stuart Elliott (1999) reports, some of the world's largest advertisers, including Procter & Gamble, are moving toward a system whereby they will compensate their advertising agencies on the basis of "sales objectives, with agencies being paid more if a brand's sales increase and less if sales decline," or if there is a measurable increase in brand awareness or an increase in the broad distribution of a new product. The rationale for the changeover is revealing. Two main reasons recur. First, surveys of agencies and advertisers using results-based compensation describe their relationship as "less tense, with more teamwork, [a]nd 35 percent of clients using performance-based compensation said they had more respect for their agencies . . . compared with 12 percent for clients that didn't use it" (p. B6). Second, agencies operating under the traditional commission system "could take as long as [they] wanted to come up with solutions" as long as media billings were holding up, but, under the new system, "if you're an agency and your income growth is tied to the growth of the brand you're handling, you have an unbelievable sense of urgency to find solutions to problems . . ." (p. B6). From an overall perspective, success-based compensation encourages "people [to] sit down and do a much better job of really determining a situation, analyzing a problem or opportunity. . . . It has a transforming effect, because you're examining every possibility . . . to achieve your goal" (p. B6).

Although there are vast differences between the worlds of business and public or academic libraries, parallels may also be drawn. Companies that move to success-based compensation have usually identified a persistent problem. For Procter & Gamble, it was the fact that the old compensation system "could tempt agencies to focus their attention on . . . advertising that cost more to create, produce, and run in the media . . . regardless of whether [it was] the most appropriate for the task at hand, because expensive media buys generate higher agency commissions." In short, Procter & Gamble felt it was not getting value for its expenditures. With the new compensation scheme, Procter & Gamble envisions the birth of "holistic marketing," defined as "looking at all the forms of communicating, bonding with . . . customers, whatever it takes: direct mail, public relations, Internet advertising, new media, traditional advertising" (p. B6). Library reference desks have a problem, too, as evidenced by the persistence of a 55 percent, or worse, accuracy rate. To be sure, many attempts have been made to come to grips with the problem. Yet, in general, there does not seem to be a sense of urgency that the problem is sufficiently acute to call for radical solutions and completely new ways of approaching the issue. If nothing else, the implementation of success-based compensation would infuse a transformative energy into the world of reference service. Why not pay reference workers, collectively, a base rate that would foresee increases in the event of reference accuracy rates over and above a pre-determined standard, but that would also entail decreases should the reference accuracy rate fall below a minimum level? As in the example from the advertising world, good things may result from such an innovation. The result might be more teamwork and less tension. Library personnel may earn more respect from their patrons or customers, and they may finally be forced to undertake a fundamental analysis of the principles undergirding the delivery of reference service.

Some library staff are reticent about such policies. Yet, as Cheryl Elzy and Alan Nourie (1992) note, university administrators are demanding accountability from faculty members for teaching effectiveness, with the result that faculty are evaluated by students at the end of every term. These evaluations are then taken into consideration for tenure and merit pay. Why should librarians be the only faculty members who do not undergo such evaluation processes, since reference effectiveness is equivalent to teaching effectiveness? Using a different analogy, Leslie Morris (1993) compares how teachers and librarians are hired. School administrators observe teachers in their own classrooms in order to evaluate the quality of their teaching before they are hired. However, when administrators interview for reference librarians, potential candidates are asked about the courses they have taken at library school, but not about the depth of their subject knowledge. Moreover, teachers are frequently evaluated by colleagues and school principals, and written reports, used for promotion and salary decisions, are placed in their files. Why should teachers and librarians, equally valuable in the educative enterprise, be subject to different hiring and evaluation practices? An incompetent teacher is typically given warnings about his or her shortcomings, while, for example, it is almost always taken for granted or "just assume[d] that all reference librarians are familiar with the *Song Index*" (p. 2). Morris's point is that, although librarians need to be every bit as competent as teachers, they are not held to the same standards.

HOLDING LIBRARY AND INFORMATION SCIENCE SCHOOLS RESPONSIBLE FOR THEIR GRADUATES

Some states, such as New York and Texas, have adopted rules whereby at least 70 percent (in the case of Texas) or 80 percent (in the case of New York) of students who graduate from state teaching programs "must pass the state licensing exam for teachers or that teaching school can be put on probation for three years and then shut down," or lose its accreditation (Hartocollis, 1999, p. A12). It may not be that outlandish to suggest that university programs in the business of training future librarians should also be subject to such regulations. As schools and faculties of library and information science transform themselves into programs stressing information systems and computer science, what often gets overlooked in the rush to capitalize on emerging trends is educating the future librarian (or information professional) to be a person with intellectual acumen and curiosity in fields beyond those in which she or he has learned technical proficiency.

Writing in an era when computerization and the information explosion was in its infancy, Jacques Barzun (1969) succinctly identified what he felt to be necessary attributes for the "New Librarian." Instead of becoming a "technician to the computer," the new librarian must be a "reader-and-teacher" who is a "voluminous reader over a much wider range than the Ph.D." Not only must the librarian know books and their titles; he must have "a first-hand knowledge of their contents and their value" to such an extent that "he must in himself and by himself be an intelligence agency, be the glowing point of contact between his library and the inquiring mind" (pp. 3964–3965). Bringing together "the broadest assortment of subjects," the librarian becomes "a practicalist adding to knowledge by its transmission." In short, the librarian develops into a person of "reading and judgment" who wins "recognition and compensation by performing the rarest service next to life-saving, namely, the exact and expert communication of intelligence" (p. 3965). As library and information science schools cast about hither and yon for new directions and for ways to be relevant in a changing world, Barzun's advice about the skills needed for the "new librarian" may, at first glance, be dismissed as quaintly old-fashioned. However, when examined closely, it hints about the type of competencies the curriculum of a re-fashioned library and information science school might demand of its graduates.

Emphasis is placed on "the inquiring mind" of the patron. This point should be stressed. Barzun perceives the patron to be just as inquiring as the ideal librarian, who inquires each time she examines and reads the contents of a book. The word "inquiring" conjures up an image of a seeker of knowledge embarking on a quest, but the very act of undertaking a quest places the patron and the librarian on an equal footing. The only difference is that the librarian "quests" continually, while the patron does so less frequently. Often arduous, time-consuming, and fitful, the patron's quest may be relieved by someone who has read widely in, and studied the structure of, various fields and specialized areas. The librarian or information professional, in this metaphor, becomes a sort of alleviator of the distress, whether intellectual, economic, social, or psychological, that a prolonged patron quest may entail. The more knowledgeable and widely read the librarian is, the sooner the patron's quest has a chance of being completed. In this scenario, why wouldn't the librarian want to know as much as possible? And why wouldn't the school of library and information science agree to tests for such knowledge, thereby showing that its graduates do have the ability to be capable alleviators?

Barzun's advice also has the virtue of answering the objections of Kimmo Tuominen (1997), who criticizes the discourse of user-centered library service for placing the user and librarian in a hierarchical power relationship in which the user is variously treated as ignorant, as a child, and as a patient who must accept "the diagnostic interventions and the treatment propositions" offered by a librarian who is expert, certain, rational, and professional (p. 368). Frohmann (1992), too, has remarked on the ambivalence of user-centered discourse, pointing out that while users are knowledgeable enough to know that they are facing gaps in their knowledge, they are often portrayed as being ignorant about the extent and nature of the gap. Barzun, on the other hand, envisions both librarian and patron as inquiring equals, one of whom helps the other to take steps to arrive at a final destination. Both are embarking on an uncertain journey through the byways and interstices of knowledge, since every question is a complex one to the person who asks it and therefore requires of the librarian or reference staff member a serious and considered response, which, ideally, has been preceded by a serpentine thought process designed to elicit the best sources for the question at hand. It would not be inappropriate to characterize Barzun's model librarian as someone who, in speaking of herself, might say: "The more I read, the less I know." That is to say, while the librarian's absolute level of knowledge is increasing, it is decreasing in relative terms because of the explosive growth of information and discovery in all fields. Moreover, the saying suggests a real humility before the accumulated mass of existing knowledge. The more one reads and discovers, the more one realizes how much there is to know, how every piece of knowledge opens the door to two or three other areas of interconnected interest, further discovery, and intellectual growth. In sum, the ideal librarian would, on the one hand, understand the necessity of perpetual reading and self-education, and, on the other, perceive the patron as a unique, yet equal individual in need of temporary help, who certainly has the capacities to find the sought-for information independently, but has chosen, for one reason or another, to call upon the library. Love of knowledge and love of reading are definite skills to be imparted, and, when all is said and done, such skills may make a more lasting contribution to the job performance of a library worker than knowing, for instance, the most recent developments in the architecture of information systems.

Accordingly, Barzun's conception speaks to many of the same issues articulated by Dervin's (1994) communitarian vision of information flow and process. This may, initially, seem like a strange comparison to make, but the basis of Dervin's model rests on her conviction that, because the world is "ontologically incomplete and discontinuous," individuals "need to hear each other not only to comprehend their differences but more importantly to get a more comprehensive, albeit always in flux, always incomplete, and always elusive picture of what reality might be about" (p. 381). Dervin gives the example of the debate over alternative medicines. On the one hand, there is the clear, normative, and expert voice of allopathic medicine represented by "credentialed spokespeople" who tend to disparage solutions that will not maintain "the power of dominant interests in the pharmaceutical-medical establishment"; on the other hand, there is the substantial minority of people who turn to alternative ways of healing despite the seeming certainty of scientific and medical facts. Dervin's point is that, while reality is unbelievably complex and multi-form, the worldview represented by, in this example, allopathic medicine is "a portrait of simplicity [because although] there are multiple perspectives present [only] one dominant authorial voice is privileged" (p. 381). Essentially positivist and empiricist, this set of ontological and epistemological assumptions regarding knowing takes it for granted that "there is much misinformation about [and that] therefore the marketplace of ideas must be kept free so that 'truth' (good information) will surface in open exchange . . . that truth will emerge in the clash of ideas" (p. 374). In contrast, communitarian ways of knowing, here represented by alternative medicines, create a dynamic whereby "multiple voices in multiple times and multiple spaces attend to an elusive reality" (p. 382). Dervin thus suggests that the only democratic way to acquire information, whether from a system or through human agency, is to understand its "multiperspectival" nature—an understanding "which mandates a procedural circling of the reality being made, maintained, destroyed, and remade by humans as they struggle individually and collectively through their lives" (p. 383). No one viewpoint has a definite answer to a specific problem or situation. And because all "knowing is made and remade, reified and maintained, challenged and destroyed in communication, in dialogue, contest, and negotiation," explanations for all phenomena "are assumed to be assumptions—potentially useful fictions—and the question is what different assumptions allow in terms of actions and possibilities" (pp. 377–378).

How does Barzun fit into this picture? As described above, Barzun imagines the librarian as a "reader-scholar"—someone who is aware of developments in a wide variety of fields, someone who is constantly increasing her store of knowledge through unceasing reading and thoughtful study. As a result, this "reader-scholar" necessarily enters into the flux of ideas and knowledge, becomes aware of the give-and-take of competing theories and paradigms, and is able to comprehend fully the contingent nature of reality in diverse fields and subject areas. The more he reads, the less he knows, because reality and knowledge are ever-changing, transmuting, and evolving. Simply put, there is always something more to know; there is always a new refinement or extrapolation to make with regard to a way of knowing. Barzun (1969) spoke of the need for the "new librarian" to create synthesis, because "[e]verywhere else there is only juxtaposition . . ." (p. 3965). Barzun wants the "new librarian" to be a synthesizer, not someone who juxtaposes, because juxtaposition implies Dervin's positivistic and competitive "clash of ideas." Barzun (1969) believes that "the important things derived from books cannot be known in advance, therefore cannot be asked for from a 'knowledge bank' like cash for the week from a money bank. And the good books, good for all serious purposes, cannot be turned into abstracts or digests without immediately losing their worth and use" (p. 3964). The value of books or articles cannot be reduced to a digest or abstract, because that would suppose a mere accumulation of fact-based information—information that competes against other information in the marketplace of ideas.

Instead, Barzun's call for synthesis bears an intriguing relation to Dervin's (1994) depiction of a communitarian way of knowing (p. 382). She pictures four overlapping wheels, representing both diversity between cultures and persons as well as diversity within people and cultures. Each wheel contains within itself multiple perspectives—necessarily incomplete representations of reality because "our ontological world" is not able to "fully instruct us." The task of thinking individuals is therefore to "conclude that humans need to tap diverse perspectives, not merely to make peace across their differences, but as ontological necessity." The real task for humans is not to accept so-called "expert" views, but to sift and synthesize differing approaches in an attempt to bring them together in a complex wheel-within-wheel model with perspectives intersecting perspectives in such a way that a decentered, never-completed, and multiple reality results. This reality, in addition, presupposes perpetual seeking because "we must jettison the baggage of our assumptions—the belief that anything but 'expert' observations are suspect. We must find a way to think of diversity of views as a step toward never-reachable ontological completeness and as a step away from the tyranny of epistemological completeness" (p. 382). As Barzun recognized, one of the few ways by which to achieve such breadth of vision and heterogeneous knowing is to read books and articles not only for their horde of facts, but also for those nebulous, indefinable, incomplete, uncertain, and suggestive vestiges and aspects therein contained that may only become of value in an indeterminate future, after due reflection and synthesis, and after having been overlayed with the indefinable and suggestive aspects of a myriad of other books, each pulling in different directions, each contributing to, in Dervin's terms, multi-perspectivality.

To be sure, the ability to understand concepts in information systems is, and will continue to be, an integral aspect of success in the job market of the 21st century. Yet, absent an awareness of and interest in the ways in which discoveries and occurrences in, for example, archeology, contemporary politics, history, psychology, the visual and performing arts, or geology have relevance for their daily library work, staff members will remain what Barzun (1969) calls technicians working "in the ideal robotry of the future" (p. 3965). And, as Barzun (1946) remarks, while it is no great crime not to know that John Horne Tooke's *Diversions of Purley* is not a book about games, but rather a book about words and grammar, "when you pile up omissions of that character—when you ask for the *Greek Anthology,* and you are asked, 'Who made the collection?'; when the *Anatomy of Melancholy* is thought to be a medical book—you begin to have an uncomfortable sense that the person is not well-read or well-educated" (p. 116). Although Barzun is writing here from the perspective of the 1940s, Richard Abel (1999) also rues the passing of the "scholar-librarian," in part "the consequence of the 'professionalization' of library practice paralleling the professionalization of the various disciplines in the academy; and in part the consequence of the conversion of the library school into a kind of 'trade school' concerned with 'how-to' rather than 'why-to'" (p. 17).

Certainly, both Barzun and Abel are speaking specifically about academic libraries and librarians, but it would be wrong to suggest that public libraries and special libraries do not require scholar-librarians. As discussed in Chapter 6, library personnel at Highsmith, Inc. explore far-flung information sources, never knowing exactly how the material they find will be useful, but suspecting that someone will, in fact, find a use for it. They, too, are adherents of multi-perspectivality. And as the general education level of North Americans rises with the growing commitment to life-long learning, it would be foolhardy, indeed, to suggest that public library staff are answering questions and solving problems on a lower level than at academic libraries. Accordingly, all types of libraries require librarians who are inveterate readers and knowledge seekers, especially those with good memories for the voluminous amounts they have read and who are able to provide users with the range of suitable information necessary to address their particular situations. Indeed, Quinn (1999) suggests that memory enhancement techniques are a vital part of professional and competent library reference work. He urges library reference staff to conceive of their task as a "performance" with the same kinds of challenges faced by concert musicians or professional athletes in their chosen fields (p. 262). Quinn recognizes that "[e]ven if the audience is one person, 'making a good impression' by recalling information quickly and efficiently is important to a librarian's self-esteem and sense of professional self-worth, not to mention the patron's satisfaction" (p. 262). Specifically, he recommends the use of mental rehearsal and imagery training, where librarians could "mentally practic[e] answers to the kinds of questions they typically encounter in the reference situation or in using a complex source or database" (p. 262). Here, then, is a related skill that might be taught at library and information science schools.

PERSONAL COMMITMENT TO ONGOING ACQUISITION OF GENERAL AND SUBJECT KNOWLEDGE

The policy changes and proposals mentioned here are, to a certain extent, important in providing the necessary preconditions for improved reference service in libraries. Enhanced learning, self-development, and improved service cannot occur without a wide array of structural and financial resources dedicated to facilitating and supporting such outcomes. As Jacques Steinberg (1999) reports, many states that in the 1990s adopted strict academic goals and tests as part of the "standards movement" are acknowledging that "they have not put in place the training programs for teachers, the extra help for students and the other support necessary to meet suddenly accelerated standards" (p. A1). Because few students are meeting the new higher standards, states such as Wisconsin, Virginia, New York, and Massachusetts retrenched by setting passing grades at very low levels. Faced with the paradox of, on the one hand, encouraging high standards and, on the other, of letting students pass, for example, with a score of 220 on a high-school exit exam with a minimum score of 200 and a maximum of 280, as in Massachusetts, or with a score of 55 out of 100, as in New York, governors signed a mass pledge "to give students and teachers the very underpinnings [of support] they have requested" (p. A25).

Structural support is vital for improving knowledge levels of high-school students or library personnel. Organizational reforms such as tiered service; a significant increase in the funds allocated to improving collections in the reference area; a financial plan emphasizing the hiring of more librarians so that existing staff can each have fewer hours of reference desk duty; the establishment of, or an increase in, daily paid time each staff member can devote to improving his or her knowledge of information resources and the content of those resources; regular sabbaticals of the kind many enlightened businesses are now providing their employees, during which staff can explore new knowledge fields and interests; team-based financial bonuses for exceeding performance levels; the development of regional library consortia and partnerships that would rotate reference personnel on a regular basis, so that each staff member would gain an enhanced understanding of the resources available in the immediate geographical area—these are some of the ways that structural support can enhance library reference service.

At the same time, such initiatives can only go so far in fundamentally improving reference service if there is no personal commitment on the part of staff to dedicate, or re-dedicate themselves to a serious, major, and self-directed program of continuous learning and content-based knowledge acquisition. In one sense, each reference staff member should undertake a "standards movement" of his or her very own. At the end of the day, library reference personnel should take stock of their own levels of general knowledge about current political, economic, social, and cultural issues. If, after an honest appraisal, they deem their knowledge to be wanting, they should challenge themselves to raise their sights and improve their general knowledge of current and historical issues, on their own time, so that they can be well-prepared to handle reference questions with a high level of proficiency. In a world whose only constant is change and evolution, where knowledge and information evolve and expand at a breathtaking pace, it would be ironic indeed if library reference personnel (who, after all, are information professionals) failed to keep up with the world of knowledge through self-education. When all is said and done, reading newspapers and books is an inexpensive way to keep current and greatly increase one's general knowledge. Why not start with that? To be sure, the reference staff member who, in answer to the question about golf and CEOs discussed in Chapter 6, blithely replied that, "if you want to know such things, you should probably be reading the papers," was being dismissive and condescending. In the final analysis, however, the joke is on her, because her statement reveals a profound misunderstanding of the role of public library reference professionals—a role that, among other things, means respecting both the profession of librarianship and the patrons of the public library by continually striving to be as knowledgeable (and hence useful) as possible when faced with reference queries. The standards movement in schools is not without controversy. Undoubtedly, its extension to library staff would be even more controversial. But, as one of the organizers of the meeting at which state governors re-committed themselves to the standards movement asserted: "We understand the pain. And we're going to have to deal with it. But we're not going to deal with it by backing off" (Steinberg, 1999, A25). Likewise, reference workers themselves, with or without the structural support of library administrators and policymakers, can no longer afford to sit on the sidelines, or refrain from taking steps to increase their own levels of general and subject-specific knowledge, despite the "pain" or the loss of time for other pursuits.

In other words, reference staff, whether or not they are provided with paid time to keep current, should do everything in their power to avoid the embarrassment of not knowing about significant local, national, or world issues that may be the subject of the next reference question. Consider the following telling example, taken from a front page story appearing in *The New York Times* in conjunction with the 25th anniversary of former President Richard M. Nixon's resignation in the wake of the 1974 Watergate scandal. Although the anecdote concerns the teaching profession, it has general applicability for librarians as well. Reporting on an exhibit of photographs at the Smithsonian Institution's National Museum of American History commemorating Nixon's fall from power, Adam Clymer (1999) describes how "an elementary school principal who was just five years old when he resigned . . . wondered aloud just why the disgraced President had to go." Upon hearing about covert payments to the Watergate burglars, "she gasped. Told about his use of the Internal Revenue Service against his political enemies and how his 'plumbers' broke into Daniel Ellsberg's psychiatrist's office, she recoiled. Then she retraced her steps . . . and looked at some more of [the] striking photographs. . . . The Oregon educator said the exhibit 'fills in some of the gaps in my history.'"

Clymer's thesis is that "those gaps are hardly uncommon in a country where news organizations have treated so many scandals that followed Watergate as if they, too, were constitutional crises and where three Americans in four say Nixon's offenses were no worse than the others." In support of his view, he quotes a Florida professor of journalism, who claims that treating all scandals in the same manner and "with the same level of breathlessness that Watergate deserved has done nothing but reduce the amount of oxygen to our brains." Later in the story, Clymer remarks that "with the events in Watergate often given short shrift in the last few weeks of a high school survey of American history, the principal's ignorance was not unusual." But, as a subsequent letter to the editor observed, "what does it say about our educational system that an 'educator' can become a principal and be so unaware of the facts about one of the most significant events of our time" (Howard, 1999)? While it is easy to blame external forces such as the media for the principal's lack of knowledge, ultimately the responsibility for not knowing rests with the principal herself.

One reason teaching gets so little respect is precisely because of incidents such as the one described here. Reduced respect often leads to reduced expectations. Standards start to slip. Shrugging, people begin to accept that Watergate is no longer something everyone knows about. As Clymer's article demonstrates, the search for explanations leads anywhere but to the individual concerned. Could this have happened to a librarian? One certainly hopes not, yet the results described in the previous chapters give pause. Reference staff simply do not seem to realize the importance of keeping up with current events. Would librarians be embarrassed if the individual highlighted in the Watergate story had been a fellow librarian? One would certainly hope so, and one would also hope that each of them would try to make sure that such a situation wouldn't happen to him or her personally. To be sure, not all the world's knowledge and information may be gleaned from a newspaper, but the act of reading newspapers may be thought of as a leading indicator of a general interest and concern about cultural and social issues. It may be perceived as an avenue towards a more in-depth understanding of key trends and discoveries. Librarians have a clear responsibility both to themselves and the profession to ensure that they are as knowledgeable as possible by constantly reading, and then reading some more. As Margaret Stieg (1980) points out, "it is a pity that most Americans define education in terms of courses taken and don't feel that they can know something unless they have taken a course in it," especially because individual purposive reading is often the best continuing education program that a librarian can take (pp. 2547–2551).

For their part, library education programs have a responsibility to engender an attitude in their graduates that "[r]eference sources are only a bridge to the world of knowledge" and not knowledge itself, that the "effective librarian must operate in that world [of knowledge]" (Stieg, 1980, p. 2550). Otherwise, library programs risk having happen to them what many leading economics departments are experiencing today. As Michael Weinstein (1999) reports, students in these departments are desperately searching for "the economic substance in graduate economics programs," which currently "emphasize teaching students how to prove theorems, misleading them into thinking that economics is a deductive exercise, the mere application of mathematical logic" (pp. A17, A19). The problem has become so acute that a special conference sponsored by the MacArthur Foundation and organized by the Social Science Research Council was recently held in order to help students "find their way toward applied economics—analyzing problems that real people face." Weinstein's description of an informal lunch session in which he discovered the woeful state of their general knowledge about real issues is instructive:

> [T]he students at [the conference] seemed surprisingly unfamiliar with many current economic issues. . . . One of the guest lecturers referred to the earned-income tax credit as the E.I.T.C., the country's most successful anti-poverty program next to Social Security. "What's that," one student asked. Nor could many of the students distinguish Medicare from Medicaid or demonstrate familiarity with simple facts about the American economy. They had studied the theory of financial markets, but not its connection to the crisis sweeping through Asia. Many of these students admitted that they do not read newspapers. Nor do they see much of a connection between knowledge of economic reality or Government policies and their chosen course of study.

While the analogy to library programs is not exact, there are sufficient parallels. To a large extent, librarians are taught the theory of reference service. There is concentration on the process, method, and tools of reference work, while subject knowledge is often neglected. To put it simply, library students, just like their colleagues in economics programs, are not accustomed to reading newspapers, to understanding the connection between general knowledge of how the world works and how that knowledge can serve the interests of the public. As a result, their level of cultural literacy is not what it should be. Nor is it overly stressed in library programs that reading newspapers, or simply reading as much as one possibly can in order to acquire as much general knowledge as one possibly can, is useful and, indeed, praiseworthy.

And although it was not librarians who did not know, in the above examples, about the E.I.T.C., the difference between Medicare and Medicaid, or the Watergate scandal, this lack of general knowledge reflects the same malaise apparent when telephone reference questions were asked, as discussed in Chapter 6. Obviously, not every librarian or reference staff member can know something about everything, but a careful reader of newspapers would certainly have no problem in identifying any of these three topics, or, for that matter, hundreds of others. As Walter

(1925), Wyer (1930), and Hutchins (1944) knew, newspaper reading not only opens up new vistas for busy librarians, but also contributes to what Stieg (1980) saw as value-added reference work: "[I]t may not be measurable, but the word gets around that Ms. X is especially knowledgeable" (p. 2551). Accordingly, daily careful reading of major newspapers such as *The New York Times*, *The Globe and Mail*, and *The Washington Post* can be a helpful starting point for improved reference service.

Along with teachers, librarians, theoretically, represent knowledge and access to knowledge for millions of citizens. They are asked countless reference questions every day. Often, their salaries are not merit based, but rather depend on longevity. Complacency about their skill sets may set in, or worse, they may not even realize, like the principal from Oregon, what they do not know. Regular certification and re-certification procedures, together with pay scales geared towards rewarding excellence, may serve as a catalyst for not only significantly raising the general and subject knowledge levels of teachers and librarians, but also raising the expectations of those who depend on them for guidance and help. Whether in the classroom or at the reference desk, improvement can only start when an individual challenges herself, first, to look beyond omnipresent and ubiquitous external sources of failure and, subsequently, to look within herself and to ask, on a daily basis, "Could I know more?," "Could I read more?," and "Could more knowledge of diverse subject areas have helped me to provide better instruction or service?" To ask these questions is to know the answer. As mentioned in Chapter 1, positive or negative opinions about unobtrusive testing of library staff are really beside the point. The real virtue of unobtrusive quantitative evaluation at library reference desks lies in how much it reveals about the willingness of reference staff to assume individual responsibility for success or failure, and to devote themselves to the kind of continual self-improvement that does not start and stop with a series of short-term training and updating courses, but that extends to developing an ingrained habit of reading widely, whenever one has a free moment, in newspapers, magazines, scholarly journals, and books, whether in print or electronic form, whether in the comfort of one's own home, on the various transportation systems that one takes to and from work, or sitting on a park bench.

But does anyone have time to read so much, to be familiar with a truly wide range of subject matter? As Jennifer Prittie (1999) reports, the answer is an unequivocal yes. All that is needed is "an openness to the world" and a belief that reading is a necessity, both an end in itself and a means towards "sustaining information." Prittie quotes Michael Bliss, a university historian, as saying that "[s]ome of the most widely read people I know are lawyers and doctors." Heather Reisman, CEO of Indigo Books and Music, a Canadian book superstore on the model of Barnes & Noble, "easily rhymes off a list of voracious readers, including a bank chairman, an appeals-court judge, a design guru, and a social-policy maverick." No one could ever argue that lawyers, bank chairmen, doctors, and judges are not busy people, yet they find the time to read copious amounts. How do they do it? "I always have a ton of books around all over the place, and that is the way I get to read things," says Reisman, who picks up a book whenever she has a spare minute throughout the day. "They're in the car, they're with me whenever I go on an airplane, they're in every room of the house" (p. 18). Others read on their lunch hours, waiting for public transit, even walking between appointments or meetings. And while books play a fundamental role in the search for sustaining information, most avid readers are adamant that "newspapers are their first—and best—source of information. Most read several every day (Reisman and Gotlieb [Chairman of the Canada Council and a former ambassador] read four and five respectively), and say they would be loathe to eliminate any of them." Bliss is even more categorical about the value of newspapers: "I believe the single best way to be informed is to read newspapers regularly, every day. It's a religion in our house. We have papers galore in the morning. This, to me, is absolutely Step One" (p. 18). Library reference staff should understand that it is possible to be reading constantly, to be perpetually expanding one's general knowledge. All it takes is a willingness to accept personal responsibility for one's work, for one's library as an organization, and for the numerous individuals in the community as a whole.

FORWARD INTO THE PAST

I want to conclude by drawing attention to the comments about reference service made by S. R. Ranganathan (1961) and their relationship to what I have called the individual or personal responsibility of the reference librarian. Primarily known for his contributions to classification and cataloging theory, Ranganathan was also a prescient observer of, and commentator on, the factors necessary for the delivery of superior reference service to library patrons. However, as Marcia Chappell (1976) observes, Ranganathan's views on reference service have never enjoyed popularity in North America, mainly because of their emphasis on "a complexity of qualities possessed by an individual that results in some mysterious way from his [or her] being in tune with the cosmos" (p. 388).

Chappell draws a contrast between the "unfathomable individual qualities" Ranganathan wishes all librarians to possess—encapsulated by the word "flair"—and the American system which concerns itself "about the personal qualities of the librarian only insofar as they can be incorporated into a system" and where librarians "address themselves primarily to designing a set of procedures whose purpose is to compensate as much as possible for the individual librarian's inevitable lack of flair" (p. 388). And while Chappell concludes that there is much to praise in his "attempt to root principles and practices of reference service in a cosmic, metaphysical reality" and that these principles "can at least awaken American librarians to the limitations of their own approaches to reference service [by] act[ing] as a counterweight to their tendency to focus narrowly and restrict their attention to immediate concerns," she notes too that Ranganathan's mystical statements and arguments about reference service are ultimately not compelling because they are "finally no more than a statement of faith in intuition" and lead to a picture of actual reference practice that is "vague and superficial" (pp. 394-395).

Does Ranganathan's theory of reference work have any relevance in the 21st century? I believe it does, for the simple reason that his teachings invariably rest on the foundation of continuous hard work and purposive self-education on the part of each individual librarian. His language may be overly ornamental, as in his description of reference service as "ineffable ... indescribable ... intangible ... and it is the wholeness of the reference work that does the work" (p. 174), but, when all is said and done, Ranganathan's theory of reference service states that each reference librarian must realize that she or he is a vital link in the never-ending process of knowledge transmission which, in turn, contributes to the creation of new knowledge, individual mental development, and social progress. It is therefore the responsibility of each reference librarian to do one's utmost not to fail, not to become a broken link in the spiral towards a higher plane of universal harmony. In Ranganathan's world view, librarianship is a very high calling indeed, but it is also a calling that demands a great deal of effort. The Sanskrit words for library and librarian—*granthalaya* and *granthalayi*, respectively—embody this very concept. As Ranganathan explains, because *grantha* means "expressed thought or work" and *alaya* denotes "perfect merging, integration, at-one-ment," the combination of these two terms identifies a person who is skilled in "helping in the merging of mind and *grantha* to the point of achievement of enrichment of memory, elevation of emotions, stimulation of intellect, increase of knowledge, and release of intuition" (p. 185). This merging, however, cannot occur if librarians are complacent about what they know, if they avoid the hard work of perpetual learning, reading, and knowledge acquisition, if they fall under the spell of their current status and achievements, what Ranganathan calls the "little ego" (p. 179). The librarian thus has a sacrosanct duty thrust upon her to aid others to reach a point of higher development, and it is a duty that can only be properly executed when the individual librarian is constantly striving to be aware of, and conversant with, a broad array of social, cultural, historical, political, and economic phenomena. In other words, librarians are conceptualized as true educators. And the term *anulayasevi*—Sanskrit for reference librarian—takes this one step further, suggesting that reference work is not only "service in the merging (of works, *granthas*) ... to the limit of the achievement of the purpose sought," but also service that emphasizes patron participation ("working with the reader and not on the reader") and respect for "the individuating particularities of each reader" (p. 186). In other words, librarians recognize that each individual reader and learner is different, and that because of this difference, the advice given will also be necessarily different, much like a teacher dispenses varying levels of instruction and counsel to students at different academic levels.

The reference librarian who exhibits the "intensely personal quality" of flair, defined as "a subconscious solution found for getting over difficulties [with] the help of a dash of intuition" (p. 173) is the person who can best fill the role of the *anulayasevi*. This quality of flair, however, is built on a foundation of hard work, whereby each librarian takes it upon herself to know every document in the library "so as to make the library yield ten times more result than it would otherwise ... for the good of others" (p. 180). The ideal reference librarian is thus not only constantly striving to attain "competence of a high order," but also has a genuine "love and respect for readers, willingness to share their problems, their difficulties, and the joy coming on them with the solution of the problems..." (p. 180). In effect, the reference librarian is the "energizing principle" at the center of untold discoveries, enrichment, and illumination (p. 182).

At times overstated and wrapped in abstruse language, Ranganathan's theory nonetheless boils down to the fact that each librarian must take responsibility for his or her state of general and subject-specific knowledge in order for optimum reference service delivery to occur. Reference librarians must constantly be on the look out for ways of expanding their knowledge so that they will have more opportunities to readily transfer such accumulated knowledge to others. Failure to do so is a selfish act. Accordingly, the reference librarian not only has an individual responsibility to herself, but also to the library, its patrons, and society as a whole to facilitate intellectual and spiritual growth. And while meticulous and rigorous classification and organization of diverse materials is the necessary precursor for any attempt at reference service, excellent reference service can only be provided by the reference librarian who "eats, drinks, sleeps, and talks his long range reference problems throughout the twenty-four hours, the week, the month, the year." Unsolved reference queries are carried home, thought about during the evening hours, and again in the morning on the way to work. Until resolved, the reference problem becomes an integral part of the reference librarian's being, urging her or him to consider a plethora of possible sources.

Despite Chappell's (1976) contention that Ranganathan's theory of reference service relies overmuch on "faith in intuition" (p. 394), he does in fact provide detailed guidance as to how reference librarians should ideally go about their tasks. And, taken as a whole, his advice always circles back to one all-important, though often neglected, aspect of librarianship and reference work: the need to read, voluminously, widely, and ceaselessly. After determining the possible subjects of interest to a particular library's clientele, Ranganathan urges the reference librarian to get "a working knowledge of the subjects involved ... [through] a careful reading of a few authoritative publications and a rapid survey of the literature of the subject as a whole." In this way, "a broad skeletal knowledge of the subject, its parts, and phases" is obtained, as well as the "relationship of the parts among themselves and to other fields of knowledge" (p. 347). Of course, the librarian's reading should not stop at this point. Ranganathan specifically mentions the inestimable value for reference staff to read newspapers and periodicals on a regular basis, because "[s]ometimes research studies and investigations are reported in the newspapers at their inception [and] [s]ometimes newspapers have feature articles on important conclusions brought to light." Accordingly, a "close scanning of both newspapers and periodicals ... is really necessary for useful, intelligent long-range reference service" (p. 349) because the reference worker has to constantly anticipate the types of questions that could possibly be asked and because periodicals "provide opportunities for the reference librarian to keep himself [or herself] abreast of the world's progress in knowledge; in effect, "keeping ahead of the game [and at] the very wave-front in the advance of knowledge" (p. 350). Thus, when reading newspapers and periodicals, "the variety of questions actually brought up by enquirers and of the questions anticipated on the basis of local knowledge and contemporary happenings should get interlaced in the mind of the reference librarian" (p. 350).

Equally important for the reference worker is renewing one's acquaintance with the current holdings of the library through what Ranganathan calls "shelf-study," defined as a "repeated skipping through the old books" (p. 351). The potential of old books is "seldom exhausted" because they act "like a kaleidoscope" insofar as "[e]very change in the angle of approach yields a new pattern." Reference librarians should realize that "[w]hat the old stock can yield depends upon what we take to it in our apperception" (pp. 350–351). Simply put, the more a reference librarian knows what is contained in the library holdings, new and old, the more she can point the patron to exactly the item required. Shelf-study must therefore be thought of as "one of the corner stones in the preparation for" long-range reference service because "[a]s the enquirers, actual and anticipated, grow, our apperception grows, too" with the result that [b]ooks or passages in books, without any meaning in the past, splash out a new message when pursued—perhaps a hundredth time it may be— with a newly enriched apperception" (p. 351).

For Ranganathan, reading is a non-negotiable attribute of the successful reference librarian. Nonetheless, he recognizes some impediments to the inculcation of a culture of reading within the world of reference librarians. First, there is the "new danger" of the ever-increasing number of "library schools," which have increased "like mushroom[s]." These schools, staffed "by overworked part-time teachers or by full-time indolent misfits" take "no trouble ... to widen the basic knowledge of students" and make no distinction "between elementary and advanced courses in Library Science." As a result, employers are made "to expect anybody with elementary training to do reference service," which is like "expecting a draftsman to design a monumental building or a holder of a school-final certificate to conduct college classes" (p. 354). Ranganathan's point, I think, is that the truly superior reference librarian is born only when she has had a great deal of first-hand exposure to a wide-variety of subject-specific sources, when she really knows what is contained in those sources, when she peruses these sources again and again in order to discover new information and knowledge, and when she constantly updates her knowledge of specific fields of study by reading in newspapers and periodicals. In other words, when she possesses a detailed overview of, or broad familiarity with, the literature of a particular subject area or field. Whereas elementary training in reference service familiarizes students with basic reference books and treatises, advanced reference service requires a firm commitment to a culture of reading and valorization of intellectual study that only comes about from intensive exposure to the literature of particular academic disciplines, broadly conceived.

A second impediment is the attitude displayed by various library management authorities who fail to understand that "the library can render its greatest possible good to the community only if it provides in the timetable of the staff sufficient free time" for such necessary preparatory work as shelf-study and other forms of reading (p. 351). Far from viewing reference service as the heart of library work, managers have the tendency to look upon it as "wholly clerical ... [where] raw hands are thrown in on every pretext [and where] even these raw hands are taken away frivolously to other departments as soon as they pick up a few weeks' experience and another brand new hand is thrust in" (p. 354). Management personnel, Ranganathan believes, often laugh at the suggestion that "the reference librarian has to read ... and re-read ..." in order to provide optimal reference service. As he notes, one reason for such scorn may be because managers understand that, were they to provide time for reference librarians to read, they would also have to hire more reference staff—a circumstance that would mean the expenditure of additional funds. However, far from being an expense, scheduled reading time for librarians is really a long-term cost-saving investment, since the money saved by staffing the reference desk with paraprofessionals and clerks is "wasted, owing to the resultant loss of time and energy on the part of the senior staff" who have to subsequently cover for the mistakes and oversights of paraprofessionals "whose training does not render them sufficiently appreciative of the importance of the considerations involved, frequently in matters of detail" (p. 354).

Ranganathan was of the opinion that, for reference librarians, the value of intensive reading, outside of the narrow confines of library and information science literature itself, was self-evident. It is an open question whether such a statement could be made today. To be sure, there have been extraordinary changes within the library profession and the working life of the reference librarian since the time of Ranganathan, yet librarians still remain a vital link in the process of knowledge transmission and new discovery. On a metaphorical level, Ranganathan argued that the library and its reference librarians have a duty of care to all patrons who enter the library—care for their intellectual development, care that they leave the library with exactly the right answer, care that they find relief for their burden, whatever it may be. Duty of care can, of course, be achieved in a number of ways. Reference librarians can assume the burden upon themselves by taking personal responsibility for being as knowledgeable as possible on a wide array of topics, thus ensuring precise and detailed attention to a patron's information need. As I have suggested above, a concerted commitment to both general and subject-specific reading can be a significant component of this kind of personal responsibility on the part of the reference librarian. On the other hand, the library, as an institution, can assume a duty of care to patrons, readers, and users. With this scenario, the working model becomes the set of changes proposed for, or instituted within, the teaching profession in the late 1990s and early years of the 21st century. Having determined that the quality of education received by public school students in North America was not what it should be, various jurisdictions and entities took steps towards ameliorating the quality of the educational experience by focusing on maximizing teacher competency and instructional outcomes. For instance, as reported by Sarah Kershaw (2000), schoolwide incentive or merit pay for *all* the teachers in schools that achieve certain educational benchmarks was under serious discussion, despite decidedly mixed results in the past. As Kate Zernicke (2000) reports, the American Federation of Teachers, the second largest teacher's union in the United States, supports national teacher testing and the creation of "a national core curriculum for what teachers need to know," in addition to a proposal whereby prospective teachers would have "to major in the subject they wanted to teach" (p. A20). Antonella Artuso (2000) reports on a plan by the Ontario provincial government in Canada not only to make beginning teachers pass a qualifying test (much like a bar exam for lawyers) before they are allowed to enter the classroom, but also to undergo recertification every five years by doing written tests upon the completion of a round of professional development programs. And Tamar Lewin (2000) comments on the fast-growing trend where school boards and school districts hire superintendents and principals who are not career educators, but rather high-profile outsiders from the fields of business, law, government, and the military. Bringing with them "new leadership and an outside perspective," these new administrators are instituting new policies and programs because of a sense that "educators have failed the schools," that "school districts need to change how they conduct themselves if [they] are to improve student achievement, and that kind of change does not usually come from those inside the system" (p. A20).

Libraries are just as critical to national well-being as schools, and libraries, as this book has argued, are having difficulty in delivering top-flight reference service. And while the analogy between schools and libraries is far from perfect, there are enough similarities to wonder whether the new ideas circulating in the educational realm would not also be a breath of needed fresh air in North American public and academic libraries. Why not have library directors who are not librarians, so long as they can raise reference service levels by rethinking the fundamentals of reference service delivery so that, finally, the 55 percent rule is no longer the rule? Why not have incentive and merit pay plans for entire reference departments that achieve consistent reference success rates substantially above 55 percent? Why not recertify reference librarians on a regular basis, according to the models proposed, for example, by Hernon and McClure (1987), one of which calls for sustained on-site educational programs at libraries delivered by educators from library and information science schools (or others) who develop "a *program* of training sessions, learning activities, independent studies, projects or other learning opportunities ... to accomplish the objectives of the program" [original emphasis] (p. 158)? Why not follow the lead of the Medical Library Association, which, in order to assure "continuing competence," requires recertification of librarians every five years either by the "completion of 35 contact hours of approved continuing education, or a passing score on the current Certification Examination of the Medical Library Association" (Hernon & McClure, 1987, p. 153)? Or why not adopt a wide-ranging list of subject competencies that each reference librarian must possess, along the lines of the list implemented by Texas A&M University (Benefiel, Miller, & Ramirez, 1997)?

Just as teachers have resisted many of these ideas or have only reluctantly embraced them, librarians too have a great deal of difficulty finding these suggestions palatable. But, just as states, provinces, and school districts all across North America were driven to adopt far-reaching and frequently unpopular changes because many teachers and schools were failing in their duty to deliver an acceptable education to students, reference librarians should realize that it is in large part due to their inability to provide high-quality reference service, as demonstrated again and again by unobtrusive research conducted in the past 20 years, that diverse proposals of the kind mentioned in the previous paragraph have been put forward. Is there a way to avoid worrying whether such measures come into being? Ranganathan, I think, provides a very useful answer. If reference librarians truly consider themselves as indispensable links in knowledge and information transmission, as key actors in the process of individual and social progress, then they will realize that they have a profound responsibility to the patrons and the community in which they work. And once this is understood, an internal impetus may develop within the individual reference librarian to be worthy of this important position, mission, and charge. A sense of personal responsibility for delivering the very best possible reference service may ensue. And once this sense of personal responsibility comes to the forefront, reference librarians may well realize the importance of constant reading—reading of subject-specific books, reading of newspapers and periodicals, reading for the sake of reading, and reading for the sake of having a storehouse of knowledge with which to feel more comfortable dealing with reference questions. Thus, having assumed personal responsibility for their own continuing competence and ongoing intellectual growth, they will be sanguine about any implementation of stricter standards for librarians, should it ever come to pass that such measures as certification and recertification of reference librarians become common currency

REFERENCES

Abel, Richard. (1999). The national enquiry into scholarly communication—twenty years after. *Publishing Research Quarterly, 15,* 3–19.
Aldrich, Duncan. (1998). Partners on the Net: FDLP partnering to coordinate remote access to Internet-based government information. *Government Information Quarterly, 15,* 27–38.
Allan, Frank R., & Smith, Rita H. (1993). A survey of telephone inquiries: Case study and operational impact in an academic library reference department. *RQ, 32,* 382–391.
Altman, Ellen. (1982). Assessment of reference services. In Gail A. Schlachter (Ed.), *The service imperative for libraries: Essays in honor of Margaret E. Monroe* (pp. 169–185). Littleton, CO: Libraries Unlimited.
Aluri, Rao. (1993). Improving reference service: The case for using a continuous quality improvement method. *RQ, 33,* 220–36.
Archibold, Randal C. (1998, November 1). Getting tough on teachers. *The New York Times Education Life,* 22–25, 30–31.
Artuso, Antonella. (2000, May 12). Teacher tests on the books. *The Toronto Sun,* 3.
Barringer, Felicity. (1998, November 3). Paid newspaper circulation in U.S. continues to decline. *The New York Times,* C7 [National].
Barzun, Jacques. (1969, November 1). The new librarian to the rescue. *Library Journal, 94* (19), 3963–3965.
———. (1946). The scholar looks at the library. *College & Research Libraries, 7,* 113–17.
Beamish, Rita. (1999, May 20). Citizens' electronic inquiries get governments' attention. *The New York Times,* D8 [National].
Benefiel, Candace R., Miller, Jeannie P., and Ramirez, Diana. (1997). Baseline subject competencies for the academic desk. *Reference Services Review, 25.* 183–93.
Benson, Allen C. (1995). *The complete Internet companion for librarians.* New York: Neal-Shuman.
Brown, Janet Dagenais. (1994). Using quality concepts to improve reference services. *College & Research Libraries, 55,* 211–19.
Bruni, Frank, & Schmitt, Eric. (1999, November 19). Bush rehearsing for a world stage. *The New York Times,* A25 [National].
Buchanan, Leigh. (1999, January). The smartest little company in America. *Inc., 21,* 42–54.

Buchman, Susan. (1999, November 9). Letter to the editor. *The New York Times*, A30 [National].
Budd, John M. (1997). A critique of customer and commodity. *College & Research Libraries, 58*, 310–21.
Budd, John M., & Raber, Douglas. (1998). The cultural state of the fin de millénaire library. *Library Quarterly, 68*, 55–79.
Bundy, Mary Lee, Bridgman, Amy, & Keltie, Laurie. Public library reference service: Myth and reality. *Public Library Quarterly 3* (3), 11–22.
Campbell, Jerry D. (1992). Shaking the conceptual foundations of reference: A perspective. *Reference Services Review, 20* (1), 29–35.
Canada. Transport Canada. Administrative Services. (1986). *You asked us: Typical questions and answers handled by the inquiry desk of the Transport Canada library and information centre*. Department of Transport: Ottawa.
Chappell, Marcia H. (1976). The place of reference service in Ranganathan's theory of librarianship. *Library Quarterly, 46*, 378–96.
Charles, John, & Mosely, Shelley. (1997). Keeping selection in-house. *Library Journal, 122* (4), 30.
Chen, Ching-chih, & Hernon, Peter. (1980). Library effectiveness in meeting consumer's information needs. In *Library effectiveness: A state of the art: Preconference on library effectiveness* (pp. 50–62).Chicago: American Library Association.
Childers, Thomas. (1970). *Telephone information service in public libraries: A comparison of performance and the descriptive statistics collected by the state of New Jersey.* Unpublished doctoral dissertation, Rutgers University.
———. (1979, October 1). Trends in public library I&R services. *Library Journal, 104 (17)*, 2035–2039.
———. (1980, April 15). The test of reference. *Library Journal, 105 (8)*, 924–28.
———. (1984). *Information and referral: Public libraries*. Norwood, NJ: Ablex Publishing.
———. (1987). The quality of reference: Still moot after 20 years. *Journal of Academic Librarianship, 13*, 73–74.
———. (1997). Using public library reference collections and staff. *Library Quarterly, 67*, 155–73.
Choo, Chun Wei. (1994). Perception and use of information sources by chief executives in environmental scanning. *Library & Information Science Research, 16*, 23–40.
Choo, Chun Wei, & Auster, Ethel. (1993). Scanning the business environment: Acquisition and use of information by managers. In M. E. Williams (Ed.), *Annual Review of Information Science and Technology, 28* (pp. 279–314). Medford, N. J.: Learned Information, Inc. for the American Society for Information Science.
Clausing, Jeri. (1999, May 17). U.S. to offer search service that links its on-line sites. *The New York Times*, D1, D6 [National].
Cleveland, Harlan. (1985). *The knowledge executive: Leadership in an information society*. New York: E. P. Dutton.
Clymer, Adam. (1999, August 9). Time (25 years) and scandal fatigue blur the fall of Nixon. *The New York Times*, A1, A12 [National].
Coleman, Vicki, Xiao, Yi (Daniel), Bair, Linda, & Chollett, Bill. (1997). Toward a TQM paradigm: Using SERVQUAL to measure library service quality. *College & Research Libraries, 58*, 237–51.
Continuing Library Education Network and Exchange Round Table. American Library Association. (1986). *Self-assessment guide for reference*. St. Paul, MN: Office of Library Development Services.

Cove, J. F., & and Walsh, B. C. (1987). Browsing as a means of on-line text retrieval. *Information Services & Use, 7,* 183–88.

Crowley, Terence. (1968). *The effectiveness of information service in medium size public libraries.* Unpublished doctoral dissertation, Rutgers University.

Czopek, Vanessa. (1998). Using mystery shoppers to evaluate customer service in the public library. *Public Libraries, 37,* 370–75.

Daniel, Evelyn H. (1987). The effects of identity, attitude, and priority. *Journal of Academic Librarianship, 13,* 76–78.

D'Aniello, Charles A. (1989). Cultural literacy and reference service. *RQ, 28,* 370–80.

Dervin, Brenda. (1992). From the mind's eye of the user: The sense-making qualitative-quantitative methodology. In J. D. Glazier & Powell, R.R. (Eds.), *Qualitative research in information management* (pp. 61–84). Englewood, CO: Libraries Unlimited.

———. (1994). Information—Democracy: An examination of underlying assumptions. *Journal of the American Society for Information Science, 45,* 369–385.

———. (1997). Conceptual models for network literacy. *The Electronic Library, 15,* 363–68.

Devlin, Brendan. (1997). Conceptual models for network literacy. *The Electronic Library, 15,* 363–68

Dewdney, Patricia, & Ross, Catherine Sheldrick. (1994). Flying a light aircraft: Reference service evaluation from a user's viewpoint. *RQ, 34,* 217–30.

Dolan, Elizabeth, & Vaughan, Liwen Q. (1998). *Electronic access to federal government documents: How prepared are the depository libraries?* Ottawa: Canada Communications Group.

Douglas, Ian. (1988). Reducing failures in reference services. *RQ, 28,* 94–101.

Dowd, Maureen. (1999, November 7). Name that General! *The New York Times,* Week in Review, 15.

Duke, Deborah C. (1994). "Night owl": Maryland's after-hours reference service. *Public Libraries, 33,* 145–48.

Dunn, Kathleen, & White, Myra. (1991). Experimenting with reference referral in a multitype environment. *College & Research Library News, 52,* 363–65.

Durrance, Joan C. (1989, April 15). Reference success: Does the 55 percent rule tell the whole story? *Library Journal, 114* (7), 31–36.

———. (1992). Raising expectations—our users' and our own. *Journal of Academic Librarianship, 18,* 283–84.

———. (1995). Factors that influence reference success: What makes questioners willing to return? *The Reference Librarian, 49/50,* 243–65.

Elliott, Stuart. (1999, September 15). P. & G. to tie agency compensation to sales. *The New York Times,* B1, B6 [National].

Elzy, Cheryl, & Nourie, Alan. (1992). Letters. *College & Research Libraries, 53,* 81–82.

Elzy, Cheryl, Nourie, Alan, Lancaster, F. W., & Joseph, Kurt M. (1991). Evaluating reference service in a large academic library. *College & Research Libraries, 52,* 454–65.

Farrell, Maggie Parhamovich, Davis, Ric, Dossett, Raenn, & Baldwin, Gil. (1996). Electronic initiatives of the federal depository library program. *Journal of Government Information, 23,* 393–401.

Ford, Stephanie. (1997). Public access to electronic federal depository information in regional depository libraries. *Government Information Quarterly, 14,* 51–63.

Frazer, Stuart L., Boone, Kathryn W., McCart, Vernon A., Prince, Teresa L., & Rees,

Anne D. (1997). Merging government information and the reference department: A team-based approach. *Journal of Government Information, 24,* 93–102.

Friedman, Thomas L. (1999, November 7). George W.'s makeup exam. *The New York Times,* Week in Review, 15.

Frohmann, Bernd. (1992). The power of images: A discourse analysis of the cognitive viewpoint. *Journal of Documentation, 48,* 365–386.

Gebhard, Patricia. (1997). *The reference realist in library academia.* Jefferson, NC: McFarland & Company.

Gebhard, Patricia, Anthony, Art, & Peete, Gary. (1978). Networking in the microcosm: Reference referrals. *RQ, 17,* 197–201.

Gers, Ralph, & Seward, Lillie J. (1985, November 1). Improving reference performance: Results of a statewide study. *Library Journal, 110* (8), 32–35.

Gross, Melissa. (1995). The imposed query. *RQ, 35,* 236–43.

———. (1998). The imposed query: Implications for library service evaluation. *Reference & User Services Quarterly, 37,* 290–99.

Harless, David W., & Allen, Frank R. (1999). Using the contingent valuation method to measure patron benefits of reference desk service in an academic library. *College & Research Libraries, 60,* 56–69.

Harris, Howard. (1996). Retraining librarians to meet the needs of the virtual library patron. *Information Technology and Libraries, 15* (1), 48–51.

Harris, Katherine G. (1963). Reference service today and tomorrow: Objectives, practices, needs, and trends. *Journal of Education for Librarianship, 3,* 175–187.

Harris, Roma M., & Marshall, Victoria. (1998). Reorganizing Canadian libraries: A giant step back from the front. *Library Trends, 46,* 564–80.

Hartocollis, Anemona. (1999, September 18). New York state regulators toughen standards for teachers. *The New York Times,* A12 [National].

Hawley, George S. (1987). *The referral process in libraries: A characterization and an exploration of related factors.* Metuchen, NJ: The Scarecrow Press.

Heckart, Ronald J. (1998). Machine help and human help in the emerging digital library. *College & Research Libraries, 59,* 250–59.

Hernon, Peter, & Altman, Ellen. (1998). *Assessing service quality: Satisfying the expectations of library customers.* Chicago: American Library Association.

Hernon, Peter, & McClure, Charles R. (1978). Library reference service: An unrecognized crisis—a symposium. *Journal of Academic Librarianship, 13,* 69–71.

———. (1982). Referral services in U.S. academic depository libraries: Findings, implications, and research needs. *RQ, 22,* 152–63.

———. (1986, April 15). Unobtrusive reference testing: The 55 percent rule. *Library Journal, 111* (7), 37–41.

———. (1987). *Unobtrusive testing and library reference services.* Norwood, NJ: Ablex Publishing.

Hernon, Peter, Nitecki, Danuta A., & Altman, Ellen. (1999). Service quality and customer satisfaction: An assessment and future directions. *Journal of Academic Librarianship, 25,* 9–17.

Howard, Donald. (1999, August 11). Letter to the editor. *The New York Times,* A19 [National].

Hults, Patricia. (1992). Reference evaluation: An overview. *The Reference Librarian, 38,* 141–50.

Hutchins, Margaret. (1944). *Introduction to reference work*. Chicago: American Library Association.

Janes, Joseph, & McClure, Charles. (1999). The Web as a reference tool: Comparisons with traditional sources. *Public Libraries, 38,* 30–39.

Jardine, Carolyn W. (1995). Maybe the 55 percent rule doesn't tell the whole story: A user-satisfaction survey. *College & Research Libraries, 56,* 477–85.

Johnston, Katharine. (1996). *Beyond customer satisfaction to loyalty*. Ottawa, Canada: The Conference Board of Canada.

Jones, Dixie A. (1997). Plays well with others, or the importance of collegiality within a reference unit. *The Reference Librarian, 59,* 163–75.

Katz, William A. (1969). *Introduction to Reference Work: Volume II: Reference Services*. New York: McGraw-Hill.

———. (1982). *Introduction to reference work (5th edition)*. New York: McGraw-Hill

———. (1996). *Introduction to reference work, Volume 1: Basic information services (7th edition)*. New York: McGraw-Hill

Kemp, Alasdair. (1979). *Current awareness services*. London: Clive Bingley.

Kershaw, Sarah. (2000, April 10). Long history of turmoil surrounds incentive pay for teachers. *The New York Times,* A23 [National].

Kristoff, Nicholas D. (2000, March 3). Rival makes Bush better campaigner. *The New York Times,* A15.

Kuhlthau, Carol C. (1993). *Seeking meaning: A process approach to library and information services*. Norwood, NJ: Ablex.

Lancaster, F. W. (1977). *The measurement and evaluation of library services*. Washington, D.C.: Information Resources Press.

Larson, Carole A., & Dickson, Laura K. (1994). Developing behavioral reference desk performance standards. *RQ, 33,* 349–57.

Lewin, Tamar. (2000, June 8). Educators are bypassed as school system leaders. *The New York Times,* A15 [National].

Mackey, Terry, & Mackey, Kitty. (1992, May 15). Think quality! The Deming approach does work in libraries. *Library Journal, 117* (9), 57–61.

Management of Reference Services Committee. Reference and Services Division. American Library Association. (1994). Information services policy manual: An outline. *RQ, 34,* 165–72.

Massey-Burzio, Virginia. (1992). Reference encounters of a different kind: A symposium. *Journal of Academic Librarianship, 18,* 276–86.

McClure, Charles R., & Hernon, Peter. (1983). *Improving the quality of reference service for government publications*. Chicago: American Library Association.

McIlroy, Anne. (1998, February 12). One-third of stores selling tobacco to minors. *The Globe and Mail,* A1, A10.

Mendelsohn, Jennifer. (1997). Perspectives on quality of reference service in an academic library: A qualitative study. *RQ, 36,* 544–57.

Moberg, David. (1999, February 21). Going bananas. *In These Times, 23* (6), 14–16.

Morris, Leslie. (1993). Unobtrusive reference testing vs. obtrusive reference testing. *Journal of Interlibrary Loan and Information Supply, 3* (3), 1–3.

Murfin, Marjorie E. (1995a). Assessing library services: The reference component. In Evaluation of Reference and Adult Services Committee, Management and Operation of Public Services Section, Reference and Adult Services Division

(RASD), American Library Association (Eds.), *The Reference Assessment Manual* (pp. 1–15). Ann Arbor, MI: The Pierian Press.

———. (1995b) Evaluation of reference service by user report of success. *The Reference Librarian, 49/50,* 229–41.

Murfin, Marjorie, & Bunge, Charles. (1984). Evaluating reference service from the patron point of view: Some interim national survey results. *The Reference Librarian, 11,* 32–35.

Myers, Marcia J. (1980). The accuracy of telephone reference services in the southeast: A case for quantitative standards. In *Library effectiveness: A state of the art.* Chicago: American Library Association.

Myers, Marcia J., & Jirjees, Jassim M. (1983). *The accuracy of telephone reference/information services in academic libraries: Two studies.* Metuchen, N.J.: The Scarecrow Press.

Newsome, James, & McInerney, Claire. (1990). Environmental scanning and the information manager. *Special Libraries, 81,* 285–93.

Noah, Timothy. (1999, August 8). People's choice awards. *The New York Times Magazine,* 42–45.

Olszak, Lydia. (1991). Mistakes and failures at the reference desk. *RQ, 31,* 39–49.

Parker, June D. (1996). Evaluating documents reference service and the implications for improvement. *Journal of Government Information, 23,* 49–70.

Paskoff, Beth. (1991). Accuracy of telephone reference service in health science libraries. *Bulletin of the Medical Library Association, 79* (4), 182–188.

Philipson, Daphne. (1999, November 9). Letter to the editor. *The New York Times,* A30 [National].

Poole, Mary E. (1960, April 15). What is reference work? *Library Journal, 85,* 1522–1524.

Press, Eyal. (1999, May 31). Texaco on trial. *The Nation,* 11–16.

Prittie, Jennifer. (1999, December 4). The age-old mind fix. *National Post,* Weekend Post, 18.

Quinn, Brian. (1995). Improving the quality of telephone reference service. *Reference Services Review, 23* (1), 39–49.

———. (1999). A multimodal approach to enhancing memory in reference service. *Reference & User Services Quarterly, 38,* 257–66.

Ranganathan, S.R. (1961). *Reference service.* 2nd edition. New York: Asia Publishing House.

Rawan, Atifa R., & Cox, Jennifer. (1995). Government publications integration and training. *Journal of Government Information, 22,* 253–66.

Richardson, John V., Jr. (1992). Teaching general reference work: The complete paradigm and competing schools of thought, 1890–1990. *Library Quarterly, 62,* 55–89.

———. (1998). Question Master: An evaluation of a Web-based decision-support system for use in reference environments. *College & Research Libraries, 59,* 29–37.

Ross, Catherine Sheldrick, & Dewdney, Patricia. (1998). Negative closure: Strategies and counter-strategies in the reference transaction. *Reference & User Services Quarterly, 38,* 151–63.

Rothstein, Samuel. (1953). The development of the concept of reference service in American libraries, 1850–1900. *Library Quarterly, 23,* 1–15.

Ryan, Susan M. (1997). Square peg in a round hole: Electronic information and the federal depository library program. *Journal of Government Information, 24,* 361–75.
Saxton, Matthew L. (1997). Reference service evaluation and meta-analysis: Findings and methodological issues. *Library Quarterly, 67,* 267–89.
Seng, Mary. (1978). Reference service upgraded: Using patrons' reference questions. *Special Libraries, 69,* 21–28.
Shapiro, Beth J. (1987). Ongoing training and innovative structural approaches. *Journal of Academic Librarianship, 13,* 75–76.
Smith, Daniel R. (1993). Collection development for telephone reference. *The Georgia Librarian, 30,* 64–67.
Steinberg, Jacques. (1999, December 3). Academic standards eased as a fear of failure spreads. *The New York Times,* A1, A25 [National].
Steinhauer, Jennifer. (1998, February 4). The undercover shoppers: Posing as customers, paid agents grade the stores. *The New York Times,* C1, C23 [National].
Stieg, Margaret F. (1980, December 15). Continuing education and the reference librarian in the academic and research library. *Library Journal, 105* (22), 2547–2551.
Swigger, Keith. (1985). Questions in library and information science. *Library & Information Science Research, 7,* 369–83.
Swope, Mary Jane, & Katzer, Jeffrey. (1972). Silent majority: Why don't they ask questions? *RQ, 12,* 161–66.
Taylor, Robert S. (1968). Question-negotiation and information seeking in libraries. *College & Research Libraries, 29,* 178–94.
Tour, Debra E. (1997). Quest line (telephone reference): A different approach to reference service. *Public Libraries, 37,* 256–58.
Tuominen, Kimmo. (1997). User-centered discourse: An analysis of the subject positions of the user and the librarian. *Library Quarterly, 67,* 350–71.
Tyckoson, David A. (1992). Wrong questions, wrong answers: Behavioral vs. factual evaluation of reference service. *The Reference Librarian, 38,* 151–73.
Tygett, Mary, Lawson, Lonnie, & Weessies, Kathleen. (1996). Using undergraduate marketing students in an unobtrusive reference evaluation. *RQ, 36,* 270–76.
Van De Voorde, Philip. (1989). Should reference service for U.S. government publications and general reference be merged? A case study. *Government Publications Review, 16,* 247–57.
Vaughan, Liwen Q., & Dolan, Elizabeth. (1998). Electronic dissemination of government information in Canada: Implications for equitable access. *Journal of Government Information, 25,* 439–52.
Vittala, Kalyani. (1999, May 27). U.S.-Canada agreement on magazines. *The New York Times,* C5 [National].
Walter, Frank Keller. (1925; reprinted 1984). In a quiet corner with a little book. *Collection Management, 6,* 28–35.
Weingand, Darlene E. (1994). Competence and the new paradigm: Continuing education of the reference staff. *The Reference Librarian, 43,* 173–82.
Weinstein, Michael M. (1999, September 18). Students seek some reality amid the math of economics. *The New York Times,* A17, A19 [National].
Whitlatch, Jo Bell. (1989). Unobtrusive studies and the quality of academic library reference services. *College & Research Libraries, 50,* 181–94.

Whitson, William L. (1995). Differentiated service: A new reference model. *Journal of Academic Librarianship, 21,* 103–10.
Wilson, Patrick. (1983). *Second-hand knowledge: An inquiry into cognitive authority.* Westport, CT: Greenwood Press.
Wyer, James I. (1930). *Reference work: A textbook for students of library work and librarians.* Chicago: American Library Association.
Yates, Rochelle. (1987). *A librarian's guide to telephone reference service.* Hamden, CT: Library Professional Publications, The Shoe String Press.
Younger, Jennifer. (1991). Total quality management: Can we move beyond the jargon? *ALCTS Newsletter, 2* (8), 81–83.
Zernicke, Kate. (2000, April 12). A national test for new teachers sought by union. *The New York Times,* A1, A20 [National].

AUTHOR INDEX

Abel, Richard, 190
Aldrich, Duncan, 28
Allan, Frank R., 155, 176n
Altman, Ellen, 26–27, 72, 73, 87, 99, 146, 172–73, 174–75
Aluri, Rao, 177–78, 180
Anthony, Art, 144
Archibold, Randal C., 175, 183
Artuso, Antonella, 202
Auster, Ethel, 151

Bair, Linda, 10
Baldwin, Gil, 28
Barringer, Felicity, 174
Barzun, Jacques, 186–87, 188–89, 190
Beamish, Rita, 28, 72–73, 76 n.9, 99
Benefiel, Candace R., 202
Benson, Allen C., 69
Boone, Kathryn W., 68
Bridgman, Amy, 155
Brown, Janet Dagenais, 178
Bruni, Frank, 16
Buchanan, Leigh, 152
Buchman, Susan, 15
Budd, John M., 12–13, 14
Bundy, Mary Lee, 155
Bunge, Charles, 79

Campbell, Jerry D., 181
Chappell, Marcia H., 197–98, 200
Charles, John, 151
Chen, Ching-chih, 1, 2, 3, 22
Childers, Thomas, 11, 43, 75 n.1, 130–31, 132, 144, 145, 155, 156

Chollett, Bill, 10
Choo, Chun Wei, 152
Clausing, Jeri, 28, 73
Cleveland, Harlan, 20–21, 23–24
Clymer, Adam, 193
Coleman, Vicki, 10
Cove, J. F., 152
Cox, Jennifer, 68
Crowley, Terence, 155
Czopek, Vanessa, 28

Daniel, Evelyn H., 2, 22
D'Aniello, Charles A., 150
Davis, Ric, 28
Dervin, Brenda, 13–14, 22, 187–90
Devlin, Bruce, 69
Dewdney, Patricia, 8, 26, 79–80, 83, 85, 87–88, 110, 126–27, 131, 132, 144, 146, 181
Dickson, Laura K., 181
Dolan, Elizabeth, 28, 62–63, 68, 70
Dossett, Raenn, 28
Douglas, Ian, 143
Dowd, Maureen, 15
Duke, Deborah C., 155
Dunn, Kathleen, 145
Durrance, Joan C., 8, 17, 26, 79, 87, 179, 180

Elliott, Stuart, 183
Elzy, Cheryl, 34, 185

Farrell, Maggie Parhamovich, 28
Ford, Stephanie, 70

215

AUTHOR INDEX

Frazer, Stuart L., 68
Friedman, Thomas L., 16
Frohmann, Bernd, 23, 187

Gebhard, Patricia, 129, 144
Gers, Ralph, 34, 144
Gross, Melissa, 171–72

Harless, David W., 176n
Harris, Howard, 182
Harris, Katherine G., 148
Harris, Roma M., 62, 174
Hartocollis, Anemona, 185
Hawley, George S., 130, 134–35, 143
Heckart, Ronald J., 176
Hernon, Peter, 1, 2, 3, 16, 22, 25, 27, 29, 32–33, 38, 40, 42, 55, 71–74, 87, 99, 131–32, 146, 172–75, 180–81, 203
Howard, Donald, 194
Hults, Patricia, 26
Hutchins, Margaret, 147–48, 149, 153, 161, 181, 182, 196

Janes, Joseph, 67
Jardine, Carolyn W., 26
Jirjees, Jassim M., 155
Johnston, Katharine, 27
Jones, Dixie A., 91
Joseph, Kurt M., 34

Katz, William A., 22–23, 33, 35–36, 149
Katzer, Jeffrey, 3, 18
Keltie, Laurie, 155
Kemp, Alasdair, 153
Kershaw, Sarah, 202
Kristof, Nicholas D., 24n
Kuhlthau, Carol C., 14, 22

Lancaster, F. W., 27, 34
Larson, Carole A., 181
Lawson, Lonnie, 8, 144
Lewin, Tamar, 202

Mackey, Kitty, 178
Mackey, Terry, 178
Marshall, Victoria, 62, 174
Massey-Burzio, Virginia, 179, 180

McCart, Vernon A., 68
McClure, Charles R., 16, 25, 29, 32–33, 38, 40, 42, 55, 67, 71, 74, 131–32, 180–81, 203
McIlroy, Anne, 75 n.2
McInerney, Claire, 151
Mendelsohn, Jennifer, 4–5, 9, 11
Moberg, David, 76 n.10
Morris, Leslie, 185
Mosely, Shelley, 151
Murfin, Marjorie E., 43, 79, 132
Myers, Marcia J., 131, 155

Newsome, James, 151
Nitecki, Danuta A., 27, 73–74
Noah, Timothy, 7
Nourie, Alan, 34, 185

Olszak, Lydia, 5–6

Parker, June D., 26
Paskoff, Beth, 155
Peete, Gary, 144
Philipson, Daphne, 15
Poole, Mary E., 148
Press, Eyal, 76 n.10
Prince, Teresa L., 68
Prittie, Jennifer, 196

Quinn, Brian, 154, 191

Raber, Douglas, 12–13
Ranganathan, S. R., 197–203
Rawan, Atifa R., 68
Rees, Anne D., 68
Richardson, John V., Jr., 23, 34–35, 176
Ross, Catherine Sheldrick, 8, 26, 79–80, 83, 85, 87–88, 110, 126–27, 131, 132, 144, 146, 181
Rothstein, Samuel, 21–22
Ryan, Susan M., 28

Saxton, Matthew L., 25
Schmitt, Eric, 16
Seng, Mary, 182
Seward, Lillie J., 34, 144
Shapiro, Beth J., 179, 181
Smith, Daniel R., 154

Smith, Rita H., 155
Steinberg, Jacques, 191, 193
Steinhauer, Jennifer, 75 n.2
Stieg, Margaret F., 19, 194, 196
Swigger, Keith, 3
Swope, Mary Jane, 3, 18

Taylor, Robert S., 3, 13
Tour, Debra E., 154, 175
Tuominen, Kimmo, 187
Tyckoson, David A., 26
Tygett, Mary, 8, 144

Van De Voorde, Philip, 68
Vaughan, Liwen Q., 28, 62–63, 68, 70
Vittala, Kalyani, 76 n.11

Walsh, B. C., 152
Walter, Frank Keller, 147, 181, 195
Weessies, Kathleen, 8, 144
Weingand, Darlene E., 182
Weinstein, Michael M., 194–95
White, Myra, 145
Whitlatch, Jo Bell, 43
Whitson, William L., 179–80
Wilson, Patrick, 129, 144
Wyer, James I., 22–23, 147, 181, 196

Xiao, Yi (Daniel), 10

Yates, Rochelle, 150, 161
Younger, Jennifer, 177

Zernike, Kate, 202

SUBJECT INDEX

Accreditation, loss of, 185–86

Certification, 74, 183, 202–3
Continuing education, efficacy of, 20
Current awareness services, 153–54

Environmental scanning, 151–53. *See also* Knowledge executives

Government documents reference service in Canada: differences due to city size, 48–49; differences due to geography, 46–47; differences due to presence of separate government information area, 52–53, 68; differences due to type of depository library, 45, 48; differences due to whether question dealt with legislative or executive branch of government, 56–58; impact of busyness on accuracy, 49–52; overall accuracy level, 44, 67–68; recommendations for improvement of, 71–75; role of Depository Service Program, 28; time spent answering questions, 53–55; types of sources used, 62–67; use of web sources, 69–71

Individual reference questions used: Abandoned communities, 165–67; Africa, 125–27, 136–37; Architect, 161–63; Auditor-General, 114–15, 140; Barley, 108–9, 141; Book, 107–8, 135–36; CIA report, 159–60; complete list of, 41–42, 156–57; Credit unions, 165; Crime, 115–16; CRTC, 106–7; Elgar Symphony, 160–61; Endangered plants, 163–65; Firearms, 112–14, 140; Fish, 124–25, 141; Fuels, 111–12, 139–40; Garbage, 121–22, 137–38; Gasoline additive, 170; Golf, 168–69; Lyrics, 109–10, 138–39; Magdalen Islands, 116–18, 141; Native artifacts, 170–71; over-all responses to, 102–6, 157–59; Photo, 122–24, 135; Refugee, 119–21, 141; Ritalin, 167–68; Rules, 118–19; Sailing solo, 169

Knowledge executives, reference librarians as, 21–24. *See also* Environmental scanning

Newspapers, reading of, 147–51, 174, 193–97, 200

Performance-based compensation, 183–85
Proxies: negative comments about reference service made by, 80–87, 92–96; positive comments about reference service made by, 87–92; recommendations made by, 96–98; use of, 32–34

Reading, 147–51, 174, 193–97, 199–202
Recertification, 74, 202–3
Reference service: alternatives to,

219

72–73, 99; public expectations of, 8–10; ready reference, 2, 11–12, 14–17; relative popularity of, 1–4

Reference service evaluation, competing philosophical models of, 6–8, 18–19

Reference service failure: examples of, 80–87, 94–96; individual solutions to, 181–83, 191–97; reasons for, 79, 177; structural solutions to, 178–80

Reference service improvement, ways of: certification, 183; increasing staff knowledge levels, 181–84; loss of accreditation for LIS schools, 185–86; performance-based compensation, 183–85; personal responsibility, 18–20, 181–83, 191–97; reading newspapers, 147–51, 193–97; recertification, 74

Reference service success, examples of, 87–92

Reference staff: collaboration among, 90–91; knowledge levels, 4–5, 92–96, 181–84, 186–91; mistakes made by, 5–6; personal characteristics needed, 22–23, 88, 181, 197–200

Referrals: detailed analysis of, 133–41; philosophy of, 130–32, 142–43; rate of, 58–61; recommendations, 144–46

Standards movement, 191–92; in libraries, 192–96

Telephone reference service: growth of, 154–55; efficacy of, 155–73

Unobtrusive evaluation: criticism of, 12–14, 24–25; debate about, 10–12, 13–14, 25–27; value of, 15–17, 196

About the Author

JURIS DILEVKO is a member of the Faculty of Information Studies at the University of Toronto.